2

THE FAIL-SAFE SOCIETY

The
Fail-Safe Society

❧❧❧

Community Defiance
and the End of American
Technological Optimism

Charles Piller

UNIVERSITY OF CALIFORNIA PRESS
Berkeley • Los Angeles • London

University of California Press
Berkeley and Los Angeles, California

University of California Press, Ltd.
London, England

Published by arrangement with Basic Books, a division of
HarperCollins Publishers Inc. All rights reserved.

Library of Congress Cataloging-in-Publication Data

Piller, Charles.
The fail-safe society : community defiance and the end
of American technological optimism / Charles Piller.
p.   cm.
Originally published: New York : Basic Books, 1991.
Includes bibliographical references and index.
ISBN 0-520-08202-8
1. NIMBY syndrome—United States.   2.   Land use—
Government policy—United States—Citizen participation.
3.   Science and state—United States—Citizen participation.
4.   Technology and state—United States—Citizen
participation.   I. Title.
HD205.P54   1993
333.73'13'0973—dc20   92-24104
                                                       CIP

Printed in the United States of America

9 8 7 6 5 4 3 2 1

The paper used in this publication meets the minimum
requirements of American National Standard for Information
Sciences—Permanence of Paper for Printed Library
Materials, ANSI Z39.48–1984.   ⊗

To Surry and Nate

Contents

⸺ ଷଷଷ ⸺

Preface

Several years ago, while working as a newspaper reporter, I began to cover a controversy concerning the efforts of a major public university to convert a large office building into a biomedical research lab. Some members of the local community objected. They feared that toxic chemicals, radiation, and dangerous microorganisms would silently, invisibly escape from the lab and contaminate their homes. Faculty members and administrators carefully explained that their research could ultimately save millions of lives. They offered reasoned, apparently well-supported arguments that the labs presented, at worst, a negligible health risk.

Still, many neighbors rejected the reassurances. With a dazzling combination of community organizing and legal maneuvering, the local community stopped the project cold. These neighbors were not polite. They shouted down the university's bland bureaucrats at every opportunity. Their contempt—even hatred—for their enemy was palpable. They looked irrational, and their fear seemed out of proportion.

Yet, as I researched the subject, I realized that these are not the tactics or attitudes of a lunatic fringe. Abject distrust of and refusal to compromise or tolerate any new environmental insult—large or small—have become commonplace among local communities throughout the nation. I wondered how such an extreme response had become so typical. And why now?

During the last 15 years, the relationship between the general public and those who create, manage, and profit from science and technology has gradually soured. A litany of ecological disasters and technical failures—from Love Canal and the space shuttle *Challenger* explosion to the Chernobyl nuclear meltdown—has turned many Americans away from technological optimism. More important, Americans have lost their faith that those who control technology will do so competently and in the public interest.

Increasingly, communities around the nation and throughout the world are learning a bitter self-reliance. They are saying "not in my backyard"—Nimby—to a wide range of technological ventures, from the demonstrably deadly by-products of the nuclear weapons complex (such as radioactive-waste dumps and incinerators) to the inevitable trappings of industry (such as airports, factories, power lines, and oil refineries) to the relatively benign manifestations of basic research (such as biomedical laboratories).

Urban planners, politicians, university administrators, and corporate executives recognize Nimbyism with painful familiarity. These managers are fed up. They blame local obstructionism on a minority of selfish malcontents who churn the ignorant fears of a scientifically illiterate public. Yet, as I studied a wide array of Nimby battles, it gradually became clear to me that the more local activists learn about a given technology, the more skeptical they often become. And I saw that locally based opposition crosses racial, geographic, economic, and educational boundaries. Nimbyism may be extreme, but it is a mass phenomenon, not the product of a few determined spoilers.

Therefore, I tried to go beyond the conventional approach—advice on how to quash, moderate, co-opt, or appease Nimby forces to minimize their disruption of science, technology, and economic growth—to probe a deeper question: What does the ascendancy of belligerent local obstructionism tell us about the way science and technology is managed in our society?

I argue that Nimbyism is caused not by selfishness or ignorance, although these factors may play a role. Rather, it is the manifest rage of victims, the desperation of the powerless. These people feel that they can do little to influence major environmental problems caused by ineptitude, corruption, and greed at the highest levels of business and government. But they recognize that they can often limit the dangerous side effects of technological miscalculations in their own neighborhoods. Without trust, people withdraw consent from those who run society. Nimbyism demonstrates a gradual withdrawal of consent at the grass-roots level.

By effectively stalling a wide range of projects, Nimby groups are beginning to shift the burden of proof about safety and necessity—from the potential victims of technological ventures to those who administer or profit from them. In individual cases, Nimby groups may be reactionary and shortsighted. They often push problems to other backyards. But Nimbyism is merely a symptom. It has grown out of a scientific and technological enterprise that tries to function like a world apart from the people it affects, spinning out risks and benefits without attention to their fair and equitable allocation.

The Fail-Safe Society offers a framework for creating the political conditions that could allow meaningful public involvement in scientific and technological decision making. Only by democratizing such decisions can local obstructionism give way to flexible, discriminating approaches to risks and benefits that can be supported by society as a whole.

I am indebted to Jim Bellows, Gary Fields, Marion Nestle, and David Noble, whose incisive analysis of the manuscript added coherence and richness to my initial efforts. Andy Evangelista, Niels Schonbeck, and Keith Yamamoto also provided pivotal suggestions on selected chapters. Two books proved inspirational in my work: *Environmental Hazards,* by Sheldon Krimsky and Alonzo Plough (Auburn House, 1988); and *The New Politics of Science,* by David Dickson (Pantheon, 1984). I am grateful to the many people who agreed to lengthy interviews without which I could not have completed this book.

Thanks also to my literary agents, Katinka Matson and John Brockman, on whose advice and good sense I rely; to Steve Fraser and Richard Liebmann-Smith of Basic Books, whose clear and probing questions contributed greatly to the final product; and to the numerous friends and relatives who gave me the confidence and support I needed to complete this lengthy endeavor.

Finally, I thank my wife, Surry Bunnell, whose keen insights and unflagging belief in each person's essential thoughtfulness and flexibility helped shape my outlook from the beginning.

Oakland, California
November 1990

1

Technological Optimism Gives Way to Fear and Suspicion of Modern Science and Industry

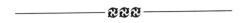

There is no society on Earth that has empowered the citizen the way we have. —William Ruckelshaus, former administrator, Environmental Protection Agency, 1988

In 1989 two scientists at the University of California at San Francisco (UCSF) won the Nobel Prize, the greatest in a constant stream of awards to the institution's professors. UCSF's medical and biochemical researchers, magnets for hundreds of millions of dollars of federal funds, are recognized as among the world's most prolific and influential. As a preeminent AIDS research and treatment center, in 1990 the university hosted the Sixth International Conference on AIDS.

With the respect, gratitude, and admiration of the nation and the world, UCSF seems to have it all. Yet the price of success has been war. Since 1985, UCSF has been fighting a bitter battle to install basic biomedical research laboratories in a large office building in the Laurel Heights neighborhood, two miles from its main campus. UCSF desperately needs the space to decompress its overcrowded labs.

Surrounding neighborhood organizations have resisted the UCSF plan tenaciously and with considerable success in the courts of law and public opinion. Activists accuse the university of arrogant disregard for local concerns; of using its ample political influence to muscle the equivalent of an industrial plant into their tranquil neighborhood. The protest leaders insist that the new labs will silently release deadly chemicals and biological organisms, in what would amount to a carcinogenic experiment on the local community. Hundreds of angry supporters back them up. "We object to the basic concept of locating a biomedical research laboratory in the midst of a highly populated urban area," said the attorney for the residents. "This sort of research is among the most hazardous and should be performed outside population centers to minimize the risk."

Exasperated UCSF scientists and administrators challenged the opposition to provide any credible evidence that biomedical research activities have ever endangered a nearby community. They commissioned studies that showed the main UCSF laboratory complex to be harmless to its neighbors. Research planned for the new labs could dramatically reduce the suffering of millions of people around the world, they added, urging politicians, businesspeople, and the scientific community to join the fight against "scientific illiteracy" and irrational opposition to progress itself. Campus leaders predicted dire consequences if their opponents prevailed: Research institutions of all kinds could be faced with impossible burdens to prove that their work is benign. It raises the question, UCSF Chancellor Julius Krevans says, whether "activities of this kind, which have gone on for 40 years at this institution and at similar institutions throughout the country, are simply not acceptable to society."

The Laurel Heights residents represent the leading edge of an increasingly powerful trend in which community groups militantly lash out at what they see as unwarranted, unfair intrusions of technological dangers. They battle scientists, engineers, bureaucrats, and executives who view the very same project as reasonable, beneficial, even essential for the welfare of society as a whole. The phenomenon is contemporary, but its roots trace back hundreds of years.

—————— ⚉⚉⚉ ——————

The Machine Breakers

From 1811 to 1816, an organized movement of weavers sabotaged the industrial heartland of England. Now infamous around the world, the Luddites smashed thousands of textile frames, power looms, and other manifestations of the tide of industrialization sweeping their industry.

The times were desperate. Nineteenth-century England was mired in economic depression. Textile manufacturers were convinced that only by introducing new technologies on a mass scale to increase efficiency—by rapidly mechanizing their industry—could they help pull England out of crisis. Mechanization would push up unemployment, but for the worthy cause of industrial progress and growth. The Luddites disagreed, and widely destroyed the machines they saw as stealing their jobs.

Although the Luddites were the best coordinated and best known of their kind, they were not the original machine breakers. Recorded examples go back to the seventeenth century, and later outbreaks, such as the smashing of threshing machines by English peasants during the Swing Riots of the 1830s, also exerted chilling pressure on industrial development. Yet, the Industrial Revolution slowed only briefly. For their efforts, the Luddites gained a dubious immortality. Their name has come to be identified with the most backward, selfish human tendencies; with opposition to progress itself. Luddites are almost universally despised and pitied as mindless obstructionists.

Today's opponents of new technologies and the intrusion of technological miscalculations and side effects are often identified by an acronym some have raised as a banner: *Nimby*—"Not in my backyard." Around the country, Nimby groups fight everything from polluting factories and military testing sites to toxic-waste dumps and biomedical research laboratories.

"A new and corrosive popular mistrust of scientists and their work [is generating] political constraints that are already cutting into the growth of our science, cutting into the capacity to help us resolve our . . . problems," Stanford President Donald Kennedy warned thousands of scientists in the keynote address at the 1989 Annual Meeting of the American Association for the Advancement of Science. He castigated a recent explosion of "science-bashing, fear-mongering single-issue campaigns." Kennedy challenged his colleagues to battle openly antiscience forces—creationists, animal liberators, activists against genetic and fetal-tissue research, and obstinate no-growth opponents of new research facilities. "The United States has entered an anti-intellectual phase in our history," Rockefeller University President and Nobel Laureate David Baltimore agreed.

Other critics of locally based resistance to technological imperatives have become strident in their condemnations. "The Nimby syndrome is a public health problem of the first order. It is a recurring mental illness which continues to infect the public," says the Southern California Waste Management Forum, a group consisting of industry and government officials. "Organizations which intensify this illness are like the viruses and bacteria which have, over the centuries, caused epidemics such as the plague."

Industry and government officials have begun to call Nimby activists "the new Luddites." The meaning of that accusation and its implications for how society addresses the Nimby phenomenon hold far-reaching implications for technological development.

———————— ଷଷଷ ————————

Nimby Origins

As the fruits of science and technology—cars, airplanes, electric lighting, telephones—became accessible to the masses in the United States early in this century, Americans began their love affair with science. Over a period of decades, technological advances convinced the public that science (or the gadgetry spawned by science and engineering) would yield continual improvements in the quality of everyday life.*

In October 1957 the National Association of Science Writers commissioned the first major postwar survey of U.S. public views of science. It came at a critical juncture; two weeks before the launch of the Soviet *Sputnik* satellite—the dawning of the space age. The survey revealed a nearly spiritual reverence for science and technology. Nearly 90 percent of those polled agreed that the world was "better off because of science"—for its contributions to medicine, to rapidly rising living standards, to American economic dominance, and for winning the Second World War. Eighty-eight percent called science "the main reason for our rapid progress." Only 12 years after atom bombs vaporized Japanese cities, during an increasingly frenetic nuclear arms race, 90 percent of the sample could not name a single negative consequence of science.

Technological optimism had become the province of everyday people, not just the scientific intelligentsia. *Sputnik* served as a wake-up call for America to intensify its commitment to scientific progress. Technical advancement became intrinsic to the national sense of self. The 1950s and early 1960s were times of intoxicating glory and growing wealth—no problem was too difficult, no job too big when our scientists and engineers rolled up their sleeves. The emerging revolution in electronics, the polio vaccine, the laser, and John F. Kennedy's vow in 1961 to place a man on the moon by the end of the decade spoke to the aspirations and the dreams of millions. American technology delivered.

During those heady times most people discounted signs that rapid

---

*Christopher Lasch, in his book *The True and Only Heaven, Progress and Its Critics*, describes how a 1950 issue of *Life* magazine, which reviewed the first half of the twentieth century, personified and reinforced those beliefs. "Economic history was reduced to the history of technology," Lasch says. "Throughout the whole issue— and throughout almost every other issue of *Life* that ever reached the newsstands— a celebration of technological progress, in short, alternated with sentimental retrospect: and it is exactly this counterpoint that seems most clearly to characterize the historical imagination of our time."

technological advancement carries significant social and ecological costs. But the signs were evident. For example, in 1959 about 3,000 Japanese fishermen rioted over the massive release of mercury from a fertilizer plant into the bay at the city of Minamata. Their livelihoods were destroyed when scores of people died after consuming poisoned fish. In 1961 health authorities banned thalidomide, a tranquilizer for pregnant women, after it caused grotesque birth defects in over 2,500 babies.

Then in 1962, the publication of *Silent Spring* by Rachel Carson made the ecological consequences of our technological society difficult to ignore. Carson's pioneering study, a seminal work in the history of environmentalism, argued that chemical pesticides, particularly DDT, could cause serious, global, possibly irreversible damage. The government eventually banned DDT. But perhaps more importantly, observes science journalist and historian David Dickson, Carson built her case against DDT "into a generalized critique of the narrow focus of contemporary science and technology, of their apparent blindness to broad social and environmental effects."

During the 1960s, concern over technology's unwanted by-products moved from vague rumblings to active demands that government exert strong controls on scientists and industry. Environmentalism quickly gained popularity in the fertile ground of the decade's social and political unrest. But not until the 1970s and 1980s did an onslaught of environmental and public-health disasters shock and awaken America's heartland. The most vivid examples include the following:

1976: A chemical plant explosion in Seveso, Italy, near Milan, released a giant cloud laced with dioxin—one of the deadliest substances ever created—which settled over some 4,000 acres. Thousands of pets and wild animals died; hundreds of people developed blurred vision and the highly disfiguring skin rash chloracne. More than 700 townspeople were evacuated from their homes, some for years. Birth defects soared.

1978: President Carter declared Love Canal, New York, a federal disaster area. Part of the town, whose name would soon become a synonym for America's growing toxic-waste problem, had been built on top of a dump containing 22,000 tons of waste chemicals. For years, enraged and terrified residents complained of childhood cancers, miscarriages, immune dysfunction, and a host of other disorders. By 1980, the federal government had relocated 2,500 residents, and had razed a school and 237 homes, while hundreds more stood empty. Many residents fled for their lives.

1979: A partial meltdown of the reactor core at Three Mile Island nuclear power plant near Harrisburg, Pennsylvania, riveted millions of Americans to their television sets. The plant released a plume of radiation over hundreds of square miles. A complete meltdown, which could have laid waste to much of the state, was narrowly averted. Over the next few years the public heard of thousands of safety violations and emergency shutdowns caused by human and mechanical errors at U.S. nuclear plants.

1983: All 2,200 residents of Times Beach, Missouri, were evacuated from their town by the Environmental Protection Agency (EPA). EPA purchased Times Beach—now a ghost town—for $33 million. A decade earlier, waste oil laced with dioxin had been sprayed on city streets to keep the dust down, killing scores of pets and livestock. Residents suffered internal bleeding, nervous disorders, and birth defects—all mysteries until the dioxin connection was discovered. Many still suffer from those symptoms.

1984: A storage tank exploded at the Union Carbide chemical plant in Bhopal, India, sending a cloud of deadly methyl-isocyanate gas into the atmosphere. More than 2,000 impoverished residents of the town were killed, while tens of thousands of others became blinded or crippled.

1986: The space shuttle *Challenger* exploded moments after takeoff, killing seven astronauts, including a woman slated to become the first teacher in space. During the following weeks, other rocket failures set the U.S. space program back years.

1986: A meltdown of the reactor core of a Soviet nuclear plant in the town of Chernobyl, 80 miles from Kiev, turned hundreds of square miles into a radioactive wasteland. Thousands of residents were evacuated, and the safety of Kiev water supplies remained gravely in doubt for weeks. Radioactive fallout contaminated animals and crops throughout Europe, and radiation followed the jet stream around the world.

1987–1988: Leading scientists confirmed earlier fears that chemical pollution is destroying the ozone layer of the earth's upper atmosphere, which reflects deadly solar radiation. They predicted massive increases in skin cancer rates. Meanwhile, a vast buildup of carbon dioxide and other gases—a side effect of decades of burning fossil fuels and destroying the earth's forests—was shown to increasingly hold in the atmosphere's heat, leading to a potential greenhouse effect. Experts warned that even with immediate and drastic antipollution controls, the planet could slowly warm, melting parts of the polar ice caps and causing massive flooding that could change the contours of the continents.

This litany of problems shook public confidence in expert wisdom. It eclipsed the technological optimism of the 1950s and 1960s. Pervasive discouragement and fear turned to outrage as human errors, carelessness, and greed were uncovered at the root of many technological debacles, while a steady stream of lies, half-truths, and cover-ups about the dangers of new technologies came to light.

"In Bhopal, Union Carbide officials considered their safeguards against a major leak so foolproof that they never considered a worst-case scenario," notes Sheldon Krimsky, a science historian at Tufts University. "The *Challenger* disaster disclosed how the imperative to push forward . . . can be used to disregard information about risks. Unsolved problems in the safety area were subordinated to scheduling demands. This shows us, in the clearest terms, that the desire for profits is not the only cause for folly and irresponsibility."

While most people still strongly support scientific research and the development of new technologies, they suspect the arrogance of those who manage science and technology. National public opinion polls consistently reflect this growing doubt. A 1980 survey indicated that 80 percent of the public agreed that "people are subject to more risk today than they were 20 years ago." In 1983 and 1986 polls, a fourth or more of the public expected that in the future, science and technology would do more harm than good for the human race; or that technology's risks outweigh its benefits. According to another 1983 poll, three-fourths of American adults agreed that due to the development of weapons of mass destruction, "science and technology may end up destroying the human race."

Shortly after the 1979 incident at Three Mile Island, 90 percent of urbanites and 50 percent of nuclear engineers said they were unwilling to live or work within three miles of a nuclear power plant. (The poll also indicated that only 24 percent of urbanites and 56 percent of chemical engineers were willing to live within 10 miles of a toxic chemical waste dump.) And 29 percent of Americans wanted to stop building nuclear plants, while 14 percent called for "a permanent shutdown of existing plants." In 1986, after Chernobyl, those numbers rose to 52 percent and 28 percent, respectively.

The public wants action. Since 1980, an overwhelming majority of Americans has endorsed stricter occupational safety and health rules and consumer protections. A 1990 *New York Times/CBS News* survey indicated that 74 percent of the public agreed that "protecting the environment is so important that requirements and standards cannot be too high, and continuing environmental improvements must be made regardless of costs." The willingness to spend money—always one of the greatest hurdles—had become a secondary issue.

To be sure, these concerns go beyond skepticism of scientists and engineers. Public opinion reflects considerable cynicism about those who directly or indirectly manage our national affairs in general and technology in particular. In a 1984 survey, Congress earned only a 13 percent public-confidence rating; the executive branch,

19 percent. The press received the blessing of only 17 percent of the public; organized labor, 9 percent.*

In the same survey, business drew a 32 percent rating, but another poll indicated that only 19 percent of Americans agreed that "business tries to strike a fair balance between profits and the interests of the public." Other polls have shown that by an overwhelming margin, Americans believe business and industry routinely lie to the public. Studies conducted in 1990 suggest that such views are particularly prevalent among young people, who are increasingly disengaged from active participation in public affairs. (Polling data on public confidence in institutions has been somewhat variable, but only the military and organized religion consistently enjoy the strong confidence of at least half the American people.)

———————— ෴෴෴ ————————

Nimbys Are Everywhere

With the decline of confidence in all kinds of officialdom came a parallel decline in the willingness of local communities to accept passively environmental health hazards caused by official ineptitude or corruption. The civil rights and antiwar movements of the 1960s breathed a sense of defiance and strength into a broad segment of the American public. The growing stature of the consumer rights movement—epitomized in Ralph Nader's successful confrontations of unfair, cavalier, or dangerous government or corporate prac-

---

*Liberal political analysts bemoan low voter turnout in U.S. elections as evidence of "apathy," implying a kind of laziness on the part of the electorate. The dearth of confidence in public officials and the media (which normally convey conventional political perspectives) suggests that many voters see little value in voting when their everyday reality contradicts the posturing, propaganda, and hype that is the staple diet of American politics. "Truth has given way to credibility, facts to statements that sound authoritative without conveying any authoritative information," says Christopher Lasch, historian and author of *The Culture of Narcissism*. "The 'flight from politics,' as it appears to the managerial and political elite, may signify the citizen's growing unwillingness to take part in the political system as a consumer of prefabricated spectacles."

tices—inspired people around the nation. Many communities recognized that they could effectively resist powerful institutional forces at the local level. Meanwhile, the environmental movement had begun to inform popular consciousness.

When residents of Love Canal militantly refused to accept the chemical pollution of their community in 1978, they were by no means the first grass-roots opponents to technological miscalculation. But by capturing national attention, Love Canal launched Nimbyism as an identifiable social force largely generated by these changing social conditions. Communities across the country nervously surveyed their backyards and discovered their own Love Canals. Since then, Nimbyism has mushroomed wherever local communities feel threatened by technology. (The overall Nimby phenomenon, which extends to many aspects of modern society beyond scientific or technological hazards, is described in chapter 6.)

Who exactly are Nimbys? In 1984 the California Waste Management Board, a state agency, published an influential report that predicted the most likely opponents of the development of solid-waste burning power plants. The report suggested that well-educated, liberal, young, and affluent professionals and homemakers living in western and northeastern U.S. cities are most resistant to such plants, and by extension, prone to other Nimby causes. Corporations began to see rural, politically conservative, less-educated populations in the South and Midwest as prime candidates for a host of technologies viewed as relatively risky.

In reality, Nimby groups are becoming ubiquitous. Urbanites, who suffer the aesthetic, practical, and ecological problems of high-density living, react quickly to intrusive development. No surprise there. But during the past decade, construction of toxic-waste dumps—the technology most likely to be met by Nimby opposition—has been halted everywhere, regardless of the ethnic, racial, geographic, or class characteristics of proposed sites. Poor blacks, who may see environmentalism as a luxury, became a driving force against toxic dumps as they gradually recognized that their neighborhoods were preferred as dumping grounds. In Brooklyn, a group of Hispanic youths aged 9 to 28, calling themselves "The Toxic Avengers," have united to fight "environmental racism." Many rural communities, even in staunchly conservative areas, have arisen with equal vigor, suggesting that resistance to hazardous technologies relates directly to proximity.

The basic Nimby attitude goes beyond organized groups, though. Whether the matter is health, peace of mind, or protection of property values, few Americans (activists or not) care to live beside chemical-waste dumps, airports, petrochemical refineries, nuclear power plants, or other standard features of a modern industrial society. Nimby groups are accordingly pluralistic and varied in their goals. Yet disparate communities are unified in defiance of experts and technocrats as the ultimate arbiters of technological risk and change. And regardless of their demographic traits, Nimby battles share common characteristics: Nearly all begin with the frustrated rage and fear of people who perceive themselves as victims and who see their quality of life threatened. Nimby groups are indigenous and highly focused on preserving the home environment. Activists quickly become adept at street demonstrations, petition drives, legal actions, and lobbying. They are combative and indefatigable. Their zeal often takes on an aura of proselytic self-righteousness. Indeed, Nimby groups have been compared to creationists, antiabortionists, and other religious or ethical movements that have gained immense followings by offering what they describe as a spiritual critique of medical or scientific teachings or practices. Although links between Nimby groups and right-wing religious movements are otherwise tenuous, they share irreverence for official versions of reality offered by scientists and technocrats. Ironically, Nimbyism is partly a reaction to the effects of the quasi-religious faith in science that emerged in this country following the Second World War.

A recent *Newsweek* article blamed Nimbyism as a major stumbling block for solving environmental problems: "Once the public went along with anything: now it opposes everything." The article described a Washington, D.C.-area community that rejected the dumping or incineration of water-treatment sludge, then opposed a plan to turn the sludge into fertilizer. "Never mind that it would be inconsistent for the public to demand that sludge not be dumped or landfilled or incinerated, then also demand that sludge not be recycled. In the Nimby Era, these are the kinds of problems municipal officials face."

Nimby groups counter that planners and bureaucrats—midwives for the urban nightmare and bunglers of virtually every major pollution problem—are in a weak position for moralizing. And the technical means of safely disposing of toxic materials—whatever the method—are often unreliable at best. "People are left with what amounts to a territorial instinct," says Michael Edelstein, an expert on the psychological effects of toxic-waste exposure. "Pollution will occur. Victims will suffer. The challenge is to avoid being one of those victims."

Risk Factors

Society will always be compelled to accept a multitude of risks—technological, political, and social—to achieve prosperity, defend against enemies, cure dread diseases, and solve social problems. Risk is an essential ingredient of a dynamic culture. It is the functional alternative to stagnation.

This book examines in detail three cases characterized by divergent objective risk levels: (1) nuclear weapons manufacturing by a secretive government factory, (2) the environmental release of genetically altered microorganisms in a corporate agricultural experiment, and (3) basic biomedical laboratory research at a public university. The miniscule effluents of a biomedical research lab hardly seem comparable to the thousands of tons of nuclear waste that will remain deadly for hundreds of thousands of years, generated by the bomb plant; or even to the remote, yet uncertain possibility of an environmental disaster caused by the mutant microbe.

Yet the Nimby groups in each of these cases—like a multitude of others across the nation—reacted with equal fear, equal determination. This record suggests that Nimbyism almost inevitably suffers from local myopia. Nimby resistance to projects that offer significant societal benefits and pose relatively trivial environmental risks often consumes millions of dollars and ties up hundreds of people in interminable political and legal disputes, while major causes of environmental degradation go virtually unnoticed.

Conventional wisdom, as promoted by those who introduce, manage, or profit from science and technology, holds that Nimbyism is the product of selfish ignorance about risk and that Nimby groups should be stamped out before they irreparably harm our ability to extend society's technical reach and advance our standard of living. When I began this book, in a basic way I agreed with this view. I saw Nimbyism as a vexing problem to be solved. In individual cases, of course, a Nimby response is certainly understandable or justifiable—even noble. But as a trend, I reasoned, Nimbyism is poison for a society that aspires to democratic processes and social cooperation. I saw this as the central question of the book: How can Nimbyism be eliminated without sacrificing legitimate aspirations for local control and personal safety?

As I examined the roots of the Nimby phenomenon and began to understand the bitter intransigence of disenfranchised communities, I grew to recognize that by labeling Nimbyism as the problem I had obscured more central issues. It is not risk per se, but how hazards have been generated and distributed that has led to the Nimby era. In a society that boasts a strong democratic identity, the demand for local participation in technological decision making is hardly surprising, even if the degree of outrage over inept technological choices has startled scientists and technology's managers. (Ironically, democratic aspirations derive partly from the scientific culture itself, with its commitment to open communication and diverse participation in the definition of natural laws.)

What does the prevalence of Nimbyism tell us about the way science and technology are administered in our society? The similarity of the Nimby response across educational and income levels, racial and geographic lines, points away from ignorance and selfishness as the roots of Nimbyism. It suggests a more fundamental cause—the dominance of an autocratic, profligate, and often irresponsible system for managing the scientific and technological enterprise. Communities all over the country, in anger and despair, have mounted organizational barricades around their backyards. They have adopted Nimbyism as the only practical alternative to powerlessness.

2
Control over Science and the Evolution of Public Fears

The distinguishing feature of hegemonic ideologies is that they require no proof or argument; their validity is assumed, understood, and ratified by convention, norms, and accepted bounds of discourse. Thus, those who challenge this dominant set of ideas typically are the ones who must bear the burden of proof that, in this setting, actually defies argumentation and evidence. —David Noble, historian, Drexel University

A deep rift has opened between local communities, and the creators and purveyors of technology. People who are directly subject to known or possible technological hazards emphasize caution. They tend to view risk expansively, encompassing ethics and social distribution of hazards as well as health and environmental impacts. For those subject to the hazard, the trigger for preventive action falls far short of definitive proof. In contrast, corporations, universities, and the federal government rely on expert evaluations of narrowly defined risks and offer measured interventions based on unmistakable evidence of hazards. Local communities often see the latter approach as callously serving the interests of industry. Technocrats may castigate such critics as irrational. (The two perspectives are described in detail in chapter 7.)

Yet political and economic goals not only drive the creation and use of technology; they also define what is rational. The Luddites, whose machine breaking is widely cited as the forerunner of this irrationality, were more astute observers of the function of technology in their economy than conventional histories suggest. Lord Byron, in an 1812 speech to the British House of Lords, gave this review of the Luddites:

> These machines were to [manufacturers] an advantage, inasmuch as they superseded the necessity of employing a large number of workmen, who were left in consequence to starve. . . . The rejected workmen, in the blindness of their ignorance, instead of rejoicing at the improvements in the arts so beneficial to mankind, conceived themselves to be sacrificed to improvements in mechanism. In the foolishness of their hearts, they imagined that the maintenance and well-being of the industrious poor were objects of greater consequence than the enrichment of a few individuals by any improvement in the implements of trade which threw the workmen out of employment and rendered the labourer unworthy of his hire.

The Luddites were not against textile frames. Their actions were a calculated effort to have their grievances redressed by attacking one of the few open targets. The Luddites focused their violence carefully. They attacked employers who caused the most hardship through a variety of business practices—including, but by no means limited to, mechanization. This was not a revolt against progress in any general sense. Indeed, most of the machines in question were far from new, having been widely used for decades before the Luddites emerged. Rather, as British historian Malcolm Thomis has noted, the introduction of labor-saving devices during a time of high unemployment suggests "that the depressed situation was being deliberately exploited by employers to weaken the position of [workers] by foisting the machines upon them to reduce their status at a time when they were least able to resist." Textile frames and power looms had more to do with this long-term political goal than any immediate effort to boost manufacturing profits, even less some abstract notion of progress.

No less than during the Industrial Revolution, economic conditions during modern times influence the public response to technological change. After the Second World War, until the early 1970s, the American standard of living rose dramatically. In the last 15 years, however, average American living standards have declined. Technology's dark side has come into focus. The economic underclass, which never experienced the technological "good life," and industrial workers, whose relatively high-paying jobs were eliminated by rationalization of the work process, grew understandably estranged from the ideal of technological progress. But even the millions whose material consumption continues to rise experience an eroding quality of life. In increasingly stressful urban centers, epidemics of drug addiction and crime spawn fortress-like precautions in many homes, amid endless traffic jams, smog, and polluted drinking water.

Take California's Silicon Valley, birthplace of the modern computer industry: Beginning in the late 1950s, the electronics-development boom converted bucolic orchards into industrial parks, yielding a harvest of jobs and wealth. It also paid some unintended dividends. Because affordable housing development has not kept pace with industrial growth, vast numbers of workers commute, fouling the air and freezing the area's freeways with some of the worst traffic anywhere. Billed for decades as "clean and light," electronics plants have leaked large volumes of more than 70 toxic chemicals into local groundwater. EPA says that groundwater cleanup in one Silicon Valley city, Mountain View, could take 300 years.

According to a 1985 poll, more than half of Americans feel that they have "hardly any" or "not much" control over the risks faced in daily life. A 1989 poll indicated that 58 percent feel a sense of powerlessness and alienation from society's mainstream. More important, as the inability of political and industrial leaders to solve technology's inherent pitfalls grows painfully obvious, many Americans have concluded that technology is increasingly out of control. The most widespread manifestation of that conclusion is fear.

"Society's becoming extremely risk-sensitive," says Donald MacGregor, a risk analyst with nonprofit Decision Research in Eugene, Oregon. "We're in a kind of frantic search for security." In short, a fail-safe society. (From 1979 to 1989, deaths due to accidents in the United States have declined by 21 percent, despite the increase in population, according to a 1990 study by the National Safety Council. People are becoming more cautious, the agency concluded.)

Yet as life expectancies rise year by year, a growing number of experts see public fears as out of proportion. "We are becoming a nation of chemophobes," says Elizabeth Whelan, founder of the American Council on Science and Health, an industry-backed group. "People have developed this fear of technology, all wrapped up in nostalgia for an earlier life, a simpler life. . . . But it's total naivete. Everything is made of chemicals."

Chemical pollution, like other problems of technology, is no myth, of course. Of the tens of thousands of synthetic chemicals used in consumer goods, or contaminating our air and water, only a handful have undergone in-depth safety testing. Still, many Americans lack perspective on the relative danger levels of different technologies, experts agree. For example, some people perceive high-level nuclear waste as being comparable to radioisotopes used for biomedical research.

Some lawyers, businesspeople, and scholars see an insidious bias toward safety in the law. To the extent that risk perceptions are exaggerated, they say, fear complicates and slows the introduction of new technologies and increases costs for thousands of consumer products and services. According to Peter Huber, author of *The Legal Revolution and Its Consequences*, "safety taxes" to protect manufacturers from losses due to increasingly common liability lawsuits make up 30 percent of the price of a stepladder and add $300 to the cost of childbirth in New York City. In 1988 a federal appeals court awarded more than $200,000 to five people for "cancerphobia"—fear of contracting cancer from industry-contaminated drinking water.

But are public fears as extreme or irrational as government, corporate, and scientific officials sometimes suggest? Of course, the world has always been a dangerous place. Natural disasters such as earthquakes and hurricanes are arguably less threatening in modern societies than ever before. And even some technology-derived hazards, such as industrial accidents and some kinds of pollution, have been greatly reduced through improved engineering. Yet the tools of modern science continually reveal new details about hazards that years, months, even weeks before had been unknown. The more danger we look for the more we find. Pollutants once thought to have been completely contained are now measured in the environment or human tissue in parts per billion or per trillion. Computer terminals have recently been found to leak potentially hazardous electromagnetic fields. Yet scientists and regulators argue back and forth about whether minute quantities of toxic chemicals or electromagnetic emissions are actually harmful.

Moreover, since the late 1970s people have come to recognize many modern hazards as different in magnitude and character from those of the past. Atomic weapons and the unearthly longevity of high-level nuclear waste; accidents or miscalculations with genetically altered microbes; ozone depletion; and ubiquitous contamination from thousands of synthetic chemicals, oil spills, and acid rain all pose risks that are latent, filled with uncertainty, and possibly irreversible and more catastrophic than anything humankind has previously wrought. Moreover, the breakneck pace of technological change infuses new hazards throughout society almost as soon as they are created.

──────── ಐಐಐ ────────

Government Control

People do, however, tend to generalize realistic fear of extreme hazards to relatively benign or well-administered technologies. This nondiscriminating fear can be explained, in part, by the alienation felt by the general public from the process of scientific and technical creation, and by the alienation of scientists themselves from the goals and products of their own work. The evolving administration of American scientific research during the postwar era describes how these conditions emerged.

The towering role of the federal government in research began when thousands of scientists and engineers put aside their traditional distrust of government interference during the Second World War to join a variety of urgent projects. These included the Manhattan Project to build the atom bomb, and work on antibiotics and radar—all successful efforts that elevated the prestige and public profile of the scientific community. After the war many scientists were enthusiastic about continuing the flow of federal funds, and the question of how such a relationship could be effectively forged was high on the governmental agenda.

A panel of scientists headed by Vannevar Bush, President Franklin Roosevelt's chief science advisor, tendered the central argument in that debate. Its 1945 report, *Science—The Endless Frontier,* proposed general conditions under which scientists would be willing to work more closely with government in the postwar era. Bush argued for a secure funding base for the scientific community along with the political independence to set its own research agenda without overbearing government interference. Any agency designed to disperse funds would ultimately be under the control of Congress and the president, but Bush insisted that universities and other research institutions retain "internal control of policy, personnel, and the method and scope of the research." Unlike other endeavors,

Bush argued, science could only be vital and successful if its practitioners were self-directed.

Considerable initial opposition formed against this proposition, from those who saw it as leading to a dangerous concentration of power derived from public funds without accountability to society. But in 1950, the government formed the National Science Foundation to disburse funds largely on the basis of Bush's suggestions. Funding trends reflected this shift in policy. From 1940 to 1960, the federal government's share of funding for all scientific research conducted in this country rose from 19 percent to 57 percent (with most of the balance coming from private industry).

As public funding of scientific research increased, however, calls for more public control over researchers and their decisions began anew. One important manifestation of this concern was the push in the 1950s and 1960s for government-funded scientists to find practical uses for their work more rapidly. This battle centered on the Department of Defense (DOD), which had long been the dominant user of federal research funds. (By 1986 DOD absorbed 72 percent of federal research and development funds. Development refers to the practical applications of research findings, short of actual production.)

The largest military research agency, the Office of Naval Research (ONR), was formed just after the Second World War in order to increase the "general fund of scientific knowledge." Scientists consider *basic* research, the intellectual focus of most university labs, to be "value free." It rarely has immediately foreseeable applications. ONR's founders, like Vannevar Bush, believed that a general program of basic research would best serve long-term military needs as well as preserve the military's reserve of intellectual capital. But pressing problems of the Korean War in the early to mid-1950s prompted ONR to add a major *applied* research program. With this came a gradual yet sweeping shift away from DOD's liberal attitude toward basic research. Competition with the Soviets stimulated new policies designed to focus defense research on identifiable problems even more closely. "In contrast to the early postwar era, when unsolicited proposals were judged simply on scientific merit," notes Stanton Glantz, an authority on military research funding, "proposals now had both to pass a scientific test and to fit into the military's research plan." This second tier of review solidified the commitment to targeting even so-called basic research.

This system of research support worked fairly smoothly until the late 1960s, when anti-Vietnam War activism renewed public attention to DOD's presence on university campuses. Senators J. William Fulbright and Mike Mansfield began to see the sheer magnitude of military research spending as an unhealthy influence on nonmilitary scientific pursuits. Academia was growing too dependent on defense contracts, they argued. Meanwhile, the escalating war had become an increasingly expensive proposition, and Congress faced a budget shortfall. To reign in DOD's jurisdiction and to hold down government spending, the senators promoted new restrictions on military research that were attached to the 1969 military budget authorization. The Mansfield Amendment, as those restrictions became known, forbade spending on "any research project or study [that lacks] a direct and apparent relationship to a military function or operation."

Ironically, the amendment had little concrete impact on Pentagon spending because the kind of targeting that had gained ascendancy during the previous 15 years had already brought the bulk of DOD-funded research into line with Mansfield's intent. But the amendment threatened to have a profound effect on researchers' attitudes. By 1969, on campuses around the country, "opponents of DOD projects argued, on political and moral grounds, that individual responsibility required scientists to take a moral stand against U.S. policy in Indochina by refusing to work on such projects," Glantz and physicist Norman Albers wrote in *Science* magazine. "Backers of DOD projects argued that the DOD supported projects solely on their scientific merits and that investigators . . . were simply engaged in an unbiased search for scientific truth which happened to be funded by the DOD."

In 1971 Glantz, Albers, and several colleagues studied this debate at Stanford University, a major military contractor. At Stanford, where defense contracts provided a majority of funding in some fields, DOD goals decidedly influenced overall research directions. In many cases, however, the Pentagon's goals for the work differed greatly from those envisioned by individual researchers. This disparity in perspectives arose because DOD intentionally excused researchers from the obligation to define personally the military applications of their work on contract forms. This effectively shielded university scientists from directly confronting the philosophical and moral questions associated with their work.

In her ground-breaking book, *A Fragile Power: Scientists and the State,* University of California sociologist Chandra Mukerji explains that by and large, university scientists depend on soft-money government grants or contracts. She calls them an "elite reserve labor force" of the state.

Few scientists view this dependence as a corrupting influence. Indeed, most academic scientists design and conduct their studies free of direct or continuous oversight by the government, and see this as a sign of their autonomy. The peer-review system, in which respected scientists judge their colleagues' research proposals and recommend funding for the most worthy among them, preserves scientific merit and integrity. Agencies presumably award grants on the basis of science, not politics.

"The sense of control over their *intellectual* lives is perhaps what makes soft-money scientists so adamant in insisting that the government gives them money for research and leaves them almost entirely alone to pursue their work," Mukerji writes. "Designing their own research proposals may [be] a valued right to scientists, but it is hardly the same as being able to set one's own research agenda, when so many proposed projects are not funded," she adds. The vast majority of scientists hustle for money. Most of those who survive have learned to adjust their research interests into favored directions. Influence over the broad programmatic directions of science remains inaccessible to all but a small group of the most respected and politically active scientists.

"[Soft-money researchers] have not examined carefully how basic research done for purely scientific purposes could fit government needs," Mukerji says. DOD's goals for its Stanford contractors are a case in point. And government-funded scientists tend to overlook their general contributions to the state. These include serving as advisors and, most importantly, honing strategic technologies and expertise to the highest level, for use by the state in emergencies (such as during wartime) or routinely (such as determining where to dispose of radioactive waste). Yet scientists do not see themselves playing a political role, per se.

"Having scientists believe in the ideal of scientific autonomy and try to realize it in their labs has made them better advisors in two ways," according to Mukerji. "[They are] more politically disengaged and more creditable as detached advisors. . . . That is why the push by scientists for intellectual control of their labs and long-term control of their research agendas through peer review has not been opposed by the state—just limited by it," she argues. "The state has as much interest in this 'purity' as scientists themselves."

Evidence that the public is increasingly prone to irrational fears about the course of science and technology takes on a new tint when it becomes clear that vast numbers of academic scientists themselves are detached, by circumstance or design, from the long-term views of those who finance their work.

The Fight over Checks and Balances

Doubts about who controls research and development form part of a more general tension between the corporate, scientific, and government managers who seek efficient promotion and exploitation of science and technology (whether for high-minded goals or profits), and those who want to open scientific and technological development to broader public involvement.

This tension has led to attacks on other basic assumptions of the scientific community. Biophysicist Robert Sinsheimer, formerly chancellor at the University of California at Santa Cruz, has pointed out that in the 1930s, when a prescient physicist suggested that atomic research could lead to weapons of mass destruction, the prospect was dismissed out of hand by many leading scientists. Sinsheimer links this episode to the "Galilean imperative"—the need to "unravel every mystery, penetrate every unknown, explain every process. Consider not the cost, abide no interference, in the holy pursuit of truth."

J. Robert Oppenheimer, who directed wartime development of the atomic bomb, revealed the power of this imperative in comments about building a much more powerful hydrogen bomb. Oppenheimer opposed the H-bomb on moral and practical grounds—such a horrendous device hardly seemed necessary in light of the destructive power already in hand. And he doubted the project's technical feasibility. Yet, when the bomb was built without his help, Oppenheimer acknowledged: "When you see something that is technically sweet, you go ahead and do it and you argue about what to do about it only after you have had your technical success."

Oppenheimer's comment shows poignantly that the scientific community has devised excellent ways to evaluate technical merit, but neither scientists nor society as a whole have developed parallel means of judging social worth or advisability. Scientific questions are readily answered. But methods to reconcile conflicting values that arise around technological choices lag behind.

Social upheaval during the Vietnam War era—amid signs of environmental degradation—prompted new questions about the conduct and philosophical foundations of science, and generated demands for greater public participation in decisions about science and technology. One important manifestation of these demands was a far-reaching debate over the use of human subjects in research. In the 1960s examples of gross abuse of prisoners, children, and the poor were exposed, leading to the development of stringent federal guidelines to protect subjects' rights. (While university researchers were implicated in some cases, CIA and DOD committed many of the worst abuses in "mind-control" experiments that came to light in the 1970s.)

During the 1970s government oversight of scientific research mounted steadily. Many scientists viewed the growing bureaucracy surrounding grant applications, maintenance of lab safety, and environmental impact statements, combined with seemingly endless legislative reviews of the ethical and practical applications of scientific research, as a frightening turn against intellectualism. "Freedom of inquiry is being stifled . . . because of nameless fears always directed to what is new and bold," as Harvard ethicist Sissela Bok described that view. Regulation can certainly waterlog important work in a sea of procedures. "Paradoxically, it can then allow genuine abuses to slip by unnoticed in the flood of paperwork required and minute rules to be followed," Bok added.

A 1967 study by a blue-ribbon committee from the National Academy of Sciences—the nation's premier scientific society—made it clear that scientists felt their prerogatives were being trampled. While agreeing that the scientific community should increase the direct social relevance of research and technology, it warned against diluting scientists' control over their work. "Real dangers are involved," the report notes, "when the nonscientist attempts to impose his own value system on what should be largely scientific decisions." In this vein, genetic-research pioneer David Baltimore described efforts to establish a review commission on recombinant DNA research as a battle between "free inquiry" and "the fist of orthodoxy."

In response to (and in an effort to moderate) demands by the popular social movements of the 1960s for curbs on technology's side effects, the federal government established wide-ranging mechanisms to attack pollution as well as occupational and consumer hazards. The most important and controversial new federal agencies were EPA, which issued hundreds of rules covering air and water quality, and the Occupational Safety and Health Administration (OSHA). (Although designed for industry, the new regulatory structures imposed many indirect restrictions on the conduct of research. This deeply troubled scientists, who saw the regulations as ill-suited for and unduly constraining of laboratory research.) By establishing these social regulations, Dickson observes, "the government was implicitly endorsing the legitimacy of public demands for direct social control over the way science was produced and applied."

Corporate America resisted each new environmental rule with protracted political and legal struggles, warning of wholesale bankruptcy if industry submitted to dubious protections that were not well founded scientifically. As the costs of most regulations proved only a fraction of these dire predictions, continued industry resistance signaled the larger stakes of strong social regulation. Just as broad research directions had come under the general sway of the government through the funding apparatus, the regulatory regime "threatened to significantly shift the balance of power over technological decision-making into the hands of the state," Dickson points out.

Regulatory zeal held sway until the late 1970s, when a more placid social environment, combined with an economic downturn, created conditions for an effective backlash against social regulation. In the name of increasing industrial "competitiveness" and preserving jobs, the regulatory edifice of the 1970s was largely dismantled. Although President Carter initiated "regulatory reform," the Reagan administration's crusading ideological opposition to agencies such as EPA and OSHA sped the process despite substantial evidence that most Americans supported even more stringent environmental controls. In addition to easing enforcement, Reagan effectively gutted the regulatory agencies' ability to promulgate new rules. The administration slashed EPA's research budget—the bureaucratic equivalent of a lobotomy. It also scrapped the requirement that federal agencies consider the worst-case environmental consequences of their actions. Regulators were directed to review low-probability effects of pollutants or new technologies only when they were "reasonably foreseeable" and based on "credible evidence."

With these changes, the Reagan administration sharply boosted funding for research and development, much to the delight of the scientific community, which had initially viewed Reagan with fear and loathing. Most of the increase was allocated to the military, however, connecting the dots of the administration's agenda: Science and technology priorities would be based more than ever on military strength and stable corporate profits. Social relevance, health, environmental, and ethical concerns would be addressed only to the extent that they did not interfere with these primary goals. As this bias became apparent, it contributed to growing public distrust for technology's managers.

The Basis of a Technological Culture

The concentration of power over science and technology in the hands of military and corporate elites—while a political phenomenon—was made possible by cultural norms established over hundreds of years. Among science's many founders and great thinkers, few articulated the emerging scientific worldview as well as Sir Francis Bacon; philosopher, scientist, and literary figure of seventeenth-century England. Bacon contributed the idea that unbiased observation and experimentation are the most accurate measures of reality. His promotion of empiricism, of inductive logic as a means of discovering universal natural laws, combined with his conviction that scientific research should have useful applications, marked a turning point away from the more expansive metaphysical approach—based largely on the marriage of religious faith and reason—that had dominated scientific thinking for centuries. Bacon's impact on the conduct of science has stood the test of time.

His vision of a technological utopia in *The New Atlantis*—describing humanity's benevolent control of nature—is an inspiration to today's technological optimists.

U.S. scientists, industry, and, indeed, our broader culture gradually adopted this linear, circumscribed, pragmatic approach to science promoted by Bacon and other British empiricists, and for understandable reasons: "The metaphysical inadequacy of science is . . . simply the price it pays for its wide acceptance," notes Robert Morrison, a biologist and ethicist. "Whatever else it may be, science is necessarily a social consensual activity, and its vision of the world, precisely because it is limited, is one that can be widely shared. Indeed, it *must* be shared, since its very validity resides in [its] reproducibility."

Science certainly depends on objective observation and reporting. Atomic structure can be watched and manipulated, chemical reactions measured, diseases studied and cured. In the service of clearly defined technical questions or problems, scientific experimentation and the knowledge it generates can be "value free." In the real world the assumptions, goals, and biases of scientists and their sponsors carry compelling practical implications. The same scientific structures and methods can lead to atomic bombs or atomic clocks, Napalm or plastic wrap, the cure for polio or biological weapons.

"There is a way to *feel* and *behave* objectively, even if one cannot *know* objectively," says Theodore Roszak, a critic of the scientific worldview. "Indeed, the capacity of people to depersonalize their conduct—and to do so in good conscience, even with pride—is the distinctive psychic disease of our age. . . ." Roszak's views may be considered hyperbolic, but the idea that the *general course* of science is based on incorruptible objectivity still enjoys wide acceptance, particularly among scientists. Many people tacitly accept the implicit extension of this idea—that knowledge based on empiricism is inherently progressive, and more accurate than knowledge based on qualitative personal history, culture, art, or spirtuality. As Jerome Wiesner, formerly presidential science advisor and president of the

Massachusetts Institute of Technology, has commented, "the only way you learn is through experimentation."

Historian David Noble argues that the cloak of rational disinterest obscures scientists' conflicts of interest (such as widespread ties to the commerical exploitation of their discoveries) to a degree that would be intolerable if applied to corporate, union, or political officials. "[The scientific] community has, for all intents and purposes, immunized itself from normal public scrutiny," he says. "So long as a scientist does not officially work for a company or government agency . . . he can rest assured that his stance of neutrality and objectivity will never be questioned by the lay public."

The conflict between the idea of objectivity and evidence that science has been steered to serve the interests of industry and the military has greatly hampered effective democratic participation in decisions about science and technology. As both explicit and subliminal recognition of this contradiction grow, more Americans feel alienated from science and technology. The rising anxiety that technology is out of anyone's control is an illusion. Corporations or military officials, who do not always consider public health and safety the highest priority, simply hold the greatest degree of control.

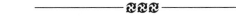

Ultraspecialization and Scientific Literacy

Today's manifestation of the Baconian ideal has also compartmentalized learning. Ever-accelerating scientific specialization has produced an unprecedented explosion of esoteric knowledge. "As with mass production technology, 'efficiency' comes to mean atomizing the project, restricting the focus of attention, and then driving one's labors on to a fever pitch of intensity," says Roszak. "But those who are not part of this expanding universe of expertise live on the margins of contemporary culture. They know technology saves their lives; they know that (somehow) science validates technology. But they watch these grandly consequential activities like spectators at an incomprehensible performance; perhaps like untutored peasants witnessing the mystery of the Catholic Mass. . . . The result is that the public appreciation of science grows ever more vicarious."

In response, every year scientists and government officials sound new and more urgent alarms about the problem of "scientific illiteracy" and its effect on the nation's future. Jon Miller, a researcher on the subject, estimates that only 6 percent of American adults meet "a minimal definition of scientific literacy"—enough understanding of scientific methods and vocabulary, as well as the impact of science on society, "to function effectively in citizenship and consumer roles." Notwithstanding the proliferation of scientific knowledge, our system of general science education is in a shambles. In standardized tests, American students routinely score below students from other developed nations, and even from some developing nations. A recent political cartoon showed children exhibiting inventions at an "international science fair." The Korean and Japanese displays were linear acceleration and gene-splicing. The U.S. entry: an ant farm.

A recent National Science Foundation poll found that 28 percent of American adults do not know that the earth rotates around the sun; 63 percent believe that antibiotics kill viruses as well as bacteria. Further, most Americans comprehend little about the controversies surrounding acid rain, recombinant DNA, the MX missile, and myriad other pressing technical questions. This mirrors the general decline of U.S. public education and the erosion of critical thinking and public understanding of world events. (Consider, for example, that after years of war in Nicaragua, pitched battles in Congress over funding rebel forces there, and almost daily newspaper headlines describing the conflict, less than one-third of Americans understood which side the U.S. government supported.) Scientific ignorance surely contributes substantially to fear of technology, and to a lack of perspective on the relativity of risk.

Scientists, educators, corporations, and politicians, fearing that the next generation will be unable to cope with, let alone compete in, our infinitely complex world, have called for better education. Although important, education alone would do little to reduce public suspicion of science and technology. Ultraspecialization means that despite lip service paid to the cross-fertilization of scientific fields, experts in one subject are generally unqualified as authorities in any others. Meanwhile, major problems involving technology or its side effects usually require collaboration by many different experts who have little more than a basic grasp of each other's work. Decisions about how and where to dispose of toxic waste, for example, depend on the skills of geologists, biologists, epidemiologists, physicists, engineers, and a host of other experts. In isolation, each specialist would be helpless to navigate the complexities of waste disposal effectively. Mass scientific literacy—the *most* that education advocates can hope for—would by no means equip nonexperts to participate in or effectively evaluate a "neutral, scientific process" to decide how or where to place a hazardous-waste site. (Decision making based on esoteric knowledge is inherently undemocratic.) A higher level of technical understanding would, however, more likely lead to a familiarity that would boost acceptance of expert judgments.

Science education is no panacea because major decisions about science and technology are only partly technical. They are also political, social, and economic judgments for which scientists and engineers hold no special credentials. The panic to educate the public depoliticizes conflicts about science and technology. Disproportional emphasis on scientific literacy suggests that most people are not presently qualified to participate in decisions about our technological society. It reinforces the dominance of scientific values and technical solutions. Says Roszak: "Where everything—*everything*—has been staked out as somebody's specialized field of knowledge, what is the thinking of ordinary people worth? Precisely zero."

———————— ෨෨෨ ————————

The Burden of Proof

For refusing to accept technical change as an irresistible prerogative of industry, society consigned the Luddites to the status of historical pariahs. Today's "mindless opposition" to modern technology and the dominant, technocratic view of its uses is similarly derided. "To be taken seriously, to be listened to (or even to be heard), one [has] now to demonstrate allegiance to technological progress, wherever it [leads]," says David Noble. "To violate this taboo [means] instantly to lose intellectual credibility."

Wiesner epitomizes this dominant perspective, suggesting that current conditions were somehow established and continued by mutual consent. "When Americans decided to have a technologically based industrial society, we were—without realizing it—making a decision to have a society that must continuously evolve at a rapid rate," he says. "There is no reasonable way of turning back to simpler days. Having committed ourselves to this style of society and having become accustomed to the level of affluence and life that goes with it, we're not prepared to turn around and go back to a totally different lifestyle"—presumably the Stone Age.

Still, the shop floors of American industry have greeted the wave of automation since the 1950s with considerable protest, including sabotage. In a well-known 1975 case, press workers at the *Washington Post,* who feared that their jobs would be eliminated by the introduction of computerized typesetting, systematically destroyed the *Post*'s entire press works. But as a modern tactic, sabotage has failed dismally. This is partly because union leaders, although they have attempted to preserve jobs, have shown little inclination to confront management control over the introduction of new technologies, even as their own organizations had been decimated by job displacement. In fact, union officials have often labeled the militant rank and file "Luddites" to discredit them and reassert control. The *Washington Post* press worker's union president called his members' action "temporary insanity," although the attack was sophisticated and obviously well planned.

Noble recounts an insight about modern machine breaking that a United Technologies plant manager offered to two researchers: "The workers out there don't think like you guys do. They don't see any inexorable technology. Survival is the thing." In this way, modern industrial saboteurs are no more antitechnology than were the Luddites. They merely want to slow down the introduction and growth of new technology long enough to review whose interest it serves. They want the right, Noble says, "to participate in the decision-making and thereby steer progress in a more humane direction."

Such efforts stand little chance of success without a shift in the burden of proof from the opponents of the technological imperative to its promoters. The burden of proof regarding workplace automation has moved little in recent years. Not so at the community level. Why has local obstructionism become a powerful influence on technological decision making, and why only during the last 15 years? The new conditions described earlier have pushed local communities beyond the limits of trust or tolerance: People have begun to recognize, with growing cynicism, that leaders and regulators have done little to contain the rapid proliferation of technological perils that are often different in kind and degree from past dangers. The public sees that military and corporate elites dominate decisions about technological change, while scientists themselves may have little influence over the broad applications of their work. Meanwhile, average citizens grow ever more removed from genuine comprehension of scientific developments. Amid growing public concern regarding environmental safety, political choices about potential scientific or industrial hazards are increasingly described as technical questions that only experts can answer. These conditions have partially shifted the burden of proof about the safety and wisdom of the scientific and technological enterprise from local communities to managers and owners. The prospect of successfully challenging the exclusive control of technological change by corporate, military, and government officials has gradually emerged.

The main function of "traditional political institutions of liberal democracy," notes Dickson, "has been to balance different political interests in a way that provides a stable environment for the growth and dissemination of technology as a tool for generating wealth and, ultimately, power." To the extent that those institutions—corporations, government, labor unions, and even environmental groups—have failed to contain the destabilizing ecological and social side effects of technology, they have fostered a noninstitutional, even anti-institutional response: *ad hoc,* grass-roots, locally based organizations often referred to as Nimby groups.

3
The Rocky Flats Radiation War

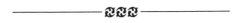

The plutonium industry is really safer than it was 15 years ago, and in five years it will be safer still. The production of plutonium involves a multiplicity of dangers; the public should be made aware of them and demand that the industry invent and apply ever better safeguards. —Donald E. Michels, Rocky Flats Nuclear Plant Official, 1972

Donald Gabel looks wearily up from the screen in the documentary film *Dark Circle.* He speaks sluggishly, with evident difficulty. Two years earlier, he was handsome and robust. In the 1980 footage, taken six months before a brain tumor killed him at age 31, Gabel's hair is almost gone, his face puffy and ghostlike. A deep surgical indentation marks the right side of his head. Gabel spent nearly 10 years as a technician at the Rocky Flats Nuclear Plant, a U.S. Department of Energy (DOE) nuclear-weapons production facility 16 miles northwest of Denver. He worked around large quantities of highly radioactive, cancer-causing materials, and during numerous accidents he was exposed to radiation, but never above levels DOE considered safe.

An autopsy revealed the presence of plutonium—a highly toxic, radioactive metal—in his ribs, liver, lymph nodes, and lungs. DOE researchers removed Gabel's brain for testing shortly after his death. But the brain was lost before it was tested. A radioactive pipe that Gabel worked near every day and that he believed caused his cancer was removed before it could be checked independently. Still, circumstantial evidence was strong enough that in 1985, a Workers Compensation officer ruled that Gabel was killed by plutonium poisoning. It was one of the first times that radiation was officially deemed to cause cancer at levels below accepted government standards.

Downwind of Rocky Flats, ranchers and suburbanites tell stories of children, parents, friends, and neighbors dying from one cancer after another. Livestock and poultry have been born dead or with grotesque malformations—no eyes, brains outside their heads, misshapen limbs. A few neighbors of the plant tested the animals or their own tumors and in some cases plutonium was detected. But scientists cannot point with certainty to a cause; no accepted epidemiological studies have been conducted.

Susan Hurst took a deep pull on her cigarette before speaking. She thought back 20 years to 1969, when she was a senior in high school in Arvada, a suburb northwest of Denver. "I regularly used to go out picnicking and swimming at Leyden Lake—about as close as you can get to that place without getting into the buffer zone." Back then, Rocky Flats was just another big factory to Hurst. She and her rebellious friends used its off-site radiation-monitoring boxes for target practice during their jaunts to the lake. Hurst didn't know that she was pregnant that warm spring. And she didn't even take notice when in May of that year, Rocky Flats suffered one of the largest fires in American industrial history.

A few months later, after Hurst had moved to California, her baby girl was born. "She couldn't keep up her body temperature and didn't have a sucking reflex," Hurst recalls, now more in anger than sorrow. "After more tests, they found out that she was missing parts of her brain. It took her three weeks to die." The doctors, Hurst adds, asked her over and over where she had spent her first trimester. Did she live in a heavily industrialized area? "All I knew was that they made Coors beer where I come from."

Hurst firmly believes that radioactive fallout from Rocky Flats killed her child. No one will ever know for sure.

The Bomb Makers

Rolling ranch land dotted by clumps of pine trees lines the road to Rocky Flats. In contrast to the scenic foothills of the Rocky Mountains that rise just over the next ridge, the plant is a nondescript mass of mostly windowless, aging industrial buildings, known by numbers, not names. Just inside the main gate, a huge safety-first billboard is followed by one that reads "National Security: Our Responsibility"—a deadly serious message. Rocky Flats is one of the nation's most closely guarded facilities. Coiled barbed wire tops each of two wire-mesh fences that surround the plutonium-processing buildings, about half the plant's area. Four guard towers, reminiscent of a high-security prison, loom overhead. Paramilitary security guards patrol the periphery in armored vehicles with mounted automatic weapons. The 250-member security force includes a SWAT team and is equipped with antiaircraft guns. Security means secrecy. Historically, plant managers have shielded all aspects of Rocky Flats operations as closely as the security guards watch its physical structures. So like Hurst, most people in the land of Coors beer knew little about Rocky Flats in its early years.

When the government announced in 1951 that a $45 million atomic plant would be built locally, Denver welcomed the economic windfall. (The plant has grown from 200 workers in 1951 to more than 5,000 today, from 20 buildings to more than 100.) Initially, Dow Chemical Company ran Rocky Flats under contract with the U.S. Atomic Energy Commission (AEC). In 1975 Rockwell International replaced Dow; AEC was replaced by the Energy Research and Development Administration, which was superseded by DOE two years later. Today, Rocky Flats is part of a 17-plant complex that designs, builds, modifies, or retires up to 4,000 warheads each year. Although the details are top secret, Rocky Flats's unique and essential role involves shaping plutonium produced at other weapons plants into smooth, softball-sized "pits," which form the core of bomb "triggers." These triggers, themselves small atomic bombs, detonate within the larger bomb assembly. In a fraction of a second they generate heat comparable to that found inside the sun, beginning the chain-reaction explosion of the bomb's main hydrogen charge. The plant also recycles plutonium from obsolete warheads, using acids or high-voltage electrical currents to strip the metal from other materials and to purify it.

Up to four tons of silvery-white plutonium normally cycle through Rocky Flats each year. Plutonium primarily emits radioactive alpha particles, which do not penetrate skin. If plutonium enters the body through inhalation or wounds, however, gram for gram it is one of the most toxic substances on earth. Scientists disagree about whether there is any "safe" dose of plutonium. Certainly one millionth of a gram, and possibly as little as 31 *billionths* of a gram, can cause cancer or chromosomal mutations.

Once inside the body, plutonium continuously bombards neighboring cells with intense radiation. With a half-life—the time it takes to lose half of its radioactivity—of about 24,000 years, plutonium 239 (the primary isotope used in weapons production) remains deadly for more than 250,000 years. Scientists do not know how to deactivate or destroy it, except by this slow decay.

Because of its toxicity, plutonium must be handled through highly automated, lead-lined glove boxes. Because plutonium ignites spontaneously on contact with moist air, these boxes are filled with inert gases. Rocky Flats uses state-of-the-art ventilation and filtration systems, and remote-control devices for keeping plutonium and other toxic substances away from its workers and the environment.

———————— ☙☙☙ ————————

Spontaneous Combustion

On 11 September 1957 Rocky Flats experienced its first major fire. In stories buried in the back pages of the *Denver Post* and *Rocky Mountain News*, AEC officials said that "no spread of radioactive contamination of any consequence" occurred, that no one was injured or contaminated on or off the plant site. In the political climate of the 1950s, these reassurances were enough.

In the late 1970s, however, partially censored information was released in response to a lawsuit filed by local landowners. A report by the landowners' attorney, Howard Holme, indicated that the fire erupted spontaneously at about 10 A.M. in Building 71, a primary production facility. It may have been caused by air entering a leaky glove box and igniting the plutonium inside. Soon after, an explosion ripped through the building's ventilation system, which burned all night and destroyed the paper HEPA (high-efficiency particulate aerosol) filters, which had not been cleaned for four years. "I looked up at the stack and a column of smoke 80 to 100 feet high was coming from it and it was very dark in color," reported the shift captain.

Despite gross contamination of the building and the absence of filters to hold back plutonium from the environment, limited production resumed two days later at Rocky Flats in order to meet a deadline. Because stack radiation monitors had been melted and destroyed, plant managers could not read radiation levels until a week later. They said 30 pounds of plutonium (enough for about three nuclear weapons) burned, while some critics estimated the figure at 10 times that amount. Rocky Flats steadfastly maintained that only a trivial amount of plutonium escaped into the environment, yet the first day the monitors were back in place, emissions exceeded federal standards by a factor of 16,000—the equivalent of a 50-year release in a single day. No one was warned about the event—and some scientists believed nearby ranches and schools were grossly contaminated.

On 11 May 1969 Rocky Flats experienced another major fire. The $45 million blaze sent at least 2,200 pounds of plutonium up in smoke, enough for 220 warheads. Production halted for six months to allow cleanup—the closest the nation had ever come to a unilateral nuclear freeze. Although the 1969 fire also burned through the HEPA filters, Rocky Flats officials insisted again that little or no plutonium was released.

Since it was founded, the Rocky Flats Plant has experienced hundreds of smaller fires and accidents that contaminated workers and released radioactivity. One of its worst problems has been haphazard waste management. From 1954 to 1968, uranium-laden oil was burned in open pits, and thousands of barrels of toxic solvents laced with plutonium were dumped on a hillside, gradually leaking into the water table; samples at some locations registered 1,000 times the safe drinking-water limit for solvents in 1988. Independent scientists, including Edward Martell, a plutonium expert at the National Center for Atmospheric Research in Boulder, said their own measurements showed contamination of local soil hundreds of times higher than natural background radiation levels.

After 1969 some Denver-area residents began to view Rocky Flats with suspicion. But initially there was little organized opposition. Politicians expressed patriotic resignation. "If you've got to have nuclear devices," then-Colorado Governor John Love concluded in 1969, "you might as well have the work done here as any place else."

———————— ଧଧଧ ————————

The Carl Johnson Findings

In December 1974 Carl Johnson, health department director for Jefferson County, which includes Rocky Flats, was asked by a county commissioner to investigate the soil of a proposed housing development two and one-half miles east of the plant. Was the soil hazard-free, as plant managers claimed, or a latent killer, as a growing body of independent scientists feared? Johnson embarked on a series of studies that would make him a folk hero among the plant's critics and an irresponsible fear-monger among its supporters. He sampled area soils for plutonium contamination and conducted the first epidemiological studies designed to determine whether neighbors of Rocky Flats had suffered ill effects from the plant. His answer: terrible effects.

According to Johnson, Rocky Flats had been causing downwind cancer rates to jump in a pattern wholly consistent with soil contamination, which he measured at up to 380 times background at off-site locations. He found leukemia deaths among Jefferson County children to be below the national average in the years before Rocky Flats opened, above the national average shortly after the plant opened, and twice the national average in the years following the 1957 fire. Moreover, Johnson claimed that the incidence of several kinds of adult cancers was abnormally high just outside the plant's downwind boundaries, gradually dropping as he checked farther away. Some of these conclusions were published in leading peer-reviewed journals. The media, politicians, and members of the community began to voice serious concerns about the plant.

Johnson's findings were criticized by Rocky Flats managers and other scientists, however. They questioned his soil-analysis methods and attacked his studies for failing to assess the impact of urbanization on overall cancer rates. In 1981 Johnson was dismissed as county health director. But after his studies, Denver would never again ignore Rocky Flats.

———————————— ଔଔଔ ————————————

The Rocky Flats Mall

Only three things matter in real estate, the saying goes, location, location, and location. In 1951 the windswept plain 16 miles northwest of Denver had all that and more. An Atomic Energy Commission site-selection team chose Rocky Flats over dozens of other areas for development as a bomb factory. Close to outdoor recreation, Denver services, and Boulder (University of Colorado) scientific talent, the land was cheap, sparsely populated, and used for grazing only.

AEC checked the winds at Stapleton Airport, just northeast of Denver, which showed most currents coming from the south. That was the first mistake. At the plant site, prevailing winds—including the periodic Chinooks that can blow with gale force—rush down the eastern slope of the Rockies from the north and northwest, directly toward Denver. For its second mistake, AEC failed to consider that others would also find the site appealing. By 1970 Jefferson County was the 13th fastest-growing county in the United States; Boulder County, just north of the plant, was 25th. By 1987 Denver had become a major commercial hub, tripling the region's 1952 population to nearly two million. Arvada, directly downwind from the plant, grew from a sleepy town of 3,600 in 1971 to 97,000 in 1987. Rocky Flats is closer to a large population than any other DOE weapons installation. By comparison, the greater Denver metropolitan area could be dropped into the grounds of another DOE weapons plant, the Idaho National Engineering Laboratory, yet leave hundreds of square miles to spare.

With Johnson's early warnings fresh in mind, landowners near Rocky Flats filed three lawsuits against Dow, Rockwell, and DOE in 1975 for a total of $23 million, claiming that plant fallout had rendered their land useless for improvement. While the suits traveled slowly through the courts, local and federal officials took a fresh look at development near Rocky Flats. In the mid-1970s a 6,166-acre environmental and security buffer zone was established as a permanent open space around the plant's 384-acre core. In 1978 the federal Housing and Urban Development Department (HUD) temporarily stopped processing subdivisions, mortgage insurance, and other housing assistance within a seven and one-half mile radius of Rocky Flats. In 1979, after repeated requests by the Environmental Protection Agency (EPA), HUD began to require that all home buyers purchasing federal mortgage insurance within a 10-mile radius of the plant be warned about plutonium contamination. "However, according to the information supplied by the Department of Energy, the soil contamination in the area in which your prospective residence is located is below the limits of the applicable radiation guidance," the HUD notice indicated dryly.

HUD also noted that the property was covered by the Colorado Radiological Emergency Response Plan. In 1980 the state distributed information on that plan to people within the 10-mile radius. The plan outlined emergency evacuation procedures for homes within four miles of the plant—a circle enclosing portions of Great Western Reservoir and Standley Lake, drinking-water sources for Denver's northwest suburbs. "Extensive safety precautions taken at Rocky Flats make the release of hazardous amounts of radioactive material extremely remote," the state's brochure reassured home buyers. It did not mention soil contamination or previous accidents. In 1981, HUD withdrew its own warning in favor of the state brochure. The state stopped giving out the brochure soon after. Subdivisions have crept closer to the plant ever since. On the farthest edge of Westminster, immediately downwind, many homes sport solar collectors. Standing on the roof next to their clean-energy generators, residents can almost hit the buffer zone with a stone.

The landowner suits were settled out of court in 1985 for about $10 million. The plant also agreed to reduce radioactivity on the properties to the Colorado standard for plutonium in soil, established in 1973. Acquisitive municipal officials and developers saw the settlement as a green light, getting the jump on less-organized critics of development.

In early 1985 the nearby town of Broomfield, which had acquired some of the land in question, announced a plan to build an 800-acre recreation area after Rockwell plowed the plutonium-tainted soil 10 inches under ("Public to Frolic on Plutonium," a newspaper headline noted.) In February 1987 Arvada approved annexation of land near the plant for development of homes and commercial enterprises within the four-mile evacuation zone. Then, tiny Superior, population 230, annexed and announced plans to develop a 1,570-acre tract just north and west of Rocky Flats. In a 1988 move that would more than double the town's size, Arvada proposed to annex a tract south and west of the plant, reaching the borders of the buffer zone. In 1989 the downwind city of Westminster topped them all, announcing that it was exploring annexation of the plant itself, should DOE ever vacate. ("Imagine a great subdivision: Rocky Flats Estates. . . . Ponder the possiblity of a fine shopping center: Rocky Flats Mall," a local paper suggested, only half in jest.)

Local officials and residents alike had incentive to brush aside doubts about the plant. With 6,000 workers and a yearly budget of half a billion dollars, the plant represented 1 percent of the state's manufacturing economy and created at least 6,000 subsidiary jobs. "People are very concerned about Rocky Flats pollution, but they're more concerned about their livelihood," said Westminster resident and plant critic Glenna Smith. "The economic argument has absolutely brainwashed a lot of people." (After the oil bust of the mid-1980s, Colorado's economy took a nosedive. Unemployment rose while property values plummeted, making the economic argument in favor of the plant more compelling than ever.)

In light of these factors, pacifists, rather than the immediate downwinders, initiated opposition to Rocky Flats. (Back in the 1970s, one activist recalled, "It was unfashionable for ordinary citizens to be against the plant." Indeed, on occasion, plant supporters organized counterdemonstrations.) In 1974 peace activists formed the Rocky Flats Action Group. The coalition conducted a public-education campaign about the plant. They argued for conversion of Rocky Flats to peaceful uses. Because of the plant's central role in plutonium processing, (it receives plutonium from Washington State and South Carolina, then sends it to Texas for bomb assembly), Rocky Flats gradually became a focal point for the nation's growing antinuclear weapons movement. The high point of these organizing efforts came in 1982, when more than 20,000 people rallied at the state capital, demanding nuclear disarmament and Rocky Flats's dismantlement, and listening to singers Jimmy Buffett, Judy Collins, and John Denver. A year later, an estimated 17,000 protesters attempted to encircle the plant with linked arms. The effort fell short due to lack of organization, rather than bodies—some protesters were stacked three deep, unable to locate gaps in the human chain.

While this was the last of the big demonstrations, the protest movement pressured the media and politicians to take some initiative about plant hazards, and slowly problems came to light. In September 1984 millions of pounds of radioactive soil just outside the buffer zone was scraped up and sent to a Nevada dump. Rocky Flats officials discounted the hazard, but photos of shovel-wielding workers in antiradiation regalia did little for the plant's image. In 1985 then-Congressman Timothy Wirth revealed that Rockwell covered up design flaws in a new plutonium-recycling facility; corrections were predicted to cost $600 million. By 1986 politicians such as Ohio Senator John Glenn were calling Rocky Flats pollution and mismanagement a national scandal.

For local residents, drinking-water quality became a major concern. The plant sits directly on top of Walnut Creek, which feeds the Great Western Reservoir, and beside Woman Creek, which flows to Standley Lake. After concerns about water quality were first raised in the 1970s, Rocky Flats built a series of holding ponds that catch run-off from the plant so it can be tested for radioactivity or toxic chemicals. The ponds serve as a warning only, however. The plant still has no means of safely draining millions of gallons of water to prevent its eventual release. A series of well-publicized scares about increased plutonium contamination in the water in 1985 and 1986 left local residents jittery. Soon after, DOE provided a few details about how several areas of the plant were dangerously contaminated with plutonium, uranium, and deadly solvents.

In late 1986 highway officials proposed a new beltway to serve the sprawling metro area's commuters and to aid development. Proposed routes for W-470 were immediately south and east of Rocky Flats, directly through the highest soil concentrations of plutonium and americium, a highly toxic decay product of plutonium. Critics, including state health officials, said that the major construction effort would churn tons of dust into the air, resuspending radioactive particles in the process. High winds, which routinely force the closure of Highway 93 on the plant's western edge, would assure wide dispersal of dust. Highway officials had neglected to consult with the health department or Rocky Flats before proposing the route.

Then in January 1987 Rocky Flats announced plans to incinerate thousands of tons of mixed radioactive and chemical wastes in a "fluidized-bed" incinerator—a device that employs 1,000-degree Fahrenheit, smokeless, flameless chemical reactions. The technology was not new, but it had never been used on mixed waste. A test burn was scheduled for the coming spring. The community flared up immediately. Waste burning was hardly new; the notorious open-pit burning of uranium chips in the 1950s and 1960s was the most flagrantly hazardous episode. Yet this untested process, coming during a period of growing doubts about Rocky Flats's operations, sparked an unprecedented furor.

———————— ଝଝଝ ————————

Burning Issues

In Cherry Hills Village, just south of Denver, luxurious homes with spacious grounds, some surrounded by large fences and stately gates, private tennis courts, and stables grace tree-lined avenues. An unlikely setting for antinuclear activists. Yet this is the home of Jan Pilcher, a tall, red-haired woman in her early 40s who carries a commanding presence, speaks with authority, and has been a thorn in the side of Rocky Flats managers for more than a decade. She would never live much closer to the plant, Pilcher explains. Too dangerous.

In 1957, when Pilcher was nine, her family moved to Denver.

She lived on the city's western edge during the first major Rocky Flats fire. At that time, no one paid much attention to Rocky Flats—certainly not a child. During the height of the cold war, Pilcher went through weekly "duck and cover" drills at school. The city passed out evacuation maps; food stockpiles and bomb shelters were widely discussed. Her grandparents lived on the Utah–Nevada border, in the fallout zone for open-air bomb testing. Pilcher recalls being shaken awake by a blast during a visit there when she was very young. It may have been a fantasy; she's not sure.

After college, Pilcher traveled around the world. Partly because of her opposition to the U.S. war effort, in 1971 she worked as an assistant in Vietnamese hospitals and saw the effects of the war firsthand. When she returned home she ran across a series of articles that linked the atmospheric testing of nuclear weapons to higher rates of childhood leukemia. She developed an insatiable appetite for information on the health effects of radiation, fed by her alarm over a short-lived effort in the mid-1970s to use atomic bombs to harvest oil from shale on Colorado's western slope.

In 1976 Pilcher joined the Rocky Flats Action Group, becoming a mainstay in lobbying, public demonstrations, and educational events about the plant for about six years. Then she married, took on a public-relations job for the Colorado ski industry, and pulled back from activism. But she couldn't stay away for long. By 1985 Pilcher had quit her job and taken over full-time coordination of Rocky Flats activities at the local American Friends Service Committee, a hub for peace activists over the years. She developed a slide show on Rocky Flats, then used her PR experience to rekindle interest in the issue among local politicians and media, with increasing success. Pilcher called a meeting at the Arvada Performing Arts Center in January 1987 to discuss the W-470 beltway and the incinerator. Due to a sympathetic newspaper article, the meeting was packed with citizens and local officials. People were furious about the two plans, she recalled. Buoyed by the response, she worked with Westminster homemaker Joan Seeman to establish a new organization, Citizens Against Rocky Flats Contamination (CARFC), led largely by peace activists but based in the immediate downwind communities.

By this time, to many concerned citizens, the plant's problems seemed endless and mysterious. The fluidized-bed incinerator was an ideal issue to organize around, even though it was not the most critical health hazard. (Although when the incinerator issue came up, the plant disclosed for the first time that it had for decades burned highly contaminated waste as part of its plutonium-recovery process. A suit filed by the Sierra Club has since shut down that incinerator indefinitely.)

Nationwide, few technologies motivate opposition as does toxic-waste incineration. (At DOE's Lawrence Livermore facility in California, for example, a local group killed an incineration plan nearly identical to that proposed at Rocky Flats.) "Incinerators really move people out of their houses and into meeting halls," said Tom Bernard, director of Colorado Peacenet, an antinuclear group. "A lot of it has to do with perception." Burning mixed waste at Rocky Flats appealed to fears of two types of hazards—routine emissions of minute quantities of plutonium, and the possibility of a major accident, like those of 1957 and 1969. The technology was new and untested, yet well defined, straightforward enough to understand, and, perhaps most important, preventable. The issue attracted middle-income home owners who feared further deterioration of their already depressed property values, Pilcher explained. "That scares the plant, because those are its constituents."

Rockwell saw the fluidized-bed incinerator as a means of easing the waste-storage and transport problems that had haunted the plant for years. The incinerator would shrink tons of contaminated cloth, paper, plastic, oils, and solvents to a few pounds. Banks of sophisticated filters would ensure environmental safety. "Based on our calculations, if we burned 9 days a month, 24 hours a day, there would be 0.0000000008 additional millirems of exposure to the community," according to Rockwell spokesman Gene Towne.

After a briefing by plant officials, local Congressman David Skaggs, considered a critic of the plant, endorsed the incinerator. But CARFC pressed a wide range of technical objections. The group demanded to know if the health and environmental effects of mixed radioactive-hazardous waste incineration had been studied (they hadn't), and asked for a worse-case scenario for the incinerator in full-scale operation. "Because no such large-scale continuous incineration of hazardous radioactive wastes has been embarked upon before, Denver residents are . . . a test population for the long-term health effects of subtle, daily releases of radioactive contamination," a CARFC report concluded. ("You can't have both ends of the seesaw up," an exasperated Rockwell official responded. "[Critics] don't want [waste] on the plant site. They don't want it transported. What do they want?")

CARFC, the local Sierra Club, and later other groups moved quickly to mobilize the community against the test burn, slated for 16 May 1987. A turning point came in March, when at a meeting called by Skaggs, enraged neighbors shouted plant officials down.

New neighborhood groups formed quickly. "I'm all for national defense, but I don't want my children to get cancer in 20 years," said Kathy Watson, an organizer of the Blue Ribbon Brigade— families in Arvada and Westminster who wore sky-blue ribbons on their lapels as a symbol of the clean, fresh Colorado air they demanded. Before the controversy, "the only political thing I'd ever done was vote," a typical Brigade member said.

The Colorado Department of Health, which by law had to sign off on the incinerator before it could be operated, was deluged with 1,500 critical letters. CARFC gathered more than 18,000 signatures against the plan. Several city governments went on record as opposing the test burn. Governor Roy Romer had to assign several aides to answer 1,000 angry letters and review federal and state monitoring efforts. Small businesses soon jumped on the bandwagon.

Pilcher also pulled together a group of independent experts to evaluate technical documents about the incinerator. The Boulder Scientists, as they became known, gained wide attention from regulators and the press. They said that the incinerator posed major risks of explosion, and that Rocky Flats managers had no means of monitoring or controlling emissions of vapors or gases, such as uranium hexafluoride. (HEPA filters hold back only particulates.) Joe Goldfield, the group's process engineer, was among those who first developed HEPA technology during the Second World War. He warned that the system described could suffer catastrophic failures, and he questioned Rockwell's claims of virtually fail-safe performance standards for screening plutonium. "The equipment, the plan, the monitoring, and the documentation are so flawed and deficient, so threatening to public safety that the application is beyond expectation of remedy," the scientists concluded.

In late April 1987, Romer, Skaggs, and Denver Mayor Federico Pena all came out against the test burn until further public health studies could be conducted. Rocky Flats finally backed down, agreeing to delay the test until July 6. Skaggs formed his own scientific panel to review the plan. Those experts gave the plant its first good news by conferring their blessing on June 6. The same day, however, in a further blow to Rocky Flats's credibility, the Skaggs panel revealed that the plant had already used the incinerator nine times since 1978, and had burned 24 tons of waste, including unknown, possibly radioactive materials. Later that month CARFC and the Sierra Club filed suit to prevent the test burn as a violation of environmental laws, and Rocky Flats announced an indefinite delay of the test in order to prepare an environmental assessment.

Then in late October information was leaked to the press showing that during a routine July test using common fuel oil, the incinerator caught fire for 20 minutes. Four-to-six-foot flames breached a viewing window and spewed chemicals into a nearby room after a sprinkler system failed. Rocky Flats had previously described the fire as trivial. Although plant officials have never formally ruled out using the incinerator, the fire was its swan song; unremitting public opposition has effectively killed the project.

Since the early 1970s, Rocky Flats attracted a wide range of opponents—Republican to Communist, naive to expert, guileless to opportunist. Thanks in large measure to CARFC's organizing, anti-Rocky Flats forces used the incinerator to accomplish something that had eluded them for 15 years: They made the plant a mainstream issue. For the first time, thousands of conservative home owners in the immediate downwind areas saw Rocky Flats as the enemy and were starting to raise hell about it. More significantly, the incinerator episode ignited a new oppostion that would irrevocably alter the terms of the debate—Nimbys.

—————————— ෨෨෨ ——————————

New Insurgents

In the late 1970s, when Marlene Batley moved into a new tract home a few miles from Rocky Flats, she had no idea about plutonium in the soil. When she found out, she was frightened and angry. After talking with peace activists, she set out to alert her neighbors. But fear overcame her, and two years after moving in, Batley, her husband, and their two children left. In selling her home, she traveled a remorseful full circle. She did not mention a word about plutonium contamination to the young couple with two children who took her family's place. Fearful of seeing their homes become worthless, should stories of contamination become widely known, many neighbors put faith in DOE and Rockwell reassurances, or quietly sold out and left town. Several cycles of Batleys have passed through. But by the mid-1980s, the neighborhood was ripe for a change.

At least four workers who complained about safety and environmental problems at four military nuclear plants run for [DOE] by private contractors say they were ordered by their superiors to see psychiatrists or psychologists . . . [as] part of a long campaign of harassment. (August 1989)

By then, a constant stream of revelations about environmental catastrophes had been splashed across the front pages of nearly every newspaper: The government was shown to have exposed uranium miners and GIs who witnessed atomic blasts to unsafe levels of radiation in the 1940s, 1950s, and 1960s. Prisoners and terminally ill patients had been unwittingly used as human guinea pigs for Atomic Energy Commission radiation experiments. Meanwhile, every few years top scientific experts lower the threshold for "permissible" exposure to radiation.

Near Rocky Flats, a new breed of tenacious, indefatigable Nimby activists were forged by sheer anger and fear about the dimensions of America's radioactive and toxic pollution problems; galvanized by the realization that they may already have joined the ranks of victims. Joan Seeman was among this new breed. She had recently started college to get her bachelor's degree, and even at 43 looked the part—slightly disheveled with a school-girl haircut, jeans, and sweater. Seeman moved with her family to Arvada when she was in the ninth grade, in 1961. After high school she moved to San Francisco and spent 14 years working for the Bank of America. In 1982, after marrying and having a baby, she became a full-time homemaker and returned with her family to the Denver area, buying a home in Westminster. At the time, Seeman recalls, "I absolutely had no eye for the environment at all. I didn't like camping. I liked fluorescent lights."

According to 22 comprehensive studies of safety and conditions at weapons facilities prepared since 1986 by the Energy Department . . . the department is facing what could be the most expensive and difficult industrial rehabilitation project in history. (October 1988)

Crude disposal practices, banned in the private sector a decade ago but permitted at government sites, are largely responsible for the extensive environmental damage at federal plants that make nuclear weapons. (December 1988)

Seeman's environmental awareness was sparked one Sunday morning in 1985, when a crop-dusting helicopter for a farm that abutted her property landed a few feet from her children, who were playing in the backyard. "The pesticide smell was overwhelming," she said. The farmer told her that the chemical was malathion, which she later learned was also sprayed as part of the city's mosquito-abatement program. After the local Sierra Club explained that malathion was toxic to humans, she pulled together a group of neighbors to protest the spraying at city hall.

Soon after, a neighbor handed Seeman an old HUD Rocky Flats advisory notice. "If the mosquito spraying worries you, check this out," the woman said. Going back to her Sierra Club contacts, Seeman learned about the plutonium-tainted drinking water from Standley Lake, and grew increasingly alarmed. In 1986 she saw an article by Pilcher about Rocky Flats in a local paper. The two met for coffee, and Seeman began to devour mounds of technical information Pilcher supplied. Seeman met with Carl Johnson and Edward Martell, and soon became an implacable foe of Rocky Flats. She and Pilcher founded CARFC early in 1987.

The Savannah River Plant in South Carolina, an enormous government complex that produces fuel for the nation's nuclear weapons, has experienced numerous reactor accidents that have been kept secret from the public for as long as 31 years, two Congressional committees disclosed. . . . Physicists . . . called the accidents among the most severe ever documented at an American nuclear plant. (October 1988)

From 1957 to 1963, officials at the [Idaho National Engineering Laboratory] secretly released at least 2,800 curies of radioactive iodine—about 200 times the amount released in the 1979 accident at Three Mile Island. . . . From 1952 to 1970, plutonium-contaminated wastes, along with barrels of toxic solvents and other trash, were haphazardly dumped into shallow pits in an 88-acre site, [and are now migrating into the Snake River aquifer]. (March 1990)

Seeman left CARFC after the incinerator controversy. Around the same time, Seeman and her husband bailed out—selling their Westminster home and buying another in Fort Collins, 60 miles north of Denver, in order to get away from Rocky Flats. She remained involved in anti-Rocky Flats activities, however. In early 1988 she founded the Committee Against Radiotoxic Pollution (CARP) with Westminster resident Kim Grice. A bombastic and brawny Vietnam veteran, elk hunter, and self-described "red-neck Republican," 41-year-old Grice seemed more like a Rocky Flats manager than a detractor. He moved to Westminster from his native Michigan in 1973, starting a carpet-cleaning business and looking to live out the American dream with his wife and three children. Hard work paid off, and within a few years he sold his thriving company and started a real estate firm. After attending a meeting on Rocky Flats contamination in 1986, he became convinced that the plant must be closed. He also started giving his clients the old HUD advisory notice.

> Energy Secretary James Watkins said . . . that a "culture" of mismanagement and ineptitude will have to be overcome in his department before the nation's troubled nuclear weapons manufacturing plants can be brought into compliance with environmental and health laws. (June 1989)

> Energy officials said yesterday that Watkins stood by his pledge to make safety at Rocky Flats his top priority. (March 1990)

> Colorado's Rocky Flats nuclear weapons plant will receive a 45 percent boost in operating funds if Congress accepts the 1991 budget proposed yesterday by the Bush administration. However, money for environmental restoration and waste management at the trouble-ridden plant will drop slightly. (January 1990)

Sue Hurst eventually resettled in Arvada after her baby died in 1969. Sitting in a restaurant on Arvada's north side in 1989, she sounded disjointed and confused, her comments riddled with non-sequiturs. One thing was clear, however—her rage at Rocky Flats. In the 1980s Hurst and her husband operated a roofing company in Arvada, and in 1986 Rockwell solicited a bid from them on a building at Rocky Flats, she said. "I wanted to find out what the particular building did, in order to find out what kind of dirt our crew would be digging into. . . . It's for our crew's protection." The Hursts rejected the job when Rockwell informed them that the roofers would be required to wear protective suits and undergo three days of safety training. She never learned what was in that building—"national security."

With some support from friends who were concerned about Rocky Flats, including Seeman, whom Hurst knew from high school in the 1960s, she began to investigate Rocky Flats. In late 1986 she ran across a copy of a report on Three Mile Island that described birth defects among infants born near that nuclear plant after the 1979 accident. "That's my baby!" Hurst recalled thinking. From then on, she was hell-bent on stopping the plant, joining forces with CARP, as well as working against the plant on her own.

> Thousands of people who live along the western boundaries of the Hanford Reservation, which made the plutonium for the bomb that destroyed Nagasaki, say that radioactive emissions from the plant . . . have caused an unusual number of miscarriages and other health problems. . . . The government officially disputes such statements. (October 1988)

> During the first decade of the Hanford Nuclear Reservation, the DOE plant released 470,000 curies of Iodine 131. Fifteen curies were released at Three Mile Island. During the course of its operations, about 200 billion gallons of toxic and radioactive liquids have been dumped directly into the soil, enough to create a lake the size of Manhattan, 40 feet deep. (February 1990)

In early 1988 Hurst invited her sister, Paula Elofsen-Gardine, to join her at a meeting of the Rocky Flats Environmental Monitoring

Council, an advisory committee formed by the governor. "I was stunned by what I saw happening in this meeting," Elofsen-Gardine recalled. The atmosphere seemed to smack with collusion between polluters and regulators, complete with "back slapping and good-old-boy politicking," she added. "And the way they treated the citizens so arrogantly, not wanting to allow them to ask questions." After the meeting, Hurst told her sister that she believed her baby's death was caused by plant fallout. "It just hit me all at once," Elofsen-Gardine said. "The rage. That son of a bitch has been able to stay there and keep pumping that shit out for 40 years. . . . It made me think, 'these bastards are not going to get away with it.' " Shutting down the plant and forcing the government to conduct a major epidemiological study of downwinders became her twin obsessions.

Elofsen-Gardine today lives with her teenage daughter in a one-story brick house, the same house she and her family moved to when she was six, in an old section of Arvada filled with modest, single-family homes. She converted an extra bedroom into an office, where she keeps a well-organized set of Rocky Flats archives. Elofsen-Gardine speaks articulately and forcefully—facile with the technical terms that litter the Rocky Flats landscape more thoroughly than plutonium itself. A lab technician in a Denver hospital, she has some college training in biology and chemistry and is working to finish her B.S. degree. Her first fight against health dangers came years earlier, when she worked as a laborer in a metal fabrication plant. A toxic fire affecting the plant gave her a severe lung inflammation; she reported her employer's failure to protect workers to EPA and the press. Like her sister, Elofsen-Gardine worked with CARP, and formed her own paper organization.

> Government officials overseeing [Fernald] nuclear plant in Ohio knew for decades that they were releasing thousands of tons of radioactive uranium waste into the environment, exposing thousands of workers and residents in the region, a Congressional panel said. (October 1988)

The Energy Department promised yesterday to pay $73 million to settle claims by up to 24,000 neighbors of [Fernald] nuclear weapons plant in Ohio that has spread uranium into water and air. The settlement was the first time the government has acknowledged that a weapons plant may have harmed large numbers of its neighbors. (July 1989)

Seeman, Grice, Hurst, and Elofsen-Gardine have functioned as a unit. They represent the first nonideological, self-organized group of activists who are indigenous, immediate downwinders. They are not fighting for peace or the greater environmental good. They are fighting for their lives—and to kick the plant out of their backyards.

——————— ✿✿✿ ———————

Worst of the Worst

By mid-1988, the peace, enviromental, and downwinder communities were subjecting the Rocky Flats Plant to ceaseless attacks. Meanwhile, analysts of the 17-site DOE weapons complex were beginning to estimate that cleanup would cost up to $200 billion over 25 to 50 years. Rocky Flats was by no means the largest or most expensive problem, but by July 1988, DOE floated a $1 billion estimate for the site, a figure that would rise markedly within months. Noting that plutonium had been discovered downwind from Rocky Flats "in the highest concentrations ever found in an urban area, higher even than Nagasaki" (one of the two cities destroyed by the atomic bomb during the Second World War), the Physicians for Social Responsibility issued a statement calling the plant "a kind of creeping Chernobyl." The phrase soon became an opposition refrain.

Starting in October 1988, the plant shut down operations for several months to revamp its safety procedures. Two employees triggered the action by stumbling into an unmarked room where plutonium-contaminated equipment was being cleaned and repaired. The same month, the General Accounting Office (GAO), an investigative agency of Congress, reported that DOE had failed to disclose a series of "very serious" violations at the plant that left "no margins for safety."* In December EPA fined the plant $47,500—the largest civil sanction ever imposed against a federal facility—for allowing toxic polychlorinated biphenyls (PCBs) to leak from electric transformers.

Also in December 1988, DOE concluded that groundwater pollution threatening Great Western Reservoir and Standley Lake represented the worst threat to human health of any problem facing the DOE weapons system. Plant management continued to dispute the seriousness of the hazard, even in the face of DOE's acknowledgment.

In February 1989 GAO concluded that Rocky Flats is "irreversibly contaminated" and must be isolated from the public for hundreds of thousands of years—a view DOE did not dispute, admitting that the technology to clean up the site's groundwater does not exist. Following this news, downwinders became increasingly vocal opponents to Rocky Flats.

Then in June 1989 more than 70 FBI agents, many clad in full radiation-protection suits, raided the plant in the dramatic climax of a massive criminal investigation. The FBI alleged that Rocky Flats discharged contaminants into air and water without permits and in excess of allowed limits, that it falsified records and hid evidence of contamination. Nighttime overflights, by planes armed with infrared cameras, detected activity at a Rocky Flats toxic-waste incinerator that had been shut down by EPA for safety reasons. The FBI charged that the fluidized-bed incinerator, scuttled by local uproar, was operated secretly, despite promises to end its use. Politicians, aghast at the revelations, joined community members and

---

*This was not the only problem, though. In November, congressional, FBI, and DOE investigators revealed that workers in a Rocky Flats machine shop had built $1 million worth of gifts—including a grandfather clock and gold-plated jewelry—and smuggled them out of the plant, bribing security guards along the way.

environmentalists in outright challenges of Rocky Flats's credibility. A major poll conducted after the FBI raid confirmed that a majority of Colorado citizens wanted Rocky Flats shut down permanently.

The siege continued. DOE officials revealed later in June that the plant's plutonium facilities could be badly damaged if a significant earthquake hit the Golden fault line, southwest of Rocky Flats. An official of the U.S. Geological Survey added that the plant may sit directly on top of other faults. Also during June, radioactive strontium and cesium—elements produced only in a nuclear chain reaction—were discovered in a Rocky Flats dump site. Because the plant does not have a nuclear reactor, suspicion centered on a "criticality"—a spontaneous chain reaction caused by the formation of a critical mass of plutonium or uranium, resulting in nuclear fission. A criticality accident could expose workers to a lethal dose of radiation, and in a worst case could even cause an explosion that would release massive amounts of radiation into the environment.

DOE hired independent scientists to conduct a Rocky Flats safety assessment during the summer of 1989. No accident was detected, and the source of the strontium and cesium remained a mystery. But the scientists' report revealed that several *kilograms* of plutonium were lodged in ventilation ducts *downstream* of the supposedly secure HEPA filters designed to keep the plutonium inside glove boxes. Much of the information for this report followed anonymous tips from employees who feared reprisals if they spoke openly. The estimate of plutonium lodged in the ducts was later upgraded to an astonishing 28 kilograms. The cause of the buildup was also revealed: Workers used screwdrivers to poke holes in clogged HEPA filters, rather than halting production to change the filters. Plant officials said that the problem was under control, and presented no danger. Meanwhile, they considered leaving the plutonium in place, rather than increasing the risk of a criticality accident by cleaning it out.

In mid-September 1989 Rockwell executives threatened to close Rocky Flats unless granted immunity from prosecution related to the FBI probe. DOE already paid fines levied for transgressions of environmental laws as part of its contractual obligation, but Rockwell officials began to see jail terms looming on the horizon. A week later Rockwell sued the federal government for putting it in an impossible position—if the company complied with environmental regulations it would never be able to meet DOE production quotas, and would thereby default on its operating contract. The day after the suit was filed, Rockwell resigned as Rocky Flats manager. (EG&G, a DOE contractor based in Massachusetts, took over in January 1990.) In October, for the first time, DOE acknowledged that bad management was the root problem. Yet because Rockwell had met production quotas, DOE had paid the company nearly $27 million in bonuses during its last three years as plant manager.

The Rocky Flats Plant was closed in November 1989 for its annual safety check. Two months later class-action lawsuits were filed against Rockwell and its predecessor, Dow Chemical, on behalf of 60,000 landowners and residents living near the plant, and 10,000 current and former plant workers. The suits requested payments of at least $550 million to compensate for emotional distress and loss of property values, and they called for independent health studies. By January 1991, amid new disclosures that DOE managers still considered production a higher priority than safety, the plant had yet to be reopened.

———————————— &&& ————————————

Science and Credibility

The new lawsuits demanded epidemiological studies. Despite Rocky Flats's obvious environmental problems, they argued, evidence that the plant had caused health problems among downwinders was basically anecdotal—a worrisome sense that too many neighbors were dying of cancer, too many babies were born with defects. Common sense suggests a link. But in the absence of carefully conducted studies, it is not possible to determine conclusively whether problems were caused by Rocky Flats pollution or simply occurred by chance. Plant managers claimed, not without plausibility, that critics exaggerated the seriousness of environmental problems out of fear, scientific illiteracy, or the advancement of their own political agendas.

Unfortunately, the science of epidemiology is ill suited for problems of this size and complexity. At issue: assessing the effects of nearly 40 years of secret emissions of plutonium on millions of people. The primary risk from plutonium is cancer that develops over decades. Even if the amount of radiation released could be calculated—a difficult "dose reconstruction" similar to one now being attempted at DOE's Hanford facility in Washington State—many downwinders have since died or moved away, making it difficult or impossible to evaluate the doses they received or other cancer risk factors that might be relevant (such as family predispostion, smoking, or exposure to other forms of industrial pollution). It was just such concerns that led many experts to discount the Johnson studies discussed earlier.

Moreover, any study would have to review the wide array of other risks created by Rocky Flats, not just plutonium. For example, Rocky Flats was the largest emitter of carbon tetrachloride, a potent carcinogen, in North America. "My hunch is this—the airborne emissions of plutonium were very bad in the '50s and '60s," says Robert Alvarez, staff investigator for the U.S. Senate Governmental Affairs Committee and a leading expert on the DOE weapons complex. "After the 1969 incident they got religion [and reduced plutonium emissions], but the other stuff they've been discharging has never even been controlled." Expecting independent researchers or state health officials to conduct unequivocal epidemiological studies is unethical and immoral, Alvarez contends, because the burden of proof falls on the very people who were exposed, while DOE has done nothing to monitor the effects of its emissions on downwind populations. "It's an invisible, indiscriminate, random sort of violence being perpetrated on these people."

Many neighbors of Rocky Flats clearly share these sentiments, not only because of the hazards but also because of the way plant officials handled local concerns from the beginning—with denials, bland reassurances, and cover-ups under a banner of national security. My own difficulties in getting DOE's side of the story are a case in point. Happy-talk public-relations people from Rocky Flats rejected complaints about plant safety out of hand, portraying critics as sadly misinformed or politically motivated. Yet plant managers were unable to offer a more sophisticated argument efficiently or effectively. In the fall of 1989, when I arranged many of the interviews for this chapter, it took weeks to gain approval from Washington, D.C., to speak with David Simonson, DOE plant manager. When I finally met with him in December of that year, Simonson was unable to cast any light on the situation. He had only been on the job for a few months and had little perspective on Rocky Flats's history of communication with its neighbors. A few months later, Simonson was replaced by the next in a string of administrators, vividly showing the instability and disarray in the plant's chain of command.

Opponents of Rocky Flats fail to understand the relativity of risk, Sam Iacobellis, a top Rockwell executive, said in 1989. They have a much greater chance of dying in an auto accident than in a nuclear accident. David Simonson, then-DOE plant manager, agreed. "The difficulty is getting the public to look rationally at the risks," he said. "If the public were to consider the real risk involved with Rocky Flats, they would find that it's not as great as they think."

Given the secrecy in bomb production, however, the public has never had the opportunity to appraise the real risks. Judging by what DOE has been compelled to reveal in recent years, there is ample cause for rational concern. Take worker illnesses: Rocky Flats boasts about a worker-safety record that shows a disabling-accident rate far below that of most other U.S. industries, and it insists that exposures to small amounts of radiation are harmless. Yet Bruce DeBoskey, lawyer for Donald Gable and other Rocky Flats employees or their widows fighting worker-compensation claims, recently released the records of 14 workers at the plant who suffered cuts, burns, and puncture wounds on the job. Some absorbed so much plutonium that their blood cells mutated. Thirteen died of cancer.

Unlike epidemiological studies on whole regions, studies involving work-related illness are quite feasible, particularly because nuclear-industry workers wear radiation monitors and records are kept on lifetime radiation doses. DOE's Los Alamos National Laboratory studied the incidence of cancer among Rocky Flats workers employed between 1952 and 1979, and published the results in 1987. Researchers found a general excess of brain cancers. They also compared workers with a plutonium body burden of 2 nanocuries (equivalent to 31 billionths of a gram) or more to those with a body burden of less than 2 nanocuries. The first group suffered higher rates for all causes of death, including many forms of cancer. Two nanocuries is 5 percent of the occupational standard for maximum permissible body burden of plutonium. Gregg Wilkinson, chief author of the Los Alamos study, was pressured by his superiors to withdraw his paper before publication in the *American Journal of Epidemiology*. When he refused, Wilkinson claims he was intimidated by DOE superiors. Ultimately, Los Alamos constrained his efforts to get any more substantive work accomplished, and he quit, Wilkinson says. He contends that other DOE researchers have experienced similar coercion. (Studies of workers at other weapons plants, released in 1989, vindicated Wilkinson's findings.)

Yet Rocky Flats workers were comparatively lucky. A U.S. Senate report revealed in 1989 that the Atomic Energy Commission knowingly exposed thousands of unwitting bomb workers of the 1940s and 1950s to unsafe levels of radiation in order to achieve production quotas. At Hanford, some workers absorbed every six months what is now considered the lifetime permissible limit of plutonium. Others working with spent reactor fuel received the yearly limit for radiation in an hour, although top AEC officials had been warned by their own experts to restrict radiation exposures carefully.

DOE's position, that there is no scientific proof that its plants have done great harm, "isn't science," says Alvarez, principle author of the Senate report. "It becomes a belief system. And that is a form of corruption of science—perhaps one of the more dangerous forms of corruption of science.

──────────── 𝕰𝕰𝕰 ────────────

Nimbys and Mainstream Activists

The unremitting scandals at Rocky Flats since 1987, and the ascendancy of locally based activism in the downwind community, are hardly coincidental. Rocky Flats's lies and deceit incensed downwinders. Nimby fury changed the tenor of the debate.

"You Don't Have to Be Jewish to Get Gassed in Denver." This bizarre message, which seems almost calculated to offend just about everyone, is from a picket sign Sue Hurst boasts about carrying at public hearings about Rocky Flats. Mainstream activists shudder when the Committee Against Radiotoxic Pollution contingent begins its antics: Outrageous, provocative, uncompromising confrontation—personal attacks on bureaucrats, shouting down speakers at meetings, and the general willingness to alienate anyone who does not share their zeal. This approach epitomizes Nimbyism.

Mainstream activists praise the Nimbys for meticulous research that has often uncovered important new data. Hurst and Elofsen-Gardine have produced hundreds of pages of fact sheets; press releases; letters to regulators, politicians, and the media; and case studies of different aspects of Rocky Flats pollution. The reports are rambling and colloquial, yet packed with valuable information. Combing public documents and using the Freedom of Information Act to mine new veins of records, Hurst and Elofsen-Gardine have identified and publicized numerous discrepancies between what Rocky Flats officials said about contamination and emissions and what plant records revealed. Grice and Seeman have spent endless hours pouring over Rocky Flats reports and hounding regulators;

they have become fountains of information about the plant's history and hazards.

Yet Nimbyism has given the environmental and peace communities a headache. "I'm a conservative," Grice explains. "I believe we still need nuclear weapons as a deterrent, but we don't need to make any more. What we need is a better delivery system." With such views, little wonder that he is shunned by many peace activists.

Grice gained a reputation as a wildcard in the Rocky Flats debate, taking his uncompromising position and abrasive style to every forum, shouting down plant managers and politicians at every opportunity. He and his allies carried signs saying "Skaggs and Romer are Nuclear Wastes." HUD briefly considered taking CARP to court when the group distributed thousands of copies of its old advisory notice on a CARP flier entitled "Living within a Radioactive Fallout Zone." CARP mailed the fliers to Fortune 500 companies, including some that Governor Romer was actively courting to move operations to Colorado. Some antinuclear and environmental activists saw Grice and CARP as dangerously prone to exaggeration or misrepresentation.

"You can't do name-calling and slamming and yelling at public officials, and disrupting public meetings, because then it's hard for people like me to get in for appointments to see the governor, because he associates us with them," Pilcher says. "Guerrilla warfare was a tactic for the '60s and '70s, but I don't think it works now. People are too sophisticated."

The Nimby opposition sees calls for tactical compromise and moderation as ineffectual—and they find justification for this view every month Rocky Flats remains in place. Nimbys regard civility toward those they view as criminals or apologists as tantamount to collusion.

Seeman's experience with the Committee Against Rocky Flats Contamination during the fluidized-bed incinerator controversy left her contemptuous of antinuclear activists. "Forming CARFC was pretty traumatic for me," Seeman says. "I was Johnny-Joe citizen, drinking, breathing, being absolutely inundated with Rocky Flats—

my kids were drinking this crap—while a lot of the movers and shakers who came in from Denver were more removed. I was not sitting around anyone who was directly being affected by Rocky Flats the way I was." She obviously did not view Pilcher's home in Cherry Hills Village as a downwind zone. Seeman's anger rises quickly to the surface as she describes her feelings about the political agenda of pacifists: "[The peace activists] didn't want to just shut [down] the plant, because they wanted to keep it to decommission bombs, their other goal. I don't give a damn about decommissioning bombs—you're not going to do it in my backyard. . . . But if you say 'relocate' [the plant] you have every antinuclear person on your back. They will absolutely excommunicate you." (Mainstream activists consider this comment absurd, suggesting the depth of the division between them and the Nimbys.) "The antinuke people certainly didn't want any confrontation, not with Skaggs or any other politicians," Seeman bitterly insists. "They said, 'We don't want to upset Skaggs because we might need him for another issue.' . . . Instead, they wanted me to compromise myself and my family."

"Kim, and Joan, and Sue, and I have been willing to stand up there and say, 'What the hell are you doing to us!' Nobody else will do this. They want to sit there and play nicey-nicey," says Elofsen-Gardine. "We have been very stringent about the politicians and the polluters being made accountable to the public. That's ruffled some feathers. . . . I think we have run rings around the antinuclear groups and that's why they're pissed [at us]," she added. "Because we get a big bang out of a small gang. And it makes them look bad."

But Pilcher argues that the emotionalism of the Nimby approach has wreaked havoc in local political organizing by scaring off middle-class property owners around the plant—people who must be tapped to get the attention of Rocky Flats managers and politicians. Nathaniel Miullo, a widely respected EPA point man for Rocky Flats waste management, believes that this emotionalism also "increase[s] the anxiety and stress level for the public beyond what is needed and accurate for this site."

The Nimbys counter that a calm, reasonable approach plays into plant managers' hands—blunting the fear and anger that make people want to fight.

Some mainstream groups see alliances with workers and their unions at Rocky Flats as a strategic necessity for forging the broad consensus that will force change. The Nimbys shed few tears about the plight of the unions or workers at Rocky Flats. "There's nothing for them to be afraid of," Hurst contends. "If they decided that they were going to close the plant down, they'd just be moved into different jobs [for cleanup and decommissioning]." Elofsen-Gardine adds: "This scare tactic about jobs is just nonsense." The threat of job loss has certainly been brandished like a club by developers, politicians, and plant managers. Yet, if the plant were decommissioned and cleaned up, there would certainly be many jobs for many years, but little hope that the majority of current plant employees would be qualified to do them. Still, Elofsen-Gardine and Hurst point out accurately that plant workers and their unions, who depend on stability at the plant for their livelihoods, have usually sided with plant management on the pollution issue. (Even on occupational health and safety, the union has rarely taken a leadership role.)

Mainstream activists take particular umbrage at the Nimby tendency toward sloppy presentation of technical data. "Local communities are starting to call the shots. We didn't for so long that it almost gives people a sense of giddiness," Pilcher says. "It places a tremendous burden of responsibility on the public, though, to be very well educated and accurate."

Playing fast and loose with the facts reflects a hallmark of Nimbyism. It is the product of contemptuous distrust of the "authorities." After decades of lies, errors, and gross negligence by government agencies and corporations, any voice of officialdom—including the scientists (even sympathetic ones) who generate, analyze, or certify data—sounds suspect. Such distrust can promote inflexible self-reliance tinged with anti-intellectualism. (Rigidity among Nimbys is a logical outgrowth of their sense of impending doom, according to Alvarez. "They feel betrayed, like a technological underclass.") This isolation leads to exaggerations and lapses in logic in position papers and public comments that mainstream activists believe damage the entire opposition's crediblity. For example, few scientists—even those who have actively called for the plant's immediate shutdown—are prepared to declare unequivocally that downwinders are now breathing high levels of plutonium dust, even though many experts believe this may be the case. The large-scale soil sampling that could verify the claim has simply not been done. This is certainly a reasonable position, consistent with the caution built into the scientific approach. To Seeman, however, such caution derives from scientists' dependency on government and private-industry grants. Scientists effectively sell out downwinders, she believes, by not taking a harder line on contamination. Seeman's position may be exaggerated, but it is not without a rational foundation, given the structure of research funding in this country, described in chapter 2. "I plan to continue following the scientific community and checking what they're up to, because they would compromise me and my family for the sake of science and technology," Seeman says.

Overall, mainstream activists doubt the effectiveness of provocative, alienating Nimby tactics. Yet Nimbys seem to have had substantial impact on Rocky Flats. Niels Schonbeck, one of Pilcher's Boulder scientists who Governor Romer later appointed to his advisory group, believes that Seeman, Grice, Elofsen-Gardine, and a handful of allies wield enormous power with considerable effectiveness. "The agencies have invited tactics that border on the abusive, because they have never listened to quiet, reasoned arguments," he said in 1989. "[Nimby activists] fluster the DOE and Rockwell guys. It's caused them to reveal much more than they would have. These people have had much more effect than they even realize. . . . I'm glad there are people like [Elofsen-Gardine] out there, because they keep me honest."

Miullo concurs. Despite, or because of, their tactics, Nimbys have forced a higher level of scrutiny. They may be a bit paranoid, but given DOE's history of secrecy, that's justifiable, he says, adding that the Nimby element "serves as EPA's conscience, constantly pushing the agency to do more." Moreover, the Nimby opponents of Rocky Flats have shown themselves capable of moderating their tactics to achieve a particular goal. Grice and Elofsen-Gardine participated on a broadly based group of critics that received a technical-assistance grant from EPA. During the group's formation, at least two prominent activists refused to serve with Grice. The group established a code of ethics that restricted confrontational outbursts in its name, however. It ultimately became "a formidable, effective voice" on plant cleanup, according to Miullo.

Differences in philosophy, approach, and sense of urgency define these conflicts. Mainstream activists hold "the philosophy that 'we're going to save the world,' " says Elofsen-Gardine. "Well, honey, they're going to take 50 to100 years to do that. I want to do it *now*. . . . None of these other groups live in the goddamn fallout zone. They haven't seen what it has done to our family and friends. *They don't have the rage.*"

In 1989 these differences broke into open warfare. Building on the shock of the FBI raid, Colorado Freeze Voter tried to organize a repeat of the 1983 encirclement of Rocky Flats. The group's director expected a turnout of 40,000. Other activists predicted 100,000. But Hurst, Elofsen-Gardine, and their allies, joined by some environmentalists, attacked the idea as "a horrendous hoax" and "a serious potential health risk," as demonstrators stir up plutonium in the dust around the plant. They organized an alternate demonstration at the state capital and tried to siphon off as many of the protesters as possible. Ultimately, no more than 4,500 attended the encirclement; perhaps 300 more showed up at the state capital. Activists who were not directly involved with the events called them gifts to DOE—an oblique show of public confidence in the plant's darkest hour. Rocky Flats spokespersons smugly concluded that most Coloradans do not feel the plant represents a significant health hazard. One experienced activist said that the events reflected a "fractured" movement. "There's a lot of little groups that posture, hold meetings," he said, "but don't bother doing the nitty-gritty organizing work." Seeman's analysis: "They're on one side, and we're on the other."

The long-range goals of mainstream activists are global—nuclear disarmament and better management of toxic pollution in general. The Nimbys have only one agenda item: shut down Rocky Flats. When other activists talk of the bigger picture, Nimbys see them as retreating from the fight against the plant's immediate dangers. The Nimby approach may or may not be the more effective. But the peace and environmental communities have a stake in discrediting the more militant Nimbys, who jeopardize mainstream activists' strategy and call into question the credibility of the "responsible" opposition.

————————— ✿✿✿ —————————

Beyond Rocky Flats: Nimbyism Extends Its Reach

Rocky Flats generates 75,000 cubic feet of transuranic radioactive waste each year, including clothing, glass, solvents, oils, and metals contaminated with plutonium or americium. Transuranic elements remain highly radioactive for hundreds of thousands of years. Such wastes have historically been shipped by Rocky Flats to DOE's Idaho National Engineering Laboratory. But the Idaho plant has its own massive contamination problems and was never considered a permanent repository for transuranic waste. Instead, since the 1970s, DOE has been building a test site for permanent storage: the Waste Isolation Pilot Project (WIPP), located in a massive, remote, New Mexico salt formation. DOE had originally planned to open WIPP in the mid-1980s, but encountered an array of technical problems that called into question the prospect of safely containing anything for hundreds of thousands of years. WIPP's completion date has been pushed back to the early to mid-1990s. Even if it does open, WIPP would be able to handle only a fraction of the current DOE inventory of transuranic waste.

Until 1984 DOE enjoyed complete autonomy in managing its mixed hazardous and radioactive wastes. At that time a court ruling subjected DOE facilities to the federal Resource Conservation and Recovery Act, a major environmental law that governs waste disposal. The ruling ostensibly gave the states, under EPA supervision, authority over hazardous waste, as well as mixtures of hazardous chemicals and radioactive waste. DOE initially resisted. Then, in a move that initially baffled many observers, DOE backed down and agreed to submit to state jurisdiction over mixed waste. An internal DOE memo, dated 14 July 1986, shows why the agency shifted gears: DOE officials expected to lose in court, and feared having to reveal "patently 'illegal' " waste-management practices at a time when plant officials were insisting publicly that Rocky Flats was in full compliance with environmental laws. By voluntarily accepting Colorado oversight, DOE tried to finesse the issue—appearing to take the high road on waste, while sloughing off some of the burden for cleanup on the other agencies.

Ten months later, DOE extended the same jurisdiction to all states, unwittingly starting a chain of events that led from a Rocky Flats waste crisis to a Nimby revolt of national proportions. In October 1988, emboldened by his new powers, Idaho Governor Cecil Andrus blocked a railroad boxcar loaded with Rocky Flats waste from entering the Idaho DOE complex, then shipped it back to Colorado. He announced that Idaho would no longer accept DOE waste from any other state. DOE had been promising for years that WIPP would soon open, Andrus explained. Enough was enough. Waste began to build up at Rocky Flats, approaching DOE's agreed-upon limit.

Over a period of months, other governors began to take similar stands regarding DOE's prerogatives to move and store its waste. In September 1989 White House Chief of Staff John Sununu made personal appeals to the governors of seven western states to accept Rocky Flats waste on a temporary, emergency basis in order to maintain bomb production. All seven refused. "I've been lied to, cajoled at. I've been coerced, and then I've had them drape themselves in the American flag and talk about patriotism," Andrus said at the time, sounding more and more like a community activist. "I'm just saying as plainly as I can, Idaho has done her share, and there is nothing they can say to change my mind."

In desperation, DOE prevailed upon Governor Romer to propose storing railcars filled with Rocky Flats waste at an army training site in Southern Colorado, near the little town of Trinidad, population 9,000. At the same time, a private company offered to administer the waste at a new site, also near Trinidad—one of the state's poorest municipalities. The company offered jobs, a new telephone system, hospital expansion, and an array of other perks to sweeten the deal. About 500 angry Trinidadians attended a meeting to discuss the plan. They shouted down company representatives with cries of "Get out of town! . . . Store it in your backyard!" Soon after, a citizen group initiated a petition drive to recall the county supervisor who had promoted the waste-dump idea. In 12 days they gathered 1,160 signatures. Romer quietly withdrew his alternate plan.

DOE then took everyone off the hook. After massive health and safety problems shut down Rocky Flats for months, and the plant acquired a supercompactor to reduce waste volume, DOE officials concluded that the plant could handle its own waste through 1991. But given the disarray in DOE's entire weapons complex, a new waste crisis at Rocky Flats seems only a matter of time.

———————— ଷଷଷ ————————

Nimbyism in Context

For decades, the nuclear weapons enterprise functioned as a culture apart from society, holding absolute power made possible by secrecy. The weapons complex was run by a tiny elite, unconstrained by any democratic process. "This is an industry that has operated under a very arrogant presumption"—that its importance makes its risks irrelevant—according to Alvarez. "[The industry has] been given a license to put people at risk without their knowledge and consent and without any recourse." For all its strident excess and bluster, Nimbyism has been benign, indeed, compared to the forces that have provoked it.

As the extent of radiological contamination became known, as people's worst fears were dwarfed by the reality of virtually irreversible environmental degradation, an extreme public response was inevitable. Downwinders at Rocky Flats, the Idaho National Engineering Laboratory, Lawrence Livermore, the Nevada Test site, Fernald, Hanford, and nearly all other DOE sites put the bomb makers on the defensive. As a result, DOE's absolute control over its realm ended. While it was not the only factor that cracked the nuclear-defense edifice, the "Just Say 'No' " campaign had a powerful impact. At WIPP, for example, DOE continued its dubious plans for years, until it could no longer ignore the ground swell of public anger. "There was this arrogance and presumptive position taken by this department that we're going to put waste in WIPP irrespective of what the local feelings are," said DOE Secretary James Watkins in 1990. "I'm trying to erase that."

After nearly four decades, DOE is beginning to communicate with the American people. In February 1990, DOE initiated major studies on the environmental and health consequences of pollution from its bomb-making activities. The following July, the agency reversed decades of secrecy by beginning to release to independent researchers its vast storehouse of health information on the people who worked in bomb plants from the 1940s through 1990. The records may be the best currently available raw data anywhere concerning the health effects of chronic exposure to radiation. And in January 1991, DOE announced that it would turn over the lead role for studying radiation effects on nuclear workers to the U.S. Department of Health and Human Services. Meanwhile, the Colorado Department of Health announced its own $4 million inventory of toxic chemical and radioactive substances used at Rocky Flats since the plant's founding, and plans a dose reconstruction.

Widespread, locally based opposition is calling in "the balloon mortgage payment of the arms industry," as Alvarez calls it, forcing DOE to develop ways to minimize hazardous waste for the first time. However, this is a far cry from trust. "As long as there isn't any demonstrable good faith and progress to turn this thing around, the public won't be very compromising," says Alvarez. Yet an enraged citizenry does not ensure effective solutions to environmental problems of this magnitude.

"I've gone to national meetings of activists working on other sites where everybody is saying disposal should take place at the source of generation," Pilcher says. "The WIPP people intend for WIPP never to open, and [they] swear that there will be lawsuits until the end of time to ensure that not one bit of waste will ever be put into the ground there. Then there's the Nevada Test Site people, who don't want to see one thing come from Rocky Flats to the Nevada Test Site ever again. And the Idaho people don't want to see anything coming. And I'm sitting here thinking, 'Rocky Flats is the major generator of transuranic waste and we've got all this liquid stuff storing up in tanks . . . and box cars'—*box cars now!*" Pausing in exasperation, Pilcher adds: "The implications here are absolutely horrendous. . . . I mean, we have people living right out next to the plant." Of course, isolation is relative. From Denver, the Nevada Test Site and WIPP may look like the most God-forsaken locations on earth. Nevada or New Mexico ranchers would disagree. Pilcher has a point, however: some places are safer than others or, at least, affect fewer people.

If the decision to decommission the entire bomb complex and to dismantle every nuclear weapon were made today, society would still have to contain hundreds of thousands of tons of transuranic and high-level nuclear waste. No civilization can make a reliable technical prediction about what will happen in a single millennium, yet we will have to plan and implement a strategy to contain this waste for hundreds of millennia. Where to store these wastes will be both an educated technical guess and a political decision arrived at through a political process.

Alvarez believes the communities that host DOE plants will fight to the death, and that in the near term they will stymie each other; waste will be managed at the point of generation. [Ultimately] the decisions and outcome will be shaped by the political clout of the citizens more than anything else," he argues. The best organized communities will kick their plants and waste out of their backyards. When this happens, Alvarez adds, "DOE is going to go where it feels welcome, and the only place . . . right now is [the Savannah River Plant in] South Carolina. While there is an active citizen movement there, it's nothing comparable to the opposition in other places, and you still have leading politicians basically supporting the presence of the plant." In fact, DOE acknowledged in late 1990 that it had secretly built an $86 million complex at Savannah River that is capable of taking over Rocky Flats's plutonium reprocessing functions. Yet the South Carolina site would hardly be a good technical guess for isolating transuranic waste. Savannah River sits atop one of the most prolific groundwater supplies in the eastern United States.

Nimbyism focused against the nuclear weapons industry has been empowering and democratic in an immediate sense. Yet Nimby gridlock—paralysis of society's ability to choose any adequate alternatives—presents new challenges for making political choices that are both democratic and consistent with the best technical guess.

4

Ice-Nine to Ice-Minus—A Battle over
the New Biology

The public does not have to understand what is going on in biotechnology. . . . But people need a perception that somebody is in charge and somebody is looking out for their best interests.
—Warren Hyer, Bio/Technology, June 1986

Steven Lindow understands the ravages of cold. Clad in jeans and a rumpled shirt, the bearded, stocky, 39-year-old plant pathologist at the University of California at Berkeley looks more like the farm boy he once was than a college professor. Lindow grew up on land his brother still works in Hillsborough, a small town 30 miles from Portland, Oregon. His family grew clover, wheat, boysenberries, and strawberries. "We had frost damage," he recalls. "Farmers burned a lot of fuel fighting the cold. The cost to try to prevent it was high." Watching the pathetic resistance of smudge pots against nature's icy breath made a deep impression on Lindow. He studied plant pathology in large part to try to make farmers' lives easier, "to use basic science to solve practical problems."

Lindow found his niche when as a graduate student he began studying the biochemistry of frost. With worldwide crop losses to frost measured in the billions of dollars annually, the issue commanded the attention of growers and the government. And the science of frost formation was raw and exciting. In 1975 Lindow and colleagues discovered a key piece of the puzzle: the bacteria *Pseudomonas syringae* and *Pseudomonas florescens,* nearly ubiquitous in the environment, produce proteins that serve as the nuclei of the tiny ice crystals that normally begin to destroy fruit blossoms, berry and potato plants, and a multitude of other crops at 32 degrees Fahrenheit. Grown in the absence of the catalyzing organisms, plants will not freeze until temperatures drop several degrees lower.

"When it became clear that we knew the method for frost formation, it was evident that there could be a new means of frost control," Lindow explains. After years of painstaking research, he located the genetic material that controls production of the proteins that promote frost formation. Using recombinant DNA methods, in 1982 Lindow cut out the ice-nucleating genes, creating "disabled" forms of the organisms. In the lab, he sprayed a heavy mist of the altered bacteria on plants, then subjected them to freezing temperatures. The result was a high-tech farm boy's dream come true: The plants remained impervious to the cold until temperatures dropped as low as 23 degrees Fahrenheit.

"Ice-minus," as Lindow dubbed his creation, was not the only live, recombinant product under development for environmental applications. Plants were being engineered to resist diseases and insects, and microbes were being altered to kill insect pests and reduce the need for fertilizer by increasing nitrogen in the soil. Altered microbes were also under development to concentrate valuable metals in low-grade ore and degrade toxic sludge. But ice-minus was the first to pass lab tests and be readied for release into the environment for field-testing. In September 1982 Lindow applied to the National Institutes of Health (NIH) for permission to try out his discovery on a small potato patch at a university research station in Tulelake, a little town in California's northeast corner.

Initially, lab guidelines for recombinant DNA were stringent. As scientists gained experience, though, the rules were relaxed dramatically. No special regulations for field-testing a genetically engineered microorganism (GEM) existed when Lindow designed his experiment. He faced only review by the NIH Recombinant DNA Advisory Committee (RAC), the equivalent of a supreme court for gene-splicing, and the final assent by the director of NIH. The committee, composed primarily of sympathetic biologists, unanimously approved the test in April 1983.

In October, just before Lindow's trials were slated to begin, however, he was blocked by Jeremy Rifkin, an author, activist, and tenacious opponent of genetic engineering. Rifkin threatened to seek a court injunction against the tests. A few weeks earlier he had sued NIH, claiming it had approved the field trials without adequately examining the GEM's possibly disastrous environmental effects. Lindow had been racing the onset of winter—he needed a few weeks of mild weather to prepare test plants for the ice-minus application—and Rifkin's threat, with its promise of lengthy legal proceedings, convinced Lindow that he was going to have to wait at least until spring.

───────── ଓଓଓ ─────────

The Rifkin Wild Card

Rifkin embraces the critique of society (offered by such theorists as Theodore Roszak and Herbert Marcuse) that questions the overall impact of science and technology on society. In 1977 he coauthored a popular primer on the social, political, and ethical implications of genetic engineering, just as scientists themselves were coming to grips with the power of their new tool.

"We reduce life to technological design principles and, in the end, we try to create perfect living things," Rifkin argues, calling genetic engineering "the ultimate desacralization of life." He soon became the nation's dominant critic—and spoiler—of the brave new world of biology. Rifkin does not oppose all genetic engineering and he insists that he is not antiscience: "I'm for scientific progress that's tempered by a sense of continuity."

A master speech maker and organizer, Rifkin works with litigators who use environmental regulations as bludgeons to beat back the advance of biotechnology. Loved by the media for his brash comments, and a constant subject of controversy with his legal challenges, Rifkin enjoys substantial influence. He knows how to translate complex information for a scientifically naive public. Rifkin has won support from some environmentalists, politicians, and religious leaders who agree that society should look more deeply at the moral and philosophical implications of new and powerful technologies.

Most scientists consider Rifkin a professional obstructionist. They seem to hold him personally responsible for stalling modern biology by exploiting public ignorance. Liberal Harvard paleontologist and essayist Stephen Jay Gould calls Rifkin's seminal work, *Algeny,* "a cleverly constructed tract of anti-intellectual propaganda masquerading as scholarship." Barry Commoner, biologist and eminent environmentalist, accuses Rifkin of "deliberate manipulation of the data."

Prophet or opportunist, Rifkin has shaped the genetic-engineering debate as much as any individual. And his basic concerns are widely shared—a point that scientists and industrialists ignore at their peril. Robert Mitchell, a lawyer and once (RAC) chair, has said that "if [Rifkin] didn't exist, we'd probably have to invent him."

Long before Lindow's proposed field test of a GEM, many critics of genetic engineering had warned that a lab accident releasing dangerous organisms could cause environmental damage comparable to, say, a nuclear-reactor accident. A decade of safe research eased early fears. Visions of a biogenetic meltdown were revived, however, when field experiments were first proposed. Most molecular biologists dismissed such analogies as fear-mongering nonsense, as they had in the case of lab dangers. With *unknown* potential risks, however, the discounting of worst-case scenarios out of hand might itself be considered ahistorical and anti-intellectual. Tufts University professor Sheldon Krimsky, a leading historian of recombinant DNA, offers this analysis:

> Nuclear power is in a class of modern leviathan technologies. . . . The technology transforms a single human error . . . in design, management, or risk assessment, into a situation synonymous with what would happen if a million people simultaneously made errors that threatened human life or environmental quality. The distinctive property of leviathan technologies is not their physical size, but the scope and magnitude of their impacts when they fail. . . . If biotechnology is fallible, that is, if it is capable of adversely affecting the biosphere, its effects may be irreversible. . . . Once introduced into the environment, a novel organism that establishes itself cannot be recalled. In these respects, biology has spawned a leviathan technology in gene-splicing.

In the 1974 Kurt Vonnegut, Jr., novel *Cat's Cradle,* a scientist changes the molecular structure of water to produce ice with many crystalline forms. One of these, ice-nine, freezes at tropical temperatures; it can also act as a seed, reconfiguring the molecules of any normal water it touches to freeze them solid. Attacking or retreating troops could cross rivers or swamps on solid ice, saving lives and gaining tremendous tactical advantage, the inventor confidently predicts in the novel. In Vonnegut's dismal conclusion, ice-nine is released into the environment and quickly travels the earth's infinitely interconnected water supply, freezing rivers, lakes, oceans, and groundwater solid as rock—destroying the planet.

Nearly all informed observers of recombinant DNA technology view the prospect of a wildly proliferating microbe laying waste to the ecosystem as ludicrous. Yet doubts about molecular alteration are deeply rooted in popular thinking. The unstoppable Andromeda Strain—an alien microorganism, released accidentally, that causes an epidemic of agonizing disease—represents one of science fiction's sturdiest clichés. Ice-minus, eerily linked to Vonnegut's fantasy, would soon embody this fear, becoming a major test for how society responds to unknown risk decisions in the Nimby era.

———————— ଧ୍ୟୟ ————————

Commercial Inevitability

Biotechnology entrepreneurs grasped the commercial potential for frost-protection bacteria immediately. In March 1984, with Lindow mired in a legal swamp, Advanced Genetic Sciences (AGS)—an Oakland, California, biotechnology company founded in 1979— petitioned RAC for permission to test its own version of ice-minus, called Frostban. AGS was a good vehicle to prepare ice-minus for the marketplace. The company was small enough to take risks, ambitious, adequately capitalized, and focused on agriculture. AGS already produced a naturally occurring bacterium, brand-named Snomax. The opposite of its corporate sibling, Snomax nucleates ice crystals at relatively high temperatures—a boon to ski resorts. More important, AGS was well-connected to UC Berkeley, having subsidized Lindow's work to the tune of hundreds of thousands of dollars—an arrangement facilitated by Milton Schroth, a Berkeley professor who doubled as a member of the AGS scientific board. In return, the university gave the company an exclusive contract to develop Lindow's invention commercially.

Trevor Suslow, an AGS researcher, brought the links between AGS and Berkeley's plant pathologists full circle. In 1980, at age 26, Suslow completed his doctorate in molecular plant pathology at Berkeley. The degree followed from a lifelong love of science and plants. Through college he worked at a nursery and landscape center selling shrubs and sprinkler systems, designing yards, and diagnosing disease and pest problems. "I tried to help people get products that would have a chance of being effective, rather than spending their money on a lot of snake oil," Suslow says. He soon became a troubleshooter, solving baffling shriveled-leaf mysteries and driving off intransigent infestations. Even with a Ph.D. from a leading university, however, faculty jobs in his field were more unusual than Suslow's state-of-the-art skills. Schroth was Suslow's adviser and soon brought his protégé into the corporate fold. At the time, AGS did not even own a lab, and Suslow continued to work at the university while AGS picked up the tab. Before long, Suslow, a fishing buddy of Lindow's, became the company's ice-minus expert.

A decade later, Suslow still looks boyish but speaks with a caution born of experience. "I told myself that I'd take this until a real job came along," he says, leaning back in his AGS office in Oakland, running his hand quickly through sandy-colored hair. "Nine years later I'm still here." He has remained at AGS, in part, because like many biotechnology companies, AGS models its corporate culture on the academic environment. Suslow's cluttered office, a few steps from his lab, could be a university archetype—books and reports piled high, personal computer close at hand. On the wall, pictures of his young children are posted beside diagrams of how ice-minus works. Bookshelves hold ten baseball caps, the kind worn by farmers, each with a Frostban or Snomax emblem. Only the file cabinet labels hint at the years of conflict Suslow had weathered—"Frostban legal," "Risk assessment," "Environmental use permit," and the like.

By 1982 AGS executives were convinced that the company and the industry—indeed, agriculture itself—would soon depend on effective, safe, and efficient microbial pesticides and cures for plant diseases. And the first company to field-test a GEM stood to gain enormous prestige, get a leg up on the competition, and make history in the process.

But history would have to wait. On 16 May 1984, Rifkin won an injunction against Lindow's field tests, nine days before Lindow's team was scheduled to begin the potato experiment. (Rifkin argued that NIH violated the National Environmental Policy Act when it approved the Lindow test without formally assessing its possible environmental impact. In December 1984 the agency agreed to prepare such an assessment and a month later concluded that the experiment would have no significant impact.) Federal Judge John J. Sirica warned NIH not to approve any other tests until it had formalized its process for allowing the release of GEMs. Surprisingly, RAC unanimously approved the AGS test two weeks later, apparently challenging Sirica's judgment. But NIH director James Wyngaarden stepped in to prevent a confrontation with Sirica, sending the AGS case back to a RAC subcommittee for further review.* By this time NIH was rapidly losing its grip on—and authority over—the regulation of field tests. This worried the industry, which sensed increasingly burdensome rules would follow. Rifkin saw a second line of attack. He approached the Environmental Protection Agency (EPA), which had already declared its intention to play a role in regulating GEMs. EPA responded forcefully, asserting jurisdiction over field testing in September 1984 and issuing a draft policy the following month. The agency said it would consider the release of GEMs on a case-by-case basis, and quickly entered negotiations with both AGS and Lindow.

The NIH monopoly had made little regulatory sense. By the time ice-minus came to the fore, many other recombinant agricultural products were waiting in the wings. When it initially approved Lindow's proposal, RAC was dominated by molecular biologists and "did not include a single scientific expert on ecology or evolutionary biology," commented Robert Colwell, a UC Berkeley ecologist who served as a primary EPA consultant on ice-minus. RAC had not even begun to draft polices for field testing GEMs, he added.

---

*NIH guidelines governing recombinant DNA research had always been enforceable only for the agency's grantees. Nearly all biotechnology corporations, AGS among them, voluntarily followed the guidelines to reassure the public and their investors that they would conform to the highest safety standards. "[But] because of the confused status and nature of the review process," Suslow acknowledged in a 1989 interview, after approval by RAC "we had committed to go ahead [with the field test] in any event, whether the NIH gave official approval or not." Further legal or bureaucratic delays—over guidelines that did not even hold the force of law—would have been untenable, in the company's view. "It was only because of some bad weather that that we didn't test" ice-minus in a remote California county during the summer of 1984, Suslow told me. "We were prepared to do it if we had gotten the strawberry plants to flower. You're the first person who has ever heard that. I figure enough time has passed." AGS had reason to be reticent about its foiled plans. The apparent willingness to ignore government rules would later create the company's biggest headache and color the entire public debate over field testing.

EPA's action opened the door to a rush of biotechnology rule making. Late in 1984 the White House declared its intention to reorganize biotechnology regulation, diminishing the NIH role and increasing the prominence of EPA and the U.S. Department of Agriculture (USDA). USDA quickly entered the fray, asserting its own authority to regulate certain GEMs but, like EPA, failed to provide clear guidelines on what data would be required to receive permission to test an organism.*

With the Food and Drug Administration (FDA) also forming policies on field testing, biotechnology industry executives grew restive. They envisioned vacillating bureaucrats spinning out erratically enforced rules built on confusing, apparently arbitrary policies and dubious statutory authority. Products had to be tested, and continual delays push up costs. Environmentalists were equally dismayed by what they saw as agency plodding. They feared that Reagan administration advocates for deregulation would fill the leadership vacuum and scuttle any prospect for stringent control over the release of GEMs.

------------------ ၉၉၉ ------------------

The Safety Debate

In 1985, EPA and NIH, in consultation with USDA, FDA, and other government agencies, conducted one of the most elaborate reviews of an agricultural test in history. The agencies assembled

---

*USDA's regulations were disorganized and ineffectual, according to a 1986 congressional report. Shortly after the report appeared, USDA acknowledged that in 1985, without consulting any other government agency, it allowed a Nebraska-based company to field-test the first live, recombinant animal vaccine in pigs in three different states. Neither the company nor USDA bothered to inform state health officials or solicit public comment. The following January the agency quietly approved a license to market the vaccine. When the actions came to light in April 1986, the ensuing scandal put a scare into USDA, slowed all agencies' deliberations regarding the release of GEMs, and spotlighted the pitfalls of back-room regulation and lack of cooperation between concerned federal agencies.

molecular biologists, botanists, meteorologists, ecologists, plant pathologists, and a host of other specialists. Their task: to predict whether ice-minus can be tested safely in the environment and to address several key issues.

Ice-minus, called a "deletion mutant," involves the removal of a single gene. Test proponents, including a panel of the National Academy of Sciences, argued that releasing an organism altered in such a way is no more risky than the release of natural microbes. Compared to the genetic changes seen in 10,000 years of agricultural breeding, adding or removing a single gene seems trivial. If anything, proponents added, genetic engineering is safer than crossbreeding, which confers many new traits simultaneously. "Anyone with a scientific background knows that this ice-minus bacterium isn't going to do anything harmful," said Schroth, voicing the prevalent view among biologists.

Ecologists, left out of the recombinant DNA debate before the advent of ice-minus, considered the biologists' argument cavalier and scientifically indefensible. "We know from past history that small evolutionary changes in microbes in nature can cause immense havoc," said Colwell. "Flu virus changes every few months. Plant pathologists [should] understand this. . . . A single gene change in some fungus or rust or bacteria can suddenly cause an outbreak of diseases in corn or wheat."

Ironically, up to 100 natural strains of ice-minus occur in nature. They are similar in effect, but not genetically identical to the deletion mutant. Some critics could not comprehend why AGS or Lindow did not just use the natural strains and save themselves the immense headache they were going through. By using a deletion mutant formed from the strain of *Pseudomonas* native to the test area, Suslow explained, scientists could be sure that ice-minus would occupy the identical environmental niche of the particular "ice-plus" bacteria that spawned it. Still, there was no overwhelming scientific evidence that the natural ice-minus strains could not work equally well. There were, however, compelling business reasons for using the deletion mutant, Suslow acknowledged. Engineered strains can be patented, and their production can be more efficiently controlled.

Their dangers aside, recombinant microbes could never spread off the test site and supplant ice-plus bacteria, insisted the biologists. "There is virtually no chance that artificially altered microbes will be competitive with the natural forms, which have been adapting for billions of years," four eminent Harvard and Brandeis professors wrote in the *New York Times*. ("Would corn planted at the edge of the forest take over the forest?" asked Nobel Laureate David Baltimore.) But EPA and leading ecologists argued that under plausible scenarios ice-minus could drift from the test site or be carried off by insects or birds, then successfully compete with native bacteria.

Critics also raised the specter of exotic pests that have wreaked havoc on American plant life. Over the past 350 years, according to the congressional Office of Technology Assessment (OTA), roughly 1,400 insects have been deliberately or accidentally introduced into the United States. About 800 became pests, including 156 important pests that had been expected to be beneficial or benign. Several harmful microbes have been introduced in this way. Dutch elm disease, for example, killed most American elms; an Asian fungus, accidentally imported on nursery plants, wiped out the American chestnut tree. But supporters of releasing recombinant microbes called these comparisons naive. Introducing wholly new insects or microbes into a new ecological niche, they said, is hardly comparable to inserting or removing a single gene from an organism already present in the local environment. "It was their finely tuned natural balance of tens of thousands of genes that caused problems," argued Nobel Prize-winning bacteriologist and biotechnology executive Winston Brill. Others pointed out that exotic pests, if carefully studied before their release, rarely cause significant damage.

Similarly bitter disagreements emerged about whether ice-minus could be pathogenic to plants, animals, or people, or whether it might spontaneously mutate into a more hazardous organism—with both sides citing considerable scientific data to bolster their views. A number of ecologists and meteorologists suggested that ice-minus could have far-reaching effects on weather patterns. Just as *Pseudomonas* allows ice nucleation on plants, it also promotes ice nucleation in clouds—essential for rainfall. If a large quantity of ice-minus was somehow wafted into clouds, the argument suggested, rainfall could be drastically reduced. Another phalanx of experts castigated this hypothesis.

These arguments were derived, in part, from each side's bias—molecular biologists see the world through test-tube lenses, while ecologists, by training and inclination, look for the interaction of whole systems in any problem. After a decade of successful and safe recombinant DNA experimentation in the lab, biologists grew sanguine. But the science of predictive ecology is today still in its infancy. "There is simply no consensus on how much and what type of data are sufficient to make an informed decision," said Krimsky in 1986. "Without the scientific basis for a predictive ecology, the release of novel life forms into the biosphere is metaphorically a game of ecological roulette." Moreover, according to Martin Alexander, a Cornell ecologist and EPA consultant during the deliberate-release debate, living organisms present too many complex variables to make quantitative predictions equivalent to what can be done with chemicals.

The muddled ice-minus debate made only one indisputable point: Experts can disagree about the wisdom of releasing a GEM. Notwithstanding, the EPA panel that was set up to evaluate ice-minus (it included Colwell and Alexander) approved the AGS experiment. The small-scale test "probably will not cause any harm to [people] or the environment," the panelists concluded. The equivocal language reflects the inherent caution of science—there is no such thing as zero risk. EPA gave AGS the official go-ahead in November 1985.

———————— ⚜⚜⚜ ————————

The Nimby Opposition

In a comprehensive biotechnology poll conducted in 1986 for OTA, 82 percent of Americans supported research in genetic engineering and biotechnology. Yet more than half of those polled agreed that it was very likely or somewhat likely that "genetically engineered products will represent a serious danger to people or the environment." People's general fear of uncertainty partly explains this apparent contradiction. Regarding environmental applications of GEMs, 40 percent of Americans were willing to accept a *known* high-level risk (1 in 100), while only 30 percent would accept a "very remote" yet *unknown* risk level. The substantial credibility problems of corporations and government officials (whose public confidence ratings on deliberate-release judgments were far below that of environmental groups in the OTA survey) undoubtedly contributed to the caution of those polled. When the OTA poll was taken, no community had ever faced the release of a GEM. The more immediate an unknown risk is, the more jittery the affected community becomes.

In general, new technologies are apt to be seen as more threatening than old ones, no matter how benign the former, how destructive or dangerous the latter. At Rocky Flats, residents tolerated gross mishandling of waste products that resulted in massive contamination with plutonium and toxic solvents over a period of years. Yet when a *new* incinerator was suggested—and endorsed by EPA as a relatively safe alternative to letting waste pile up—neighbors of Rocky Flats mounted fierce opposition. This story is familiar to corporate planners. State-of-the-art, relatively clean factories, waste-disposal sites, and a wide range of other industrial plants can be impossible to place in communities that live in apparent harmony with older, more polluting facilities.

Prunedale, California, in northern Monterey County just south of the San Francisco Bay Area, would soon become the test case. Prunedale's lush crops and forests typify Northern California's coastal mountain range. These low mountains are more like hills, really—human scale. Pines and madrones blanket their rolling contours, and from a rise, the ocean's waves are clearly visible. Two-lane roads pass stacked hay bales, ranches, and farms—the image jarred only by an occasional shopping strip. Elkhorn Slough—a protected wetlands and one of the most ecologically diverse areas in the nation—hugs the coast a few miles away.

Glen Church, a 30-year-old Christmas tree farmer, lives three miles from the site EPA approved for the AGS test. Church's driveway, marked by a sign in the shape of a Christmas tree, winds a quarter mile up to his nondescript ranch house attended by loud but friendly dogs. Tall, thin, clad in a work shirt and jeans, he looks the part of a farmer. Church grew up on this land, which he bought from his father, who farms trees just down the road. Both sides of his family can trace their roots in Monterey County at least back to the 1920s. A mammoth aquarium dominates his living room. Nearby, in poignant symbolism, stands a much smaller "quarantine" tank where new fish live for a month to prevent possible infection of the old.

Serious, yet with an easy laugh, Church recounted his first impression of ice-minus. In December 1985, just after AGS gained EPA's nod, he saw a newspaper article describing the experiment. "My first thought was, 'this is historical.' It doesn't take much to realize that biotechnology is going to be around until the end of time—it's like making fire. Two hundred years from now . . . everything—agriculture, industry, and our daily lives—[is] going to be tied into it." Church sounded like a technological optimist. But he was troubled by the scientific controversy that, as the test grew imminent, was leaking into the local press. In a casual conversation with his father, a former county supervisor, Church voiced these concerns. "He told me, 'You know, the county can get involved in something like this, as a land-use issue.' "

Church considers himself a political moderate. The land is everything here, however, and a farmer's protectiveness in his father's generation has given way to an identification with environmentalism in Church and his peers. He had never joined in an environmental cause, though. Until now.

On 3 January 1986, a Friday, Church drafted a letter raising concerns about the field test to the Monterey County Board of Supervisors, cosigned by a school board trustee, a former county planning commissioner, Church's father, and a nearby berry farmer. The locally based opposition to ice-minus was born. ("It's interesting, the only person who refused out of all those I asked to sign it was a real hardened environmentalist," Church recalled. "She said, 'I'm not really familiar with the issues.' ") A county supervisor, after reading the letter, confided to Church that the board had previously asked EPA and the California Department of Food and Agriculture about the test, and had been told to butt out—that the county had no jurisdiction.

Church and his allies raised the concerns that had been argued back and forth in the scientific community, and added some questions that the regulators and experts hardly gave a passing thought: Why was the test site being kept secret from local authorities and residents, and why were they being denied a role in decisions about the test? Why test ice-minus in some of the richest farmland in the country? Who would pay for the damages if something went wrong? Church walked the letter around to local reporters on Monday, 6 January. The Tuesday supervisors' meeting was packed with local and regional media. "The Board was trying to back off," according to Church. "They were basically saying that there wasn't anything they could do. My father really challenged that." The supervisors took no action, but scheduled a land-use hearing for 27 January.

"Then it exploded. It was local one day, then a little bigger, a little bigger," he said, forming concentric arcs with his arms, his voice rising. "I started getting calls from the San Francisco Bay Area. Then—*bang-bang-bang*—within a week it was the *Washington Post* and *New York Times*." Church and seven or eight other activists, their heads spinning in the glare of television lights, scrambled to respond. "The press always wanted to know, 'Who are you with?' " Church explained, "There has to be organized opposition. It started off as [loosely affiliated] individuals. But the press created the organization—the press created the need for it." Thus a Nimby group was formed: Concerned Citizens of North Monterey County (CCNMC). Like other Nimby groups, CCNMC was formed on the moment around a single issue, made up exclusively of local residents opposing a perceived threat. Within two weeks, CCNMC was drawing 100 people to meetings on little notice; soon it adopted the hyperbolic analogies emblematic of Rocky Flats and a multitude of other conflicts. "We cannot afford a biogenetic accident like Three Mile Island, Love Canal or Bhopal," Church wrote in an opinon piece in the *San Jose Mercury News*. Church also warned of bacteria designed to clean up oil spills but devour petroleum reserves, wood pulp-eating microbes that "defoliate forests and consume wood houses." The media found the scary comments irresistible, and helped thrust CCNMC to the center of the ice-minus drama.

Such analogies prove irresistible to Nimby activists and infuriating to scientists, regulators, and technocrats. This reflects a cleavage in the general approach to risk posed by technological endeavors—particularly new or experimental projects. Local communities tend to err on the side of caution, and consider past problems of any technology, however obscure their relationship to the situation at hand, as valid precedents. In contrast, the promoters of technology emphasize circumscribed, directly relevant technical criteria to evaluate safety. This is more than a conflict in approach. It represents a clash of worldviews (which is discussed in detail in chapter 7).

On 25 January 1986, Church and others from CCNMC joined Rifkin in a lawsuit meant to block the AGS test, prompting speculation that Rifkin was orchestrating local opposition. Church used Rifkin as a resource, but CCNMC was indigenous and self-directed. In Church's view, the group could succeed only as an autonomous operation, in part for pragmatic reasons: "[Rifkin] didn't have a grasp of the local situation. . . . I knew the community and I knew what was being affected," he said. "I felt that the issue had to stay in the middle of the road if it was going to win" in the basically conservative local milieu. If CCNMC became identified as antiestablishment, Church explained, Monterey County farmers would stay clear. "It begins to be seen as all these environmental kooks. . . . You can get isolated very easily."

Church's instinct to keep his group's public posture consistent with the political tenor of Monterey County is more than mere common sense. It reflects the nature of Nimbyism itself. Nimby groups draw their strength from average citizens. The ability to maintain broadly based support in the face of attacks from officials who denounce Nimbyism as a purely selfish phenomenon derives from this mutual sense of identification between activists and the mainstreams of their communities.

CCNMC packed the 27 January supervisors meeting. By then AGS had adopted a damage-control mode and offered to postpone the test, but the situation had taken on a life of its own. Just before the meeting, two sharply worded telegrams opposing the AGS test— one from 26 members of the European Parliament, the other from 28 Green party members of the West German Parliament—were sent to the board. It would have been hard for local officials in rural California not to be impressed.

The supervisors listened to a litany of opposition from a series of witnesses. Adding insult to injury, they learned that EPA rules required that the ice-minus test be conducted on a "remote" site. "For someone sitting in Washington, D.C. [Prunedale] may seem remote," commented Supervisor Barbara Shipnuck, "but [not] when you live in Monterey County." (In a congressional hearing a month later, board Chairman Sam Karas was asked by Republican Rep. Ron Packard, a biotechnology booster, to suggest a safe test site. "Belgium," Karas responded, drawing laughter in the hearing room. Packard was not amused.) Board members ordered county administrators to draft an ordinance regulating the release of GEMs, and at their 11 February meeting, over the objections of state regulators, they bowed to the cardinal rule of politics—obey your political base. The supervisors unanimously passed a 45-day moratorium on the AGS test.

The ice-minus scientists and their supporters were by then deeply worried about the community's tactics, which they attributed to a handful of selfish critics. "If the scientific illiterates win ... humanity's chances for life-enhancing breakthroughs will wither along with the spirit animating the biotech revolution," warned an editorial in the Oakland *Tribune*.

"A very vocal minority is depriving the vast majority of the population from some potentially large benefits," said Lindow. The evidence suggested that his comment was wishful thinking. Regardless of the validity of safety concerns, public opposition to the test—as demonstrated by hearings, letters to local media, and successful CCNMC organizing—was widespread.

"Somebody told them [these] bacteria multiply 30 or 100 times per day. They were absolutely fascinated by this. It was like giving a baby a rattle," commented Doug Sarojak, AGS marketing director. "We were shocked. *All* bacteria multiply at that rate or faster. It was like we had to start educating them at the very introductory level of biology." Concern over the rate of bacterial reproduction is certainly naive. Yet in light of substantive scientific disagreements about ice-minus, the community's caution, however shaky its base of understanding, was certainly understandable.

Suslow, who views himself as solidly liberal, "almost Socialist, perhaps," became a plant pathologist with the idea that he could help reduce the nation's dependence on dangerous chemical pesticides. He was aghast at being accused of plotting a heinous ecological crime. Suslow placed his opponents into three categories. Some were earnestly concerned people who wanted enough information to draw their own conclusions. I feel that we always did and would always be able to convince "[that kind of person] that what we were doing was safe and reasonable," he said. "Then there was the type that was going to be opposed no matter what, because it was a new technology. . . . They manipulated information to their advantage." The last category was made up of people who would simply jump on the bandwagon and regurgitate misinformation. Suslow told the following anecdote to emphasize his point: EPA classified ice-minus as a pesticide and required AGS to follow normal requirements for testing a novel chemical pesticide—including a head-to-foot protective "moon suit" for the person applying the organism. The agency acknowledged that the suit was a formality, not an indication that ice-minus was acutely toxic. According to Suslow, Judy Pennycook, a central member of CCNMC, was told repeatedly about the formality. Yet, at every public event, "She would say, 'If it's so safe, then why do they wear this suit?' You throw up your hands and say, 'Come on . . . !' "

Overall, however, Suslow blames the opposition to ice-minus testing on Nimbyism. "Just don't do it here first. Do it out on Mars, or the Moon," he said, letting out a short laugh. "I don't see anything in it for me . . . so why should I take the risk?"

———————— ଓଓଓ ————————

Scandal

Bad luck was becoming the dominant theme at AGS, but it was of the company's own making. As AGS looked ahead warily to a protracted struggle to win over Monterey County residents, it had no idea how bad things could get. On 26 February 1986, the *Washington Post* reported that a year earlier AGS had conducted open-air tests of ice-minus on the rooftop of its Oakland labs. An unnamed, disgruntled former AGS employee revealed that ice-minus had been injected under the bark of about 50 fruit trees in a test of pathogenicity. The whistleblower also claimed that AGS misrepresented data indicating ice-minus was harmless to the trees tested and that, in AGS greenhouse experiments, ice-minus may have escaped through open windows. Suslow, who months earlier had fired the employee for performance problems, suggested in an interview that the revelations were mostly sour grapes. Clearly the employee had his own agenda. He later assisted Church in his efforts to direct public opinion against AGS, using the pseudonym "Mr. Frost."

EPA called the tree tests a deliberate, illegal release, because the bacteria could easily have leaked out of the injection sites and been carried away by insects drawn to the leaking sap. The company's documentation seeking EPA approval had not disclosed the open-air setting for the experiment.

"If AGS is allowed to go ahead with the first legal deliberate release after flouting the law, what precedent will this set for the industry?" asked Church. Even Rep. Packard blasted the company, calling the tests "a breach of public trust" that could tarnish law-abiding companies.

AGS Research Director John Bedbrook explained that his scientists were convinced ice-minus was not pathogenic and would not multiply within the trees. Therefore, although the trees were outside, the woody tissue itself was as good as a greenhouse for containing the bacteria. And in the greenhouse tests no aerosols were used, making it unlikely that bacteria could have floated out the windows, added Bedbrook, who blamed ill-defined EPA rules, not deliberate lawbreaking, for the transgression.

Colwell, the Berkeley ecologist who had recommended approval of the AGS field test, pointed out the tautology of Bedbrook's argument. "One might well ask why they are doing the test if they are already confident that [the bacteria] are not pathogens," he said. Steven Schatzow, EPA director of pesticide programs, ridiculed the company's interpretation of EPA rules. If presented with a sequence "that talks about 'laboratory, contained laboratory, growth chamber, greenhouse, or other contained facility,' " he said, "and someone then said 'tree . . . does that go in the same group?' you or I would probably say 'I don't think so.' "

EPA fined AGS $20,000—the highest penalty ever levied for willful violations of research rules. (The fine was cut to $13,000, though, after AGS convinced EPA that it had not intentionally falsified data.) The agency also rescinded the test permit, pending new tree-pathogenicity tests, this time in a greenhouse. "We're sending a message," Schatzow said. "This is a new technology that evokes great public concern. People who want to play this game had better be careful."

Less than two weeks after the scandal broke, a local paper was tipped off about the location of the proposed Prunedale test site and ran a picture of the test grid below a banner headline. The site, located on land owned by an AGS employee, was 50 feet from the property of Gary Cowen, a local farmer whose house nearly abutted the property line. The site was a mile from an elementary school. The locals were enraged. "You don't come in somebody's backyard and test something like that," said Cowen, who pointed out that the AGS employee's home was well protected by trees and much farther away from the grid than his own.

Ironically, AGS never really intended to use that site, Suslow said in a 1989 interview. "The normal thing you would do in most agricultural experiments would be to put the test plot in a corner of some farmer's field," he explained. But all the strawberry growers AGS approached had turned the company down. "That should have been our first clue that there could be a problem," Suslow added. In order not to delay the eleborate EPA permit-application process, Suslow decided to list the property of the AGS employee, despite the fact that it was too close to houses. He assumed EPA would reject it, but in the mean time AGS could be searching for a more appropriate property. EPA, however, shocked the company by approving the site without ever looking at it. "That crystallized in my mind that EPA doesn't know what's going on here," Church said. "And the state was saying 'We just follow the EPA.' It really alarmed us how things were so chaotic in the regulatory system." The net result of these revelations was a stiffening of Nimby resistance—a growing view that the community could only rely on itself.

About this time, conspiracy theories surfaced. The prevalent scenario cast ice-minus as a biological weapon, with Monterey County residents destined to become unwitting guinea pigs. The argument rested on obscure associations traced back to Hitler's death camps. Suslow recalled a middle-aged man who approached him at a public meeting, suggesting that AGS intended to produce a biological weapon, then make a fortune by selling the antidote. "I thought he was kidding at first, but as I talked to him I realized that he was absolutely, dead serious, frightened. . . . He was livid. . . . There were tears in his eyes. Obviously, I felt that this was a disturbed individual," Suslow said. "But he wasn't the only person." CCNMC rejected conspiracy theories as too far out, as well as a distraction from what the group regarded as obvious shortcomings of the AGS test.

Regulatory disarray commonly feeds Nimbyism. At Rocky Flats, for example, Nimby activists viewed EPA and the state Health Department as little more than apologists for Department of Energy ineptitude and corruption. In such cases, cynicism about the ability of regulators to protect public interests is certainly justifiable. And Nimby groups rarely regret going around regulators to politicians in an effort to enforce local demands. But lack of faith in any and all regulatory processes promotes isolation. Nimby activists lose valuable allies when they fail to recognize that agencies such as EPA are not monolithic. They employ many indivuduals who consider vigorous public participation essential to effective technological decisions.

In the face of relentless pressure from local opponents, on 24 March 1986 the Monterey Board of Supervisors banned the field testing of GEMs for one year.

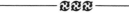

The Testing Bottleneck

Ice-minus had become a living nightmare, and not just for AGS. The entire industry viewed with alarm the delays and expenses that AGS had incurred to test a mere strawberry garden. What would happen when the testing of 1,000 acres was proposed? Industry leaders complained bitterly that the fledgling regulatory apparatus was choking off research. Dozens of field-test proposals already languished in the approval pipeline, while EPA and USDA expected hundreds more within a few years.

Moreover, the industry showed that it was not above economic blackmail. Notwithstanding his company's tarnished image, at the height of the rooftop test imbroglio AGS Chief Executive Joseph Bouckaert told the *Wall Street Journal* in March 1986: "What matters is that the research go forward. We will move forward, if not in this country then in Europe or Latin America. And that would be a great loss to the United States." This was hardly idle chatter for AGS, a multinational corporation. (Ironically, by 1990 some European biotechnology firms were moving operations to the United States to take advantage of the relatively *relaxed* regulatory environment in this country.)

A few months later Bouckaert's threat was carried out, although not by AGS. The nation's oldest biomedical research institution, the Wistar Institute of Philadelphia, tested a live, genetically altered rabies vaccine on cows in Argentina without the consent or knowledge of the Argentine or U.S. governments. When the incident came to light months later, the Argentines were outraged. According to a report in the *New York Times,* "Farm workers who handled the animals and milked them had never been told that the herd had been inoculated with an experimental virus." Argentine health officials initially believed that the workers had accidentally become infected with the altered virus, and made a formal protest to the Pan American Health Organization, cosponsor of the Wistar tests. Two days after the incident in Argentina was revealed, an Oregon State University research group went public about its own recombinant animal vaccine tests, conducted in New Zealand in April 1986.

The Reagan administration turned a sympathetic ear, and in June 1986 the White House issued a "Coordinated Framework for Regulation of Biotechnology," designed to set basic definitions, clarify vague or overlapping jurisdictions, and streamline approval of experiments. David Kingsbury, architect of the new policy, predicted it would improve oversight. However, he made the policy's primary goal apparent in his comments about the Argentina affair: "We may be overregulating and pushing companies to test their products overseas."

Significantly, the new framework assumed deletion products such as ice-minus and alterations involving "regulator genes" (those that control the functions of other genes) are inherently benign. It suggested that both categories be virtually exempted from field-test review, a reflection of the policy's general message: To commercialize biotechnology, its products cannot ultimately be regulated case by case.

While the industry and many scientists applauded the new policy as a safe, progress-oriented approach, others were startled by its sweeping oversight exclusions and saw the overall framework as a sop to industry. Critics feared most that deletion of a single gene might possibly upset the delicate balance of relationships between genes, leading to mutations, wild multiplication, or other unforeseen consequences. "It is a medieval scientific view that deletion is automatically less risky," said MIT biologist Jonathan King. (The framework also ignored some rapidly developing techniques that use chemicals, electricity, and other methods of transferring DNA, rather than the usual genetic-engineering process. Similarly, because these methods did not fit easily into preexisting categories, they were not regulated by NIH or USDA.)

———————— ཟཟཟ ————————

Lindow's Struggles

Ironically, the coordinated framework left intact laws replete with gaping loopholes on the one hand, arcane and redundant controls on the other. And because the framework had no force of law, individual agencies adopted only portions of it. But by issuing the coordinated framework, the Reagan administration sent a vital message to AGS and the biotechnology industry as a whole: Don't give up. The top policymakers want you to succeed.

Success was not coming easily, however.

As AGS slogged through another series of tests and reconsidered its options in light of the Monterey County ban, Lindow pressed forward in Tulelake. By the spring of 1986, Rifkin had lost his lawsuit against Lindow's experiment, and Lindow was following the same process as AGS to obtain a test permit from EPA. He had a lot going for him: No direct profit motive tainted his experiment, and Tulelake residents could be expected to trust professors from a well-known university. Lindow also enjoyed the university's exemptions from local planning and land-use laws. Learning from the AGS experience, the UC Berkeley public-relations team introduced the experiment to local business groups and residents. Based on sparse attendance but generally positive comments at public forums—even one on 17 April, long after the AGS scandal broke—the university saw the sleepy rural town as either supportive or apathetic.

The university team would soon learn how badly it had misjudged the Tulelake community. "People need time to process information about new technologies," Krimsky and colleague Alonzo Plough point out in a chapter of their book that describes Lindow's experience. "Local controversies do not just happen through some cognitive process. They are socially constructed."

At Rocky Flats, controversy over the plant's health effects went through several cycles over a period of more than a decade. In 1984 and 1985, for example, the attitude of downwind communities ranged from apathy to general support for the plant. Two years later, hundreds of citizens were actively organizing their communities in opposition to the proposed radioactive-waste incinerator. It was not that people suddenly became aware of the plant's existence or even of the dangers it posed. Rather, the community had become involved in a social process that identified a clear target and offered the possibility of success.

The social construction at Tulelake began shortly after Ava Edgar, a secretary in a local business, read about the 17 April forum in the paper. It sparked a vague recollection about a Tulelake Chamber of Commerce meeting she attended two years earlier, at which Lindow appeared. At that time the test sounded safe. But after reading about the environmental controversy, Edgar began to have doubts. A week later, Glen Church came up to Tulelake to give a talk. By then he had made stopping ice-minus his personal crusade. "It was the same situation as in Monterey County," Church recalled. "People were concerned, but no one was speaking out." As the situation evolved in Tulelake, the similarities to Monterey County became striking. After the Church talk, Edgar and social worker Djuanna Anderson—like Church, political neophytes—established Concerned Citizens of Tulelake, and the organized Nimby opposition in the community began. Their concerns paralleled those of Church's group—doubts about the organism being nontoxic, fear that it would drift off the test site, and skepticism about EPA's handling of the experiment. As in Monterey, the Tulelake group sought background information from Rifkin, and pored over reams of technical data to develop an in-depth understanding of the test.

Concerned Citizens of Tulelake became a model Nimby group. Its core of activists, led by Edgar and Anderson, lobbied regulators, local officials, and farm organizations, and distributed fliers directly to the community, citing the unknowns of ice-minus. "The most important thing we did was talking with people who live here—getting them involved," Edgar said in a 1989 interview. The group worked fast and furiously. "A lot of late nights, a lot of babysitters, a lot of husbands going without meals and wondering why." (In classic Nimby fashion, the Tulelake group, like its Monterey County counterpart, dissolved shortly after its purpose was obviated in 1987, when the ice-minus field tests were conducted.)

EPA, unmoved by the growing local protest, approved the Lindow test on 13 May 1986. By then the Tulelake group was well on its way to persuading 800 people—fully half of the town's population—to sign petitions opposing the test and had drawn nearly a fourth of the town to a public meeting on ice-minus. Public sentiment swung dramatically against the experiment. By early June the supervisors of both Siskiyou County, which includes Tulelake, and the adjacent Modoc County went on record opposing the test. The university responded by providing more information, and rescheduled the experiment for 6 August.

Soon after, Concerned Citizens of Tulelake, with Rifkin and a Sacramento-based environmental group, filed suit against the test. They claimed that state environmental law required UC Berkeley to file an environmental impact report before the test could be conducted. They won a restraining order on 4 August, two days before the Lindow test was scheduled to begin. Lindow knew that further delays would close the window of opportunity before the winter weather hit. The university finally gave in and agreed out of court to perform an elaborate environmental impact report—a process that would take at least six months.

———————— 🙟🙟🙟 ————————

AGS Shifts Gears

By August 1986 AGS had written off Monterey as a lost cause. The company had patched up its relations with EPA by September of that year, but decided it would start from scratch on a new test site, targeting both the Contra Costa County town of Brentwood, west of San Francisco and known for its "U-pick-'em" fruit and vegetable farms, and a location near Hollister in San Benito County, northwest of Prunedale. This time, however, the company adopted a new strategy—aggressively open outreach. AGS hired two public-relations firms—one to handle public education, the other to handle the expected crush of media. The company assumed that cultivating local support would take as much effort as the research itself. This included announcing the proposed test sites at the very beginning. AGS held public meetings, courted politicians and business groups, and produced a slick video presentation.

For Suslow, public relations became a second career. When people from the community called AGS with concerns, he would often jump into his car, go directly to the individual's house, and talk it over. To make up for the long hours spent away from home, Suslow's family would sometimes join him on his weekend rounds. "There's no question about it—I was [also] bringing them along so that people would be more comfortable with me as a person, seeing that I also had a family, that I had children," he said. "It's sad to learn that those things work, and you use them to your advantage." Suslow added: "Essentially we prepared for a political campaign—a real community campaign to provide information, convince people that what we were doing was safe, had some potential to benefit society, and that it was really a first step . . . for trying to develop effective ways to reduce the use of chemical pesticides. It was what we always tried to do, but [it] kind of got overshadowed" by the controversy.

The essential message—that ice-minus was more than safe, that it was environmentally desirable—hit home in San Benito and Contra Costa. By March 1987 both counties' boards of supervisors had unanimously approved the tests. AGS chose the Brentwood site for its proximity to the company's Oakland labs.

There was amorphous concern in Brentwood, with a rising anxiety level after the decision was made. But unlike Prunedale and Tulelake, no core of local residents stepped forward to organize the local community. The organizers were outsiders—notably the Berkeley Greens and Earth First!, the latter a radical environmentalist group. The Greens gathered the signatures of about 1,500 Contra Costa residents on petitions protesting the test, but AGS and local politicians shrugged off the petitioners as interlopers. The test was scheduled for 24 April 1987.

The evening of 23 April, Church and an environmental attorney made a last-ditch effort for state Supreme Court intervention. After that failed, they waxed philosophical over a couple of beers, then called it a night. The two had intended to wake up at 4 A.M. in order to drive from Sacramento to Brentwood and see the test take place. "But we overslept, and as it turned out it was probably better that way," Church recalled with a laugh. He didn't want to be identified with a more militant 11th-hour effort—vandalism.

The night before, saboteurs cut through the chain-link fence, eluding sleeping security guards. The intruders uprooted about 80 percent of the strawberry plants. AGS scientists hurriedly replanted them when they arrived before dawn, however. Soon a horde of reporters, photographers, and camera crews from as far away as Tokyo arrived to witness the first authorized release of a genetically altered microbe.

"[Brentwood residents are] willing to throw their bodies down . . . to prevent this test," a Greens spokesperson had confidently predicted less than a week earlier. But without indigenous leaders, locals stayed away on the morning of 24 April. Sheriff's deputies escorted a lone protester, a member of Earth First!, off the site.

At 6:45 A.M., AGS scientist Julie Lindemann donned her white, head-to-toe protective moon suit, fitted with a respirator. On the front of the suit was a picture of a snowman in a red circle with a line drawn through it. Printed below the picture: "Frostbusters." That image was splashed across the front pages of newspapers all over the world. Walking between rows of strawberries with a simple hand-held sprayer, the deed was done. (Industry officials later complained that the moon suit, which they considered an unnecessary formality, probably did as much damage to public perceptions of the test's safety as any aspect of the ice-minus episode. As a joke, or reminder, Suslow keeps a plastic statuette of a moon-suit-clad scientist in his office.)

Meanwhile, Lindow and his university team struggled through their environmental impact report and mandatory public hearings. The report did not break any new ground. There were still no sure answers on what was ultimately an untested technology. But slowly the opposition subsided. Some residents were won over. The Siskiyou and Modoc supervisors withdrew their opposition, albeit with strongly worded requests that the university take the test elsewhere. Concerned Citizens of Tulelake felt that the report, performed under duress, changed little. "At first I personally thought that the university would be more responsible," Edgar said. "I was a little naive. I thought they would be concerned about our concerns."

On 30 April 1987, five years after he ignited a historic debate, Steven Lindow finally got his chance. In the essence of anticlimax, he simply dropped bacteria-soaked potato wedges into the earth and covered them over. The spraying did not take place until the sprouts came up through the soil, weeks later. (Before the spraying, Lindow's sprouts were also vandalized. Edgar's group abhorred the action. A second round of testing by AGS was also delayed briefly by vandalism. Responsibility was claimed by Earth First! and a group calling itself "Mindless Thugs against Genetic Engineering.")

——————— ଷଷଷ ———————

The Aftermath

The experimental results could hardly have been more heartening to the battle-weary scientists. In both the AGS and Lindow tests, ice-minus successfully colonized the plants and prevented the formation of frost down to as low as 23 degrees Fahrenheit. Moreover, the scientists' reassurances about the safety of the GEM were proved correct. Ice-minus stayed within the buffer zones. No nearby residents or animals became ill. Other plants were totally unaffected.

So positive a report offered no hint of what would come next: AGS abandoned ice-minus. The company knew that much more extensive field testing on a wide variety of crops in a range of environments and in much larger fields would be essential if ice-minus could ever be brought to market. "If we have to go through a huge amount of effort to educate every community, the cost is going to be beyond us," Bedbrook said in January 1988. Soon after, AGS was acquired for $34 million by a New Jersey agricultural biotechnology firm, DNA Plant Technologies. This was down from $45 million offered only months earlier, reflecting the increasingly precarious financial situation of AGS. Frostban had cost millions and generated no revenues. The new company dropped it almost instantly.

Ironically, Suslow later began marketing naturally occurring strains of *Pseudomonas* that have the same frost-inhibiting qualities as recombinant ice-minus—the very strains critics of the tests had urged AGS to use from the beginning. Recent research has shown that multiple strains used together create a hardier, more effective product.

While Lindow did not abandon ice-minus, as of late 1989 he had no new field tests planned, partly due to the expense. (Public-relations and legal services can alone cost hundreds of thousands of dollars.)

Church blamed the media for forcing scare stories about ice-minus into the forefront. (A general lack of depth in the media coverage was largely verified in an analysis by Krimsky and Plough.) "If you say, 'maybe this test is safe, but maybe in the future other tests won't be,' " the media ignores you, politicians and regulators dismiss you, Church said. Like the Nimby activists against Rocky Flats, Church came to see fear as a potent organizing tool. "No matter what, the media looked for the splash. It corrupted the process, [but] it worked out well for us," he said. Church paused and added: "I'm sure AGS wasn't too thrilled with it." Church's personal goal was always to slow what he saw as rudderless technological progress. Even with a technology presenting low-probability risks, the more and the larger the tests, he reasoned, the greater the prospect of an eventual problem. He saw ice-minus as relatively unimportant as a product itself, but vital to the ground-work needed for more ambitious plans.

Largely true, Suslow acknowledged. "Once you've identified that you can make a deletion of this gene that didn't impair its ability to grow in the environment," he said, "you could then look toward the day when you might put new genes into that deletion site to make it a couple of times better, or to give it a specific advantage that, in truth, it might need to make it effective. That's one of the things that was always very difficult to say at the time." Meanwhile, the rest of the industry hoped that after AGS and Lindow took the heat, their tests could proceed in an orderly fashion.

Indeed, ice-minus convinced EPA that it could kill agricultural biotechnology if it did not ease up. In May 1988, after two other GEMs had been released in other parts of the country with no apparent ill effects, the agency proposed greatly relaxed rules in the spirit of the White House framework. Industry opposed the rules as still too cumbersome, while environmentalists saw EPA lurching toward a triage system—where case-by-case review of GEMs would no longer be attempted.

To a degree, the fear that EPA would end case-by-case review of genetically altered agricultural products was validated by the crippling effects of Reagan era budget cuts on EPA research, rule making, and enforcement. The agency was already hopelessly behind in virtually all areas of its authority. Although EPA increased its spending on biotechnology risk assessment to about $4.5 million in 1988 (other agencies spent far less), that sum represented less than one-thousandth of the annual public and private U.S. investment in biotechnology. Moreover, the Office of Management and Budget (OMB) apparently sided with industry when it blocked the EPA rules pending further revisions. At the time of this writing, the rules had still not been released in final form.

Tactical Errors

Tactical mistakes and miscalculations by UC Berkeley and AGS speak volumes about the pervasive insensitivity of the technological establishment to local community concerns. AGS wanted to test in Monterey County for a variety of valid logistical and scientific reasons, but it overlooked one obvious drawback: Monterey County rarely sees frost. Local farmers handle the relatively minor frost problem effectively, with rare exceptions, by using traditional frost-fighting methods—smudge pots, fans, and irrigation. There was little local incentive to face any additional environmental risk, particularly one of uncertain dimensions. Moreover, the region surrounding Prunedale is one of the most prolific vegetable-growing areas in the nation. Even a very remote chance that ice-minus would prove harmful and invasive could be expected to stir strong concerns among local farmers.

In Tulelake, frost is a greater concern. But UC Berkeley misread the situation there in other ways. When Lindow proposed the tests, the potato industry was mired in recession. By 1986 production costs rose to more than double the price of potatoes on the glutted market. Local farmers thought that the controversy over ice-minus might provoke a consumer boycott of Tulelake potatoes, just as the improper use of chemical pesticides periodically leads to the banning of some fruits. These concerns pushed conservative farmers who are not readily drawn into environmental protests—and even in this case those inclined to accept the university's stance—into the Nimby camp.

Such miscues derive in part from the idea that science-based reasoning should be the sole arbiter of technological disputes. "Legislators and regulators should not be responding to the vocal minority of antagonists or to fears that have no scientific basis," said Winston Brill in a typical industry view. "The kind of attention we received as a result of our research was unforeseeable—it's just ridiculous," Lindow said in 1986. The idea that common knowledge is illegitimate and that concern over the inherent uncertainty of new technologies is "unforeseeable" and "ridiculous" vividly portray the isolation of scientists from the public. Such comments feed Nimby furor. Nimby activists are rarely die-hard environmentalists. "Yet they have listened to diehards," the British journal *The Economist* pointed out, "because they wanted better reassurance than they got from scientists." (The financial ties of university scientists in this field also undermine their credibility. Many influential critics of government actions have much to gain financially from deregulation. Further, regulators are not free from such conflicts. Kingsbury resigned his post in 1988 after it came to light that he received payments from a biotechnology firm. See p. 131 for other striking examples.)

UC Berkeley's effort to override its opponents by enforcing its immunity from local zoning laws reflected the validity of *The Economist*'s observation. "The university is our employee. [It] should not try to put us off or belittle us," says Edgar. [It] say[s], 'We want to help,' Why then did we need a lawsuit?" Church and Edgar see the failure to solicit the public at large—as opposed to easily identifiable local authorities—as disregard for local opinion. "It was very inappropriate, very arrogant of AGS to think that they could come down here and do a test of this magnitude and just ignore the people who live in the area," Church says. "That kind of corporate rudeness should not be imposed on people."

These are not fanatical views. If anything, they are becoming mainstream. "One of the sad parts is that scientists are totally unaware of this," says Jan Reber of Perceptions International. He should know. Scientific and technological companies hire him to investigate their critics.

Suslow, chastened by his experiences, bristles when he hears industry or academic leaders talk about educating "the public." "When you look at what they're really doing, they're talking to legislators, to heads of this and heads of that," he says. "You don't really know what it's like until you go out and attend coffee klatches, go out to the Lion's Club and the Kiwanis."

The biotechnology industry is learning from its struggles, however. Some companies now realize that aggressive outreach may be the only way to reshape the jaundiced public perception of their industry. They use sophisticated public-relations specialists, as AGS did in Brentwood with substantial success, to find a way to soothe wary citizens. Only by talking with everybody—officials, regulators, and residents—can the damage of the past five years be undone, they say. Some companies even express hopefulness that the tide is already turning. This campaign to "educate the public," however, betrays the same weakness for the technological imperative that created a PR problem in the first place. It assumes that public opposition stems from ignorance alone.

"One frequently hears from the establishment side, 'If we only educated them properly and they understood all this, then they wouldn't object.' That's virtually never true," says Allan Mazur, a professor of sociology at Syracuse University who has studied technological controversy. "There's usually no correlation between how much you know and how you feel about the project." At Tulelake, the community was never solidly behind the test, even after absorbing a virtual library of data. "Knowledge . . . is the best cure for fear, if indeed the knowledge confirms that there is nothing to fear," Congressman Leon Panetta, in whose district Prunedale falls, told a congressional committee studying the ice-minus controversy.

Panetta and Mazur's comments were borne out by the 1987 Office of Technology Assessment poll. Well-educated people (including those who describe their understanding of science as very good) rated technological risks—including genetic engineering—at virtually the same levels as those with little formal education. Actually, public-relations efforts are not meant to educate but to convince. This is where the corporate strategy for biotechnology begins to make sense. The OTA poll showed that while education seems to have little effect on risk perception, people who are more knowledgeable about science and technology tend to accept risks—including the risks of biotechnology—more willingly.

———————— ଌଌଌ ————————

Science as Commodity

Biotechnology corporations, scientists, and the media usually portrayed the ice-minus controversy as a conflict between progressive stewardship and selfish irrationality. But the economic subtext often defines what is progressive and rational. Field testing, by nature, is a step toward commercialization. Correspondingly, environmental applications of biotechnology are corporate-driven. All corporate endeavors, even in research-intensive industries, must eventually show a profit or they will die. That profit imperative can distort or artificially inflate the value of a new technology. The potentially positive environmental applications of recombinant organisms demonstrate this point. Altered plants and microorganisms could replace toxic chemical pesticides, killing pests while sparing helpful or benign insects. Ice-minus was touted as a safe alternative to biocides—chemicals that wipe out ice-promoting bacteria. If proved successful and safe, such products would indeed be welcome. Yet ice-minus reveals the industry's shallow environmental logic: The use of chemical biocides has never been a major control for frost.

Other experiments demonstrate similar contradictions, such as a walnut tree engineered to produce a caterpillar-killing toxin. Self-protecting plants of this kind sound good but pose latent risks. An existing biological pesticide, *Bacillus thuringiensis* (BT), kills caterpillars with the same toxin and is harmless to plants, people, and most animals. Farmers use BT in brief, intense sprayings that wipe out breeding moths and butterflies, and inhibit the insects' ability to develop resistance to the poison. A BT-producing plant, Colwell warns, "is a simple prescription, from an environmental point of view, for breeding moths and butterflies that are resistant to BT," which would evolve during constant exposure to the insecticide.

Herbicide-resistant plants have also been produced. Chemicals kill weeds without harming crops, improving yields. Putting aside the obvious environmental flaw in this strategy—continued dependence on chemical pesticides, as opposed to developing non-polluting pest-control methods—some of the corporations working on such plants offer another clue: Monsanto, American Cyanamid, and Du Pont, promoters of the so-called environmentally sensitive strategy, are the very companies that produce chemical pesticides. In other studies, pollution-tolerant fish and plants are being engineered—a backward approach to the toxics problem.

Biotechnology may yet play an important role in aiding agriculture and improving environmental quality. But rapid routes to profit are the primary goals of biotechnology corporations, however high-minded their public statements.

The industry's early years, when new companies cropped up every month, have come and gone. Inevitably, an industry shakeout, in which weaker, smaller firms go bankrupt or are acquired by industry giants, has begun. Surveys conducted in 1989 and 1990 by the Ernst and Young accounting firm revealed that two-thirds of the nation's biotechnology executives believe their companies will be acquired in the next decade and that 40 percent are trying to attract a buyer. The harsh necessities of corporate survival often dictate the pace of research. Companies know that they must have products to sell. The profit imperative creates a compelling need to satisfy investors who have spent billions on an industry that has so far returned little. Only a quarter of the nation's biotechnology companies had posted a profit by 1989. Monsanto, which has spent more than $800 million on the agricultural applications of biotechnology, has yet to earn its first dollar from that investment.

Just as economic pressures influence the choice of products, they push the pace of field testing. Suslow felt keen pressure to test Frostban in order to pave the way for other products. "AGS must demonstrate an ability to participate in commercial agriculture," he acknowledged in 1986. The context for his comment speaks volumes—AGS lost $8.2 million in 1985, and was acquired by a larger biotechnology corporation in 1988. Arrogance, fear of foreign competition, and the exigencies of corporate survival create an urgency to field-test products independent of social value or even economic viability, not to mention the readiness of test-area communities. ("For most of the [community] people, it was simply too fast, and they didn't understand, they didn't want to be guinea pigs," Suslow says.)

The field-test issue symbolized a larger question about the environmental applications of biotechnology: Who will benefit from its advances? Judging from the history of agricultural technology, family farmers will not benefit. In the 1920s through the 1940s, machines replaced animals in American farming, vastly boosting productivity. The number of farms decreased from 6 million to 5 million. In the 1950s chemical fertilizers and pesticides revolutionized American farming. Fewer than half the number of farms at the start of the chemical era exist today. New biotechnologies could again greatly increase farm productivity. But short of major policy changes, they are likely to accelerate the demise of smaller farms that can neither afford the equipment nor accommodate the procedural changes mandated by the new technological standards. Nearly a million more farms could disappear by the turn of the century, a recent congressional report predicts. As economic forces concentrate the biotechnology industry, biotechnology could speed up the monopolization of agriculture.

Genetically engineered bovine growth hormone, which can boost a cow's milk production by 10 percent to 25 percent virtually overnight, looked like a winner for biotechnology. But small dairy farmers refuse to jump on the bandwagon. Like the potato growers of Tulelake, they worry about consumer skittishness. And like the potato glut, they face a chronic milk oversupply that hurts them at the marketplace (and costs the federal government, which subsidizes the surplus, billions of dollars yearly). Corporate farms and the four chemical companies (including Monsanto) trying to market the hormone stand to make a fortune. What would 25 percent more milk do for small farmers? Drive them out of business, many reason. An unusual coalition, including farm-state politicians, farmers, consumers, environmentalists, and Jeremy Rifkin recently persuaded a major ice-cream maker and five of the largest supermarket chains to boycott milk produced by cows treated with the drug. Wisconsin and Minnesota have banned the use of bovine growth hormone until mid-1991.

In such cases, the terms *progress* and *irrationality* obscure the context of fear and risk in Nimby battles. The real issue is control. Who will manage and profit from new technologies, and at whose expense?

To Church, who denies being against technology, part of the

answer to commercial anarchy is for communities to enforce a testing slowdown. "I think what we did was good for this community, for society, and in the long run, for biotechnology," he said recently. "Sooner or later a disaster is going to happen. The later the better for the industry, because the more [biotechnology] will be set into our ways."

Recent events showed the vulnerability of the corporate strategy for commercialization of agricultural GEMs. Although about a dozen other living GEMs have been field-tested since ice-minus, this is a far cry from the hundreds expected only a few years ago. And no corporation is close to marketing a living GEM. "No floodgates have opened here," says Rifkin, who predicts "years and years of battle in the courts and in Congress" before the first commercial-scale release occurs. Federal agencies are still squabbling over establishing rules for such a test. The sector of the biotechnology industry based on the release of altered microbes is in deep trouble. Costly delays scare off investors who the companies once had eating out of their hands. By 1988 only a handful of American companies were actively developing GEMs as products for the agricultural environment. "Putting out genetically altered [recombinant] microbial pesticides—microbial biocontrols—is going to be an extremely limited and an extremely slow process if it really continues much at all," according to Suslow. Perhaps a few GEMs will be marketed within 10 years, but he doubts even that. The regulators are not the problem, he adds; "it's largely the commitment, the cost, the time for public acceptance."

The agricultural uses of living, genetically altered organisms carry risks. The biotechnology industry's claims about the safety and social benefits of its products may be self-serving and oversold. And its priorities may be skewed. Yet, slowing or halting the technology altogether also carries risks. The 1987 OTA poll suggested that despite widespread fears, most Americans want to develop GEMs for agriculture. They believe that the industry ultimately will be an important, perhaps pivotal, force in the economy as well as a boon to the world food supply. If community opponents demand certainty that ice-minus and every other agricultural GEM will not be harmful, that potential may never be realized. More important, the conflict raises serious questions about a process of scientific and technological development that makes obstructionism the only antidote to impotence.

5

Biomedical Research and the Nightmare in Laurel Heights

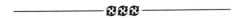

Nobody is stupid. Nobody needs a degree to understand that the wool was pulled over our heads. —Ruth Mansbach, critic of biomedical research lab expansion

Jere Goyan, dean of the School of Pharmacy at the University of California, San Francisco (UCSF), smoothes his gray beard and eases into a chair in his office. He sighs, pondering the question, "Has this been the most trying time in your career?" At issue: A neighborhood group bitterly opposes the proposed move of his school's basic research labs into a building in their area, close to campus. "No, getting beat up by the U.S. Congress was harder," he answers. That was during his stint as President Jimmy Carter's commissioner of food and drugs. But Laurel Heights has been a bear.

While writing this chapter, I was on an unpaid leave of absence from my former job as a writer, editor, and advisor for *Synapse,* the student publication of the University of California at San Francisco. *Synapse,* although administered through the official university structure, is funded out of student fees and retains formal editorial independence from university administration. In that position, I was the first to report several of UCSF's occupational-health and planning problems, described in this chapter, that were later cited by community critics in attacks against the university.

Though comfortable and attractive, Goyan's office lacks the pristine quality of the dean's office in the larger, wealthier School of Medicine. The lobby radiates a rumpled approachability: jammed faculty mailboxes, aging carpets, a "Do Not Water" sign so prominent that it destroys the aesthetic of the plant it guards. Goyan's own relaxed informality signals that he hasn't completely surrendered his working-class roots. He grew up in Eureka, California, then a sleepy logging town near the Oregon border where community spirit and local ties were strong. He came to the field of pharmacy the small-town way. "I had worked from the eighth grade on in a small drugstore in Eureka, Buxton's Drugs, and had come to the conclusion that I really liked that sort of thing." Goyan took his pharmacy degree at UCSF after a year at Humboldt State College, close to home. The idea was to return to Eureka to practice. Instead, the lure of science won him over. He earned a Ph.D., then made a meteoric rise through the ranks of academia, becoming dean in 1967 at the tender age of thirty-seven. By age fifty, Goyan was the most influential drug policymaker in the nation.

Goyan's father, who ran a filling station and drove a tank truck for an oil company, found his son's academic career baffling. After Goyan completed his pharmacy degree, Buxton's owner offered him a $10,000 salary to take over a new store—quite a sum in 1952. Instead, he chose $1,500 a year as a graduate student. Years later, as a faculty member, he made only $6,000 a year. "My father thought I was an absolute nut," to give up both money and the home fires for this, Goyan says with a laugh. It wasn't until Goyan was suddenly a national figure headed for Washington, D.C. that his father began to come around. As Goyan talks about the protracted conflict with the Laurel Heights group, he leaves the impression that he wonders if his father's doubts may have been justified after all.

Like Goyan, UCSF had humble beginnings. In 1864 local physician Hugh Toland founded a medical college, enrollment eight. The college affiliated with the fledgling University of California in 1873, quickly adding schools of pharmacy and dentistry, and taking over responsibility for clinical care at San Francisco General Hospital, the primary county medical facility. In 1895 San Francisco Mayor Adolph Sutro donated 13 acres on a central city hill, complete with stunning views of the Golden Gate. Parnassus Heights, as the area was known, would seem a misnomer decades later when it became home not to Olympian poets but to a massive scientific edifice. Over the years, UCSF's picturesque setting and proximity to Berkeley and Stanford, generous state support, and torrents of federal research funds attracted the nation's top biologists. One of the few universities anywhere dedicated almost solely to biomedical sciences, UCSF rapidly built a reputation of quality and prestige, and its schools soon ranked at or near the top of their fields. A major new hospital was constructed in 1955 and an adjacent research tower in 1958, then two more research towers in 1966 and a new nursing building in 1972.

By this time UCSF scientists were on their way to making dozens of cutting-edge discoveries involving kidney transplants, infant lung function, fetal surgery, cancer-causing oncogenes (for which two UCSF scientists shared the Nobel Prize in 1989), AIDS, and what may be the most influential biological development of our time—recombinant DNA technology, or gene-splicing.

But as early as the late 1960s the price of UCSF's success became painfully evident. Despite massive expansion, campus buildings induced claustrophobia. Famous professors had to cram each new experiment into labs already bursting at the seams. Clinicians in UCSF's tertiary-care hospitals coped with half the average space per bed at comparable medical centers. The Dental School risked loss of accreditation due to overcrowding. More growth seemed unavoidable. The Board of Regents, the multicampus UC system's governing body, approved construction of a new Dental School and a 15-story hospital, and contemplated adding yet another research tower.

─────────── ღღღ ───────────

Urban Realities

During the 1940s and 1950s, the huge expanse of sand dunes, meadows, and forests that UCSF overlooked filled up with housing and small businesses that pressed forward to campus boundaries. Harvesting a rich economic bounty from the huge medical center, for decades the community passively accepted UCSF expansion. But by the early 1970s, many neighbors saw UCSF as a growing problem—blocking their view of Mount Sutro (a wooded hill directly behind Parnassus Heights) with an ugly monolith of buildings, crowding their streets with the cars of thousands of commuting employees, displacing hundreds of people from scarce housing.

Campus leaders firmly believed that UCSF's success depended on cross-fertilizing academic programs that enjoy ready access to library and hospitals. Banishing a program from the Parnassus hub was considered tantamount to ordering its descent into mediocrity. Yet recognizing changing realities, UCSF reopened its planning process with an eye toward controlled growth. Its administration endorsed the concept of a "soft-edged campus"—creative landscaping and low-rise, terraced architecture. It announced plans to increase carpooling and declared a moratorium on the purchase of local housing through 1985.

Still, campus planners misjudged the degree of alienation caused by prior development. As it became clear that UCSF intended to build more major structures, the community's rhetoric grew incendiary. "[UCSF's] expansion juggernaut is ruthlessly crushing the nearby San Francisco residential communities," read one flier. A local resident compared campus growth to the Watergate scandal, and used a pointed analogy, labeling the medical center a wildly proliferating "cancer in our midst."

Loosely affiliated as the Mount Sutro Defense Committee, community groups took UCSF to court in October 1974, charging campus planners with violations of the California Environmental Quality Act (CEQA)—a statute modeled on, but more stringent than, the National Environmental Policy Act. CEQA, like most major environmental legislation in this country, was enacted during the sweeping regulatory tide of the late 1960s and early 1970s. By 1974 antigrowth groups and environmentalists were using the act to fight expansion projects of all kinds, not just those that were obvious polluters. The campus violated CEQA by failing to conduct a meaningful evaluation of alternatives to central-campus growth, the suit charged.

When the Superior Court sided with the plaintiffs, for the first time UCSF glimpsed the limits of its unilateral power. The court blocked all construction until UCSF redrew its environmental impact reports (EIRs) and reopened the process to community input. The campus appealed, dragging out court deliberations. In May 1976 the parties reached a compromise considered unthinkable a few months earlier: The campus population would be capped and structural growth held to 3.55 million gross square feet—allowing a new hospital, Dental School, and library, but no other major structures. The hospital would be the last campus high rise; the library and Dental School would be contoured and terraced. UCSF agreed not to expand into adjacent areas beyond campus boundaries, and to sell dozens of houses back into private hands. Mount Sutro would be maintained permanently as open space.

---------------- ଓଓଓ ----------------

An Elegant Solution?

Most UCSF administrators and professors gradually recognized that a second major site was the only long-term prospect for growth. Finding it was a conundrum. To maintain the quality and productivity of research, teaching, and patient care, the site would have to be close to the main campus. To preserve the integrity of the

1976 commitment to the community, it would have to be out of the immediate area.

Then came a godsend. In December 1984 a large building two miles from Parnassus came onto the market. Formerly headquarters for an insurance company, the well-maintained property boasted a plush 350-seat auditorium, ample conference facilities, a television studio, a restaurant, and more than 500 parking spaces; and it was surrounded by acres of meticulously landscaped lawns, perfectly matched with the adjacent, upper-middle-class Laurel Heights area. The Board of Regents quickly offered $55 million for the site. "We see this as a place where many of our campus administrative functions can be centralized and where we can also provide space for certain academic programs," said UCSF Chancellor Julius Krevans, in announcing the purchase. There was vague talk about portions of the School of Pharmacy moving to the building, now called the Laurel Heights Campus.

The site's Laurel Heights neighbors gave a mixed response. Merchants from nearby restaurants and boutiques catering to the affluent residents were ecstatic at the thought of hundreds of professionals with money in their pockets. George Carr, an attorney and president of the local home owners group, the Laurel Heights Improvement Association (LHIA), expressed caution. "Present-day students are not that desirable in large quantities in a residential community," he told the *San Francisco Chronicle* the day the sale was announced. "The thing we don't want is to turn it into another Telegraph Avenue," he added, referring to the strip adjacent to UC Berkeley, across the San Francisco Bay, to which renegades and street people have flocked since the days of the free speech movement.

Carr's comment was telling. It showed considerable unfamiliarity with UCSF, which despite its size and prestige remained obscure to those living only two miles away. Unlike most universities, nearly all UCSF students pursue advanced academic or professional degrees. The entire campus currently has only about 2,300 students—

the School of Pharmacy a few hundred—compared to Berkeley's roughly 35,000. Moreover, UCSF has no comparable tradition of activism; even mild nonconformism is rare.

The day after the *Chronicle* story appeared, Krevans wrote to Carr, inviting him to a get-acquainted meeting to assure him that UCSF planned to be a good neighbor. The letter's timing showed that, like the Parnassus episode, UCSF was behind the curve on community relations. Carr learned of the sale when the reporter called him for a quote—no one from the campus approached him until after his guard was up.

Six weeks later, when UCSF held its first public meeting to discuss the new Laurel Heights campus, 150 edgy neighbors showed up. Krevans soothed most of them by predicting that UCSF would be less obtrusive than the building's former owner. At its peak population, he said, the new campus would have 200 fewer people than did the insurance company, adding that most activity would be administrative, with some academic programs. Following the meeting, representatives of the Jordan Park Improvement Association, also near the site, called UCSF "a stabilizing influence in the neighborhood." And Carr's organization voted not to oppose the sale. Carr wrote to Krevans, reiterating the association's understanding of UCSF's commitments regarding site development: The parklike grounds would be maintained, the building would not be expanded in any way and it "will be primarily used for administrative offices; that there would be some teaching functions . . . but that it would not become a major teaching facility."

A few months later, in July 1985, UCSF announced its intention to move the basic research labs of the School of Pharmacy—so-called "wet labs" for biomedical studies—to Laurel Heights. When the implications of the plan became apparent in a draft EIR the following April, the placid relationship between UCSF and its Laurel Heights neighbors ended. The locals were incensed. They launched a multilayered attack on the EIR, beginning with general land-use complaints. For example, they predicted that deliveries for research activities—though amounting to less than 1 percent of area traffic—

would promote street congestion; Board of Regents meetings in the auditorium would draw protesters, disrupting the area's tranquil atmosphere; and 10- to 12-foot-high stacks for lab ventilation would obscure views from hillside homes. They also criticized plans to build a new loading dock and 25 parking stalls in a lawn area. For each of these concerns UCSF ordered changes in its EIR designed to solve or reduce the problem. The relatively minor complaints of Laurel Heights residents were a far cry from those voiced by the neighbors of Parnassus Heights, where the medical center dominated virtually all local land use.

The Laurel Heights neighbors harbored a more elemental concern, however—fear of toxic substances. Of course, the pharmacy researchers planned to use the tools of modern biology—recombinant DNA, toxic chemical reagents, radioisotopes, and lab animals. Inevitably, these products would generate hazardous waste. At the Parnassus campus, similar research had been conducted for decades, using far larger quantities of hazardous materials without apparent ill effects on the local environment. Indeed, universities, hospitals, and pharmaceutical companies in every urban area in the nation routinely use these methods and substances with virtually no sign of harm to neighbors—and rarely with any harm to scientists, for that matter. UCSF promised that state-of-the-art safety practices would be the rule at Laurel Heights. Still, the residents stood firm: absolutely no labs. Some of the local critics called Krevans's reassurances—that the site would be used primarily for administration, with some "academic" programs—a ruse to deter opposition to the labs until after they became a fait accompli. Carr called the lab proposal "a violation of the understanding reached between the University and [LHIA] prior to the purchase of the facility."

The university represented the issue as a simple, if unfortunate, misunderstanding. "Apparently, we did not make it clear enough that 'academic' includes a mixture of teaching and research," explained Tom Gwyn, the UCSF community relations chief. "As our plans for the specific use of the building developed over the course of the year, in consultation with our own faculty, it became clear that the best possible use was to move the basic sciences program of the School of Pharmacy. Each step of the way we tried to keep the public informed." It was certainly true that UCSF did not *promise* that the building would be primarily administrative—officials merely spoke of intentions and plans. Gwyn said in a 1990 interview that, while there was no effort to deceive, campus planners intentionally used broad terminology in order to maintain flexibility and protect faculty prerogatives.

When Carr wrote his welcome letter to UCSF, explicitly stating his understanding that the building would be an administrative center, Krevans replied that things were still in flux. "I wish to emphasize that we have not completed our decision making with regard to which specific administrative and academic functions will be located at the new site," he wrote. Krevans said nothing about what range of possibilities were being considered, however. More importantly, he responded only after a month had passed—three weeks beyond the date UCSF officially took ownership. Whether by design or accident, Carr was encouraged to believe that the views stated in his letter reflected those of UCSF, until long after a challenge to the sale could have been mounted. The Laurel Heights residents believed they had been deliberately misled.

The acrimony quickly escalated. "Most of the people I have talked to are bordering on hysteria" over the project's toxic threat, said Margaret Verges, a prominent anti-UCSF activist who lived near the site. Sensing political opportunity or the need for damage control, three county supervisors requested a delay in all development of the Laurel Heights site until after new public hearings could be conducted.

At this point, LHIA took the lead for the opposition, using every equivocation, every qualification in the university's EIR as evidence of grave danger. Of course, UCSF's EIR stopped short of saying that the labs would pose no risk—"zero risk" is a concept foreign to science. (Apparently exasperated by LHIA's high-flying fears, Krevans himself lapsed into hyperbolic nonsense in a July 1986 letter to local residents. "We will not be adding any pollution whatsoever to the neighborhood—no air pollution, no noise pollution, and no toxic waste," he wrote. "There is no danger of leaking or accidental spills.")

The UC Board of Regents brushed aside residents' complaints and approved a revised EIR in July 1986. Work to retrofit the building for labs began almost immediately. LHIA complained to the city, but as a state institution, UCSF is exempt from local zoning laws. Seeing no alternative, LHIA sued, charging violations of the California Environmental Quality Act and breech of contract claiming that Krevans had lied to the neighbors about plans to use the site as a major lab. From then on it would be war.

---------------- ଈଈଈ ----------------

Foundation for Fear

UCSF scientists and administrators saw the LHIA suit as based on absurdly exaggerated fears and selfish obstructionism. ("I am for research and I am for helping the poor and the sick, but not in this neighborhood," said one critic.) Basic research into biology and medicine, although sometimes controversial for ethical reasons, has generally presented few significant health or safety risks. The researchers found the complaints incomprehensible. Unlike patently hazardous, accident-prone technologies such as nuclear bomb manufacturing; unlike untested technologies, such as the release into the environment of living, genetically altered microorganisms; decades of experience suggest that biology labs are relatively safe.

Why such fear? A series of recent developments shows that the response of the Laurel Heights neighbors fits a general public skepticism of biological research. "Research biology is still having only a minor effect on people's well-being," acknowledged David Baltimore, a Nobel laureate in biology. In 1970, the federal government declared war on cancer, "but the victory has not yet materialized, and public disillusionment with the research enterprise is significant enough to label the so-called war against cancer a kind of biomedical Vietnam," Stanford University President Donald Kennedy said in 1981. His comment is even more relevant today.

While appreciation for complex, abstract research is difficult, aversion to potential dangers is instinctual. Fear, well fed on the kinds of ecological disasters recounted in chapter 1, generates safety concerns that the public generalizes to other technologies. And a few notable medical-science missteps have contributed their share. Take exposure to radiation: The public's proclivity to draw extreme analogies and generalizations finds fertile ground here. The radiation-safety abuses of the nuclear bomb makers, detailed in chapter 3, have been widely publicized in recent years, as have the Chernobyl and Three Mile Island nuclear power plant accidents. In all these cases, experts were found to be dishonest, negligent, inept, or just plain wrong. The lesson was clear. Many neighbors of the Rocky Flats Plant in Colorado will never accept *any* additional radiation risk, whatever the opinion of scientists. Why should they, given their experience?

In contrast, the residents of Laurel Heights have no personal experience of gross radiation mishaps. In fact average exposures to workers in biomedical labs are a fraction of the dose we all absorb from natural sources. And for many years biomedical labs have depended on radioisotopes without apparent health effects. Residents near those labs receive exposures that are so slight as to be virtually undetectable. Yet this apparently reassuring picture has little impact in the current social context. Exposures seen as appalling today were once routine in medical therapy and on the job. Every few years the standards for acceptable doses of radiation have been adjusted downward—to the point now that many experts refuse to define any exposure level as "safe." The public vividly remembers the series of miscalculations and adjustments. The resistance of the Laurel Heights neighbors, like resistance to scientific and technological endeavors by many other groups, was linked to a growing distrust of expert assurances, not just in regard to the safety of research isotopes but also to technical hazards of all kinds.

Science seeks the unknown. Danger may lie where science leads, people reason. The manipulation of genes, the building blocks of heredity, offers the prospect of medical miracles and limitless human understanding of our essential biochemical nature. Yet many people blanch at the idea of tampering with the nature of life itself. To some, cloned animals and organisms formed from the genetic material of different species represent the ultimate in human arrogance. Efforts to forecast or prevent genetically linked ailments or traits remind others of the specter of Hitlerian eugenics.

In 1974, 11 eminent biologists proposed a moratorium on certain experiments until after scientists had the opportunity to evaluate the potential biohazards of the revolutionary new technique. Two years later, based on a landmark meeting of leading scientists from around the world at the Asilomar Conference Center in California, the National Institutes of Health (NIH) established and codified safety guidelines for work with recombinant DNA. It limited the kinds of organisms that could be used and banned certain experiments involving cancer genes and toxin production.

Thousands of person-years of research attested to the relative safety of DNA experimentation, however. The guidelines were gradually relaxed to the point where virtually any experiment envisioned can now be conducted. Biologists cannot imagine their work without recombinant DNA. But the general public is less sanguine. As noted in chapter 3, in the largest national poll on genetic engineering ever conducted, more than half of the respondents expected (in 1987) genetically engineered products to present "serious danger[s] to people or the environment."

Today the pervasive fear of AIDS correlates with this caution about the biological unknown. Medical centers that treat AIDS patients and directly study the AIDS virus—UCSF is a leader in this work—may seem scary. Recent surveys indicate that education has done little to allay public fears about AIDS. Most people understand that they cannot contract the disease through casual contact. Yet many people who know better—including scientists—shun people with AIDS. (In one recent study, only 39 percent of a sample of medical researchers and other scientists said that they would permit contact between their six-year-old child and a "playmate at school with AIDS.")

Recent scandals involving illegal disposal of medical waste, including dirty syringes and blood samples that washed up on beaches, were met with widespread public outrage. In the New York area, the episodes led to stricter regulations for handling infectious waste. They also carried an ironic Nimby twist: The new rules increased the amount of waste to be burned, but strong neighborhood opposition has blocked construction of incinerators to meet the demand.

Meanwhile, major universities, including Case Western, Rutgers, the University of Southern California, Stanford, and UCSF (as will be discussed later) have experienced a wave of lab-safety mishaps. Thirty-five percent of the biological sciences departments in U.S. universities judged their air-decontamination systems "inadequate" in a 1989 NIH survey. In the same survey, 16 percent to 23 percent of hospitals and medical science research organizations rated their toxic-waste disposal capacity as inadequate. Other studies indicate that academic chemistry labs suffer 10 to 100 times as many accidents as does industry. Yet few universities sponsor formal safety training. This does not mean that those seeking careers should reject universities in favor of chemical manufacturing. Most lab accidents are minor, most legal violations procedural—posing small health risks. Industry commonly uses far higher quantities of hazardous substances, usually creating vastly greater dangers. Yet the spate of well-publicized problems contributes to a gestalt of public skepticism about the safety and wisdom of biological research.

Just as gene-splicing has spawned new organisms, the new biology has stimulated hybrids of business and academia. Pharmaceutical companies have financed university research for decades. But the biotechnology revolution has for the first time drawn large numbers of basic research biologists in American universities into the corporate fold. Lawmakers, university officials, and researchers worry openly that the pull of vast biotechnology profits may skew biomedical research, compromise its quality, or lead to the exploitation of unwitting patients as subjects in tests of potentially profitable techniques or drugs. NIH and many universities are revising conflict-of-interest rules in an effort to chill the increasingly cozy relationship between their professors and the biotechnology industry.

The U.S. government encourages industry–university collaboration, in part to justify a vast investment of tax dollars. Yet the public grows suspicious when hundreds of leading biomedical inventors cash in on the mysteries of dread disease. Commercial affiliations in academia are so pervasive (industry funded 25 percent of university research in biotechnology by the mid-1980s, according to a 1986 study) that the trend has significantly affected public perceptions. Some 60 Harvard scientists have links with 65 or more biotech corporations. Several UCSF scientists have become high-profile entrepreneurs, including Herbert Boyer, one of two scientists credited with the discovery of gene-splicing. Boyer made tens of millions of dollars as cofounder of Genentech. These links were not lost on the Laurel Heights activists, who frequently accused UCSF of eyeing the site as a way to line professors' pockets with drug-company fees.

"For most scientists, basic research continues to be a relatively low-paying profession that requires deep dedication," writes Baltimore, himself a biotech millionaire. "But when some priests act like lords, the whole clergy becomes suspect."

———————— ଷଷଷ ————————

Animal Rights Rebellion

The public's growing skepticism about biomedical research has also been fostered by the ascendancy of the animal rights movement. Concern over using animals to test cosmetics or produce fur coats is hardly surprising or new. And conditions that few would describe as humane typify livestock and poultry production. Is the scientific use of animals different in kind? Of course, there have been incidents of callousness, even cruelty toward research animals in the scientific community. Some tests are redundant or otherwise wasteful. But scientists claim a morally sound purpose for their use of animals, and the public largely agrees, according to polling data. The academic community brands activists' accusations of wholesale abuse in animal research as false and misleading. Still, in recent years animal activists have put biomedical researchers on the defensive.

For more than a century, the nation's many animal-protection societies emphasized humane treatment, never questioning the age-old belief that human needs must come first. Since the mid-1970s, however, increasingly militant activists espouse animal-human equality. The animal rights movement has grown dramatically in recent years. It exerts growing influence on the nation's roughly 7,000 animal-protection groups, which have a combined membership of an estimated 10 million.

Forget the local humane society. The Band of Mercy, Animal Liberation Front, and Urban Gorillas take actions as warlike as their names imply—vandalism, infiltration, espionage, attempted bombings, and arson that have caused millions of dollars in damage. Many research institutions have resorted to elaborate security systems, spawning an armed-camp mentality in a profession that can only thrive on openness. Animal rights activists routinely take to the streets or deluge public officials with letters and calls, in order to crack down on researchers considered particularly bad offenders. UCSF, a frequent target, had a serious run-in with animal activists shortly before the Laurel Heights controversy erupted.

Animal rights militants represent a growing discomfort about animal treatment in society as a whole. Federal regulators, increasingly responsive to the animal rights message, enacted rules in 1985 that were estimated to cost research institutions $900 million to start and more than $207 million in yearly maintenance. Leading universities have had major projects delayed or funds withdrawn in the wake of animal care scandals. Moreover, activists now use laws designed to protect the environment as a means of scuttling animal research they find reprehensible. The New England Anti-Vivisection Society attempted to block construction of a major biomedical research facility in Boston based on subsidiary concerns that it would congest traffic, tax the city's water supply, and cause pollution. In an ambitious though unsuccessful effort, a large national group, People for the Ethical Treatment of Animals, attacked all federally funded biomedical research in the San Francisco Bay Area by charging that the studies violated federal standards for air and water quality, and by making a wide range of general land-use complaints.

The use of environmental law, combined with the decentralized nature of the animal rights movement, fosters alliances between groups that share common goals. George Carr rejects the movement's philosophy, he says, and the Laurel Heights Improvement Association never officially questioned the validity of animal experimentation per se. "[But] when you're fighting a giant and someone comes to help, you accept that help, and in turn, you extend help to them," he says, describing his group's links to antivivisectionists. This experience was not unlike the symbiotic relationship between antigenetic engineering activist Jeremy Rifkin and the Nimby groups that opposed ice-minus. Rifkin gained a more credible position from which to pursue his own political agenda, while the Nimbys gained the benefits of legal expertise and political savvy. Just as the Laurel Heights group was drawn to animal rights militants, Concerned Citizens of North Monterey County and Concerned Citizens of Tulelake—conservative, nonideological farmers and workers—saw Rifkin, a sophisticated radical activist, as an ally.

In this way, Nimbyism transcends traditional political barriers. For average citizens, figures of institutional authority—politicians, university leaders, government regulators, scientists—would ordinarily seem the natural place to turn to resolve local conflicts. Radicals would normally be shunned. But the erosion of trust in official versions of reality has begun to turn conventional political affiliations upside down. Instead of turning *to* authority figures, average citizens are turning *on* them.

--------------- 𝕽𝕽𝕽 ---------------

Nimby Reflex

Given UCSF's long-standing credibility problem with neighbors of its main campus, a poorly articulated proposal for a large new lab seemed almost calculated to invoke the latent constellation of public fears and doubts about biological research. The situation was ripe for a Nimby response. The media image of Nimby groups as forged from raw self-interest suggests why Laurel Heights activists bristled at the label. But they displayed classic Nimby qualities, including self-interest. LHIA, a voluntary organization of affluent property owners, fought fiercely to protect the quality of life in Laurel Heights. The incursion of major laboratories into residential neighborhoods should simply not be permitted, Carr said in a 1989 interview—particularly not in his area or those contiguous to it. "Presidio Heights, Pacific Heights, Laurel Heights, or Jordan Park— those are some of the [most] prime residential areas in the city," he said, by way of explanation. Real estate values there are among the highest in the nation.

Carr, a private attorney, has an office on the 23rd floor of a fashionable tower in San Francisco's financial district. He hardly fits the image of a community activist. Nearing 60, rounding at the middle, Carr fills out a three-piece suit, complete with watch fob. Furniture with a 1940s look, pictures of masted schooners, and framed photos and newspaper headlines of the great 1906 earthquake complete the archaic feel of his inner office. In the lobby, an oil painting by his father-in-law shows downtown San Francisco as viewed from the Laurel Heights home Carr has owned for a decade. Like many here, he is a transplant—from Des Moines, Iowa, originally. An Irish Catholic, Carr exudes traditional family values. He calls himself a political conservative. "Some people say that I'm to the right of John Birch, but I don't believe that," he jokes. Carr speaks slowly and deliberately, as if always looking for an elusive word. He laughs easily and peppers his comments with mild profanity. He claimed San Francisco as his home when he graduated from Stanford Law School in 1955. In a city easily loved, Carr is clearly among the smitten.

"The whole idea that we're [LHIA is] opposed to science is another big cop-out and lie," Carr says, responding to UCSF's frequent suggestions that the opposition is a product of scientific illiteracy. Carr supports large-scale research such as space exploration, he says, "but you don't put the launching pad in the center of your residential neighborhood, for God's sake."

To be sure, Carr is no scientific sophisticate. For example, he suggests that UCSF uses chemicals and isotopes to explore "subatomic matter"—confusing biology with physics. But he studied science in high school and worked as a radar technician in the navy. His wife, also active in LHIA, is a physician with a research background. "My wife is much more upset than I am about the [potential UCSF] emissions in relation to our children," he says.

One word defines the issue for Carr: *control*. UCSF, exempt from municipal zoning ordinances that would prohibit similar development of the site by a private company, does what it pleases, the neighbors be damned. "I have more control over Standard Oil than UCSF," Carr says. His words could easily have come from anti-Rocky Flats activists in Arvada, Colorado, or a multitude of other Nimby groups around the nation.

Initially, UCSF officials apparently did not sense the tenacity and determination of Carr and LHIA. They saw the Laurel Heights suit as a minor irritant. Their confidence seemed justified when in September 1986 the Superior Court ruled in the university's favor. (Around this time, the portion of the suit that claimed UCSF committed fraud was split off as a separate legal action.) Chancellor

Krevans soon after announced that all School of Pharmacy basic research would move to Laurel Heights by the end of 1988. LHIA quickly appealed, however.

Carr and Kathryn Devincenzi, a young corporate attorney who grew up in Laurel Heights, oversaw the efforts of the group's legal team. Gradually, Devincenzi took over the case. Dressed in business suits, lugging a bulging briefcase, and filling page after page of yellow legal paper with notes, she looks like a typical, no-nonsense lawyer. Actually, Devincenzi is the opposite pole from the studied reasonableness practiced by all UCSF officials who deal with the public. (Like Carr and others in her group, she sees that very reasonableness as a manipulative ploy.) Crackling contempt belies her tailored exterior. As much rabble-rouser as litigator, at community meetings and public hearings Devincenzi shouts down the opposition, exposes any apparent inconsistency or error, and turns it into an organizing tool. "Without somebody like Kathy," Carr said in 1989, "the university would have won a long time ago." In this war, Devincenzi was field commander.

-------------- ??? --------------

The Siege Begins

When the state Court of Appeal agreed to review the lower court decision, the imbroglio became a potential crisis for UCSF. The main campus continued to burst its seams and restive faculty members eyed offers of spacious labs at other institutions. Before the court hearing in April 1987, two developments would lead to a siege mentality.

In March 1987 UCSF was cited for thirty-three violations of state radiation-safety regulations on its main campus. Making matters worse, the previous year many of the same labs had been cited for similar problems, and students had complained about a dearth of lab-safety training. Nearly all the violations involved training, monitoring, and documentation, rather than actual overexposures, but the lapse could hardly have come at a worse time for UCSF. Headlines in the local papers gave LHIA activists better ammunition than they could have hoped for. UCSF had staked its legal case on the strength of its safety record. It quickly upgraded its radiation monitoring and enforcement, but the damage to campus credibility was severe.

Meanwhile, UCSF had recruited a large research group led by Nina Agabian, a respected molecular parisitologist who studies some of the worst microbial killers of the Third World, including malaria and African sleeping sickness. Agabian was viewed as the cornerstone of the Laurel Heights research outpost. She was leaving her job as acting director of the Oakland, California, Naval Biosciences Lab (NBL), run jointly by the navy and UC Berkeley, and used Department of Defense funds in her own research there. (The navy closed the lab in June 1987, at which time Agabian moved her research team to Laurel Heights.) Carr, Devincenzi, and Margaret Verges charged publicly that UCSF would be conducting biological-warfare research at Laurel Heights. Exotic organisms causing incurable diseases might leak from the labs and infect local residents, they claimed.

Krevans categorically denied the claims. Agabian threatened court action against the accusers. Still, LHIA and its allies trotted out the allegations at every opportunity, attracting press attention and boosting public anxiety.

In context, LHIA's claims were not totally implausible. From the 1940s through 1969, NBL studied and "weaponized" various microbes as one of the largest labs in the nation's biological arsenal. When President Nixon renounced biological warfare in 1969, the lab shifted its work to endemic diseases that afflict sailors stationed in developing nations, and to "biological defense"—primarily vaccine and drug studies. But defensive research, arms-control experts agree, is indistinguishable from offensive research. Although NBL's safety practices during Agabian's tenure were relatively good, an expansive public record concerning the military's overall biological-weapons research program shows a cavalier disregard for public health and safety. LHIA used that record to its advantage.

Indignant denials did little to allay rising fears, partly because UCSF's statements were as arrogant as LHIA's were overblown. Krevans repeatedly pointed out that UCSF could not conduct biological- or chemical-warfare research even if it wanted to, because of the university's prohibition on classified research. Actually, UCSF had taken on a number of unclassified contracts to study chemical-warfare antidotes over the years, which activists pointed out. And in early negotiations between UCSF and Agabian, the university expected the navy to remodel Agabian's Laurel Heights lab, as part of its ongoing interest in her work. Ultimately the navy withdrew all support, but Carr, Devincenzi, and Verges refused to believe it.

---------------- ରରର ----------------

The Tide Turns

In a now volatile atmosphere, the Court of Appeal heard the case of *LHIA v. UCSF.* The arguments differed little from those offered to the Superior Court. "This sort of research is among the most hazardous and should be performed outside population centers in order to minimize the risk," Devincenzi wrote to the court. She presented little concrete evidence to support the claim, however. UCSF attorneys countered that because clinical facilities use many of the same chemicals and radioisotopes, a logical extension of Devincenzi's argument would be that people should travel to industrial parks for critical health care.

Still, the shortcomings of the university's environmental impact report were apparent. The California Environmental Quality Act aims to expose the environmental-review process to informed public scrutiny. In July 1987 the appeals judges ruled unanimously that the university failed that test miserably. "It's a significant victory for neighborhood preservation and residential viability," said Devincenzi. One local paper compared the case to David slaying Goliath.

UCSF had described the Laurel Heights project in its EIR as involving only labs from the School of Pharmacy, using about a third of the building. This was indeed the initial plan, but campus officials had made it clear that they ultimately expected to fill the rest of the building with biomedical labs. The court ruled that the law requires a review of "the cumulative impact on the environment of . . . reasonably foreseeable future projects." The court also castigated the EIR's discussion of alternatives to using the Laurel Heights building. UCSF devoted three pages in the 500-page document to a perfunctory checklist of alternate sites, all of which were rejected without meaningful analysis. (Ironically, UCSF lost to the Mount Sutro Defense Committee in 1974 by violating the same CEQA provision.) More important, the court ruled that UCSF's description of the treatment of hazardous materials—their dispersal into the environment and effects on human health, as well as proposed measures to prevent potential hazards—was useless for drawing conclusions about the project's safety.

UCSF appealed to the California Supreme Court, but at least a year would be lost even if the court ruled in the university's favor. And the case began to assume wider implications. UCSF was effectively being forced to show that small quantities of toxic substances, often diluted in the air beyond the point of detectability, did not pose significant risks to the local community. No comparable institution had ever been placed in such a position, and there was substantial doubt that the case could be proved. For many toxics, or mixtures of toxics, there are no laws that govern allowable emissions from biomedical labs, no standards from which to judge health effects, no documented evidence of harm caused by such emissions.

"If the decision stands, it will have a chilling effect on health-related research in our university and in the state of California, and will have serious repercussions all over the country," Krevans warned in a press statement. In the face of such a precedent, the university could not consider cutting its losses by finding a new site. But UCSF's position was rapidly unraveling. As the university nervously awaited its February 1988 hearing before the Supreme Court, state Attorney General John Van de Kamp weighed in with a condemnation of the environmental impact report. If accepted by the court, UCSF's arguments "would inevitably cause great detriment to the state's natural resources," he wrote. Van de Kamp warned that if approved, the EIR would offer a "road map" for circumvention of the law by other agencies. The general counsel of a coalition of 130 California environmental groups called the UCSF case "one of the most environmentally destructive legal actions" against CEQA.

The university had become an environmental outlaw. In an effort to shore up its credibility, UCSF churned out reams of press releases and slick publications extolling its contributions to the community and humanity at large, as well as explaining the vigilant safety practices of its researchers. A widely quoted, university-commissioned study indicated that UCSF was pouring $500 million a year into the San Francisco economy.

UCSF also commissioned a poll measuring public attitudes toward the university in light of the Laurel Heights affair. The results seemed to confirm frequent suggestions by campus officials that the activists were a small band of crusading malcontents. Most respondents apparently were oblivious to the battle in their midst. Only about 14 percent knew of a dispute involving UCSF; only 1 percent considered it a major problem. When informed by the interviewer that a dispute existed, a 28 percent to 44 percent majority of respondents were inclined to favor UCSF. But the poll reflected reality only dimly. Scores of committed opponents attended hearings, wrote letters, talked with their neighbors, signed petitions, and generally showed a strong base of support for LHIA's efforts. Moreover, the poll itself offered some clues to the apparent contradiction. It indicated that most Laurel Heights residents (like their counterparts throughout the city) opposed unchecked growth of large institutions. And 35 percent of Laurel Heights respondents said they tend to support those who believe UCSF's work poses serious hazards to residents.

The plans for a Laurel Heights campus were on fire, and LHIA fanned the flames by promoting worst-case scenarios with poetic license. A disaster was about to hit the neighborhood, according to one flier: "Special dangers to firemen, police, children and YOU . . . Explosions! Leaks! Toxic Spills!" Another pictured an oil derrick more than 100 feet tall and 30 feet across on top of the Laurel Heights building. UCSF had actually proposed a 30-foot-tall, 1-foot-wide tower to measure wind currents as part of an emissions-monitoring effort. The proposal was quickly withdrawn after community groups objected. The flier also claimed that most main-campus labs would be moved to Laurel Heights—an impossibility (beyond its obvious lapse of logic), given that lab facilities at the Parnassus campus are far larger than the entire new building. Despite such inaccuracies, the LHIA fliers helped undermine UCSF's links to many neighbors who had stayed above the fray.

LHIA also fomented opposition within other community organizations. With energetic outreach and relentless attacks on UCSF's credibility, the activists exploited every lapse in campus safety practices, every hint of mismanagement. This did not prove particularly difficult, given the university's habit of being its own worst enemy. For example, the Committee for the Future of UCSF was appointed "on a 'crisis' basis" by Krevans in the summer of 1987, after the Court of Appeal ruling. Its members were a who's who of UCSF—world-class researchers and top academic officers. In February 1988 the committee recommended that the campus construct a new research building at Parnassus Heights, in conflict with the 1976 agreement with the community that no new development would take place there. Neighbors could only shake their heads in disbelief when UCSF continued to insist that it was being completely open about its Laurel Heights plans.

Then in late 1987, three campus radioactive-waste disposal technicians showed radiation exposures 100 times expected levels. The mysterious cases apparently involved the mishandling of radiation-monitoring badges. Then early in 1988, the labs of two prominent USCF scientists lost small shipments of radioisotopes. In an effort to show a recently adopted get-tough enforcement posture, the university fined the violators and temporarily revoked their permits to order isotopes. It appeared to backfire, however, when outraged faculty members went public with their complaints that the radiation-safety rules and penalties were arbitrary and draconian. Later in the year, a breakdown of health and safety rules and monitoring in a campus animal facility apparently led to an increase in the number of UCSF employees who contracted Q fever, a disease of sheep that can cause flulike symptoms in humans. The problems directly violated an order by the state occupational-health agency made nine years earlier.

None of these incidents constituted a major threat to life or health. But together they created an image of ineptitude and carelessness at UCSF.

Then in late October 1988, an unusual outbreak of childhood cancer in the Noe and Eureka valleys, about two miles east of the Parnassus campus, was identified by the San Francisco Department of Public Health. Local residents suspected toxic emissions from UCSF as the culprit. Angry denials by David Werdegar, public health director, appeared self-serving to frightened locals, as Werdegar was himself on leave from his post as a UCSF professor. Devincenzi and others from LHIA exploited the issue in an effort to undermine UCSF's credibility. Follow-up studies judged the outbreak to be a chance phenomenon unrelated to any environmental factor. But that conclusion was released only after UCSF had suffered another public-relations disaster.

Reeling from this barrage of bad press, in June 1988 Krevans announced formation of a "model program for radiation safety and comprehensive environmental protection." Its cornerstone was a $1.6 million review of biological, radioactive, and chemical effluents from Parnassus campus stacks and drainpipes. Touted as "the first truly comprehensive environmental assessment . . . on any [university] campus in the country," it would be conducted by a leading risk-assessment firm. As a gesture of good faith, UCSF formed an advisory committee for the study, dominated by members of neighborhood groups bordering the Parnassus campus—including some implacable foes of its development policies.

---------------- ෴ ----------------

The Verdict

On 1 December 1988, the high court rendered its judgment on Laurel Heights. On the central issue of environmental safety, UCSF was largely vindicated. The court found the plans to mitigate potential environmental effects of Laurel Heights research to be credible and acceptable. Citing LHIA's "gross misstatements of the record," the court added: "[T]he association's fears as well as its assertions regarding radioactivity are greatly exaggerated." Accordingly, the court allowed the Agabian lab to continue its operations at Laurel Heights, including work with radioactive isotopes, pending approval of the state radiation-control agency.

However, on procedural and public-disclosure issues, the university lost big—the court threw out its EIR. The justices cited UCSF's failure to plan for use of the entire building for labs, as campus officials had clearly implied was their ultimate goal. The high court also agreed with the Court of Appeal that the discussion of alternatives to using the Laurel Heights building was inadequate. UCSF had argued that alternatives had been *considered* in detail but not written into the EIR. That argument "misses the critical point that the public must be equally informed," the court responded. (Adding insult to injury, the court awarded attorneys' fees to the opposition. UCSF itself would finance LHIA in the next round.)

"Although [the court] finds the EIR defective in some technical respects, it lays to rest allegations that there is something risky or harmful about the university's activities," said Ethan Schulman, the university's attorney. "CEQA is not designed as a tool to promote endless litigation to block projects from going forward. . . . This is a game that [Devincenzi and her allies] have been playing, and it's not a game without end. We're in the bottom of the ninth here."

Schulman was wrong. The game was nowhere near the end.

While the complex process of completing a new EIR commenced, UCSF applied for an extension of its radioactive materials permit to cover Agabian's lab. The state Department of Health Services conducted a public hearing on the matter, at LHIA's request, in April 1989. Esteemed professors testified as to the safety of the experiments. "We could drink our experiments" and suffer no injury, one claimed. Another regretted the general public's inability to understand that the minute amounts of radiation used in labs could never cause the kind of fallout seen in the Chernobyl disaster. Patients and supportive members of the community gave testimonials about how UCSF clinicians had saved their sons or daughters. Others praised the wider impact of campus research. "Surely those living within walking distance have compassion for people in the Third World," one said.

Treating opponents as misguided or selfish children is a standard approach whenever technological endeavors meet well-organized, community-based opposition. Scientists and technocrats effectively suggest that only experts are capable of rational decisions about where technology should be introduced and how it should be managed. This attitude implies that the questions facing Laurel Heights, Rocky Flats, and hundreds of similar conflicts across the nation are primarily scientific. The placement of a major biomedical lab into a residential area may pose scientific questions, of course, but the issues are more political than technical. The Laurel Heights neighbors tried to use proceedings that ostensibly involved a narrowly circumscribed scientific delineation of risk as a forum to advance their real agenda—a political one. They became increasingly enraged when they saw their political case against the lab being ignored or belittled.

Dozens of neighbors countered angrily. "We do not consider

ourselves child murderers," Margaret Verges said, noting that the issue was safe handling of radioactive substances, not the value of research, which no one disputed. ("We are being told that we should be ashamed of guarding our neighborhood," she added at a later public forum. "Well, I'm not ashamed. I'm not ignorant. I read. This is news for you UC; a lot of us read.") Devincenzi characterized comments about the neighbors' lack of perspective on radiation as patronizing and self-serving in light of the series of radiation mishaps on the Parnassus campus. Not surprisingly, the state sided with UCSF, granting a permit extension to Agabian's lab.

In October 1989 UCSF released the new draft EIR. This time, discussion of alternative sites filled 127 pages. Forced by the court to anticipate the state of the building when fully occupied by research labs, yet buoyed by the belief that they could not be effectively challenged on the health issue, the report writers outlined changes that dwarfed those described in the old report: many new exhaust stacks, substantial brick ventilation bays on the outside of the building, and a large underground animal-holding facility. The daily population of the site was bumped upward, well beyond the maximum predicted when the building was purchased. By all appearances, UCSF officials figured that they would never be able to please the community critics, so why try? Instead, they went for broke. Predictably, the plan laid out methods for mitigating most environmental impacts—pollution, traffic congestion, noise—to the point of insignificance. Only in a few cases, such as the addition of a screened area on the roof that would partially block the view of some nearby houses, was the impact of the project deemed unavoidable.

In response, the Laurel Heights neighbors seemed ready to tear the building down brick by brick. In a general plan of this nature there are innumerable loose ends, a multitude of descriptions that must eventually be refined and eleborated. And because the university had not yet decided which research programs would move to the building, the report was riddled with ambiguities and guestimates. LHIA prepared to have a field day.

By this time, UCSF had turned all its work on the planning process to Bruce Spaulding, former chief executive of Fresno County, California, and Clark County, Nevada (which includes Las Vegas), before being wooed to UCSF as a vice chancellor. Spaulding had coaxed recalcitrant citizens in those communities into accepting far larger developments than Laurel Heights. No one expected miracles, but with Spaulding as doctor, campus officals hoped the community finally might take the bitter pill. He immediately added two public-information meetings prior to the formal public hearing required under CEQA. The goal was to answer questions about the EIR and the public-hearing process, in order to help local residents make the best use of the arcane document and open the proceedings.

It may have been too late to begin building trust through openness, but UCSF sunk itself deeper into community quicksand by bringing forward some almost unimaginably inept spokespersons. Lloyd Smith is a powerful and famous doctor who helped make UCSF a world-class medical center. As a communicator to suspicious, angry community members, however, his patrician tone could hardly have been more alienating. Smith's descriptions of recombinant DNA and other technologies were so esoteric (he talked about the safety of isotopes without ever noting that they are radioactive substances, for example) as to be opaque to the uninitiated.

Overall, the droning, technocratic UCSF representatives gave exactly the opposite impression Spaulding had hoped to achieve. They appeared to dodge community concerns under a veil of calm reassurances that all was well. The anger and disgust from the community activists was palpable. UCSF's experts looked increasingly pathetic and pasty-faced as insults and accusations rained down on them from the ascending rows of the Laurel Heights auditorium.

By the time the formal public hearing was held in December 1989, the community had gathered signatures on petitions opposing the project from nearly 1,000 neighbors. Activists attempted to shout down each supporter of the campus, sometimes turning the hearing into a free-for-all event. Among the hundreds of complaints, opponents of UCSF who appeared to have scoured every page of the encyclopedic EIR attacked it for being too vague. For example, just how many cubic feet of air per minute would be moved by the ventilation system? Such questions, which could not possibly be answered at such an early stage of planning, were meant to imply that UCSF was covering up the answers.

Nevertheless, the university's official governing body, the Board of Regents, approved the EIR in May 1990, and returned the document to Superior Court for review. Six months later, in November 1990, LHIA lost the lawsuit in which it accused UCSF of breach of contract by planning to build labs in the Laurel Heights building. In January 1991 the Superior Court approved UCSF's EIR, clearing the last legal hurdle standing in the way of full development of the Laurel Heights Campus. LHIA's attorneys threatened to appeal the decision to a higher court, although their case was weak, at best, given the degree to which the legal issues in the case had already been reviewed.

Yet UCSF won a Pyrrhic victory. The university faced a cold war with its neighbors, even as the legal war appeared to be ending. And by 1991, California was mired in economic recession. The state government, chief source of funds needed for the multimillion dollar renovation of the Laurel Heights building, was battling the largest budget deficit in its history, forcing austerity measures on the entire university system. Today, more than five years after the Laurel Heights battle began, the building's ultimate disposition remains an open question.

------------------------------ ඞඞඞ ------------------------------

The Logic of Power

How did UCSF reach such a dismal state? One of the more glaring reasons involved planning. The planning process overlooked the prospect that the Laurel Heights purchase—its impact on the community aside—was not in UCSF's long-term self-interest. To understand why, recall the university's historical strategy for growth: UCSF has always relied on the notion that the core research and clinical programs of a great biosciences center must never be separated geographically. This view is not universal, however. "[It] is a heretical position around here," said Thomas Rolinson, UCSF's principal planner from 1980 to 1988, in a 1989 interview. "But the necessity of close proximity of every program to every other program is a myth. That myth is one of the best defenses you can put together in turf battles over space." (Moreover, UCSF conducts effective research at several outlying hospitals it runs.) Rolinson added that every group that was asked to move away from the central campus to outlying UCSF satellites fought tenaciously. He compared it, ironically, to Nimbyism; "move anybody but me." Two of UCSF's leading researchers, Nobel Laureate J. Michael Bishop and Biochemistry Chairman Bruce Alberts, voiced similar sentiments.) The Laurel Heights site was considered only when further growth on Parnassus became politically untenable.

In biomedical research the urgency to expand traces back to two sources. One can be called the "noble" cause—the compelling need to find cures for dread diseases and the strong empathy that draws many to the search for such cures. The other is the "Nobel" cause—the pursuit of discoveries that win awards and fame, build careers and fortunes, and ultimately draw power and prestige to an institution. Each cause feeds on growth. The most successful institutions become empires. UCSF represents its actions as based purely on the noble cause, while LHIA sees only the Nobel cause. Each cause plays a part; each can take on a life of its own that ignores its economic, political, and social contexts.

Krevans and Goyan are empire-builders. For them, the stakes are high. Krevans will retire in 1993, and despite an illustrious career, he may well be judged on his success or failure to develop biomedical labs in the Laurel Heights neighborhood. Failure would condemn UCSF to a difficult search for another suitable site, losing faculty, grants, and influence along the way. It almost inevitably would lead to further decentralization. Once seen as a visionary, Krevans could be remembered as the man whose missteps led to the prolonged battle for Laurel Heights and the ultimate dismemberment of UCSF. Goyan, too, might be dragged down.

Krevans and his senior administrator, Herbert Suelzle, figured that to win at Laurel Heights and in the inevitable expansion battles of the future, they needed a savvy operator. Bruce Spaulding was hired in February 1988, initially to rationalize an archaic budgeting and accounting system, reorganize lethargic bureaucracies, and oversee critical areas of infrastructure that had been performing badly, such as environmental health and safety. A planner by trade, Spaulding understands CEQA and knows how to grease the wheels of government and accommodate public pressure groups under the media's watchful eye. Krevans and Suelzle gave Spaulding the planning-and-growth portfolio in February 1989. When he took over, he found a one-dimensional planning process. "Instead of weighing land use, environmental and social costs and benefits, planning was capital-driven. Laurel Heights was found and purchased completely based on affordability. Fiscal considerations created Laurel Heights," Spaulding said. Other highly placed observers concur. Campus leaders created and relied on a planning system that failed to grasp the intensity of neighborhood-preservationist instincts in San Francisco, despite decades of difficulties at Parnassus Heights. "These are people who don't go into surgery without the best possible team. Yet they didn't have the right team for planning," an informed UCSF source said. "Can you take an office building in a residential area of San Francisco and turn it into labs? That critical question was never asked of city planners, community leaders, and politicians until after $55 million had been spent. And the question was only asked then in order to answer 'yes.' "

UCSF was far from unique in allowing financial concerns to dictate what amounted to decisions of social policy. More often than not, Nimby resistance to toxic-waste dumps, manufacturing plants, prisons, and even drug-treatment programs flows from decisions by corporations or government agencies to place their controversial projects in locations that fit their budgets. This is hardly surprising. But in most cases, the sponsoring organizations foment local opposition because they do not examine the conditions and needs of the area they are moving into. They fail to study the social context or talk with local residents until after angry neighbors form an opposition group and harden their stance against the project.

The Laurel Heights site represented UCSF's last chance for decentralization without pain. There was no serious talk about building a second major campus at some remote site, to fulfill UCSF's growth needs for decades to come, until after the Court of Appeal ruled against UCSF and it appeared that Laurel Heights might be lost. "The problem of crowding can never be solved by a stop-gap measure like Laurel Heights," Spaulding continued. "USCF has been growing at a rate of more than 100,000 square feet a year. In three years another Laurel Heights will be needed—then another. Or, a major campus of two million square feet of space could be created in a little over a decade—a campus big enough to form a true critical mass."

Failure to Communicate

UCSF's public-relations team boasts an enviable record for generating favorable media coverage about the campus' impressive scientific accomplishments. Yet, on the community level, the sophisticated outreach apparatus failed abysmally. Large segments of the community ended up hating UCSF, and top administrators remained so detached from the local environment that they seemed genuinely perplexed as to why the opposition was not persuaded by their reassurances. Goyan could not name a single error in UCSF's approach. Krevans acknowledged that the term *academic* could have been more precisely defined at the outset, but "other than that, I cannot think of anything we could have done differently."

What went wrong? From the beginning UCSF established a pattern of withholding key information. Krevans has insisted throughout the controversy that the movement of labs was not preordained. And indeed, no formal decision was made until after lengthy faculty discussions. Yet the prospect arose at least a month prior to the purchase of the site, according to Goyan. At that time, Goyan says, he suggested to Krevans that the Laurel Heights site could house all School of Pharmacy basic science labs. "We had to have a critical mass of scientists at the building for it to be effective," to prevent Laurel Heights research from becoming a poor relation, he said in a 1989 interview. Only the vague phrase "certain academic programs" filtered down to the public, however.

More significant, according to a highly placed campus official who requested anonymity, only a massive research complex could have justified the purchase of the Laurel Heights site. The official estimated the cost of using the building for offices and determined that without the large overhead fees generated by research grants, UCSF could never pay off the $55 million mortgage. Labs were an economic imperative, no matter what deliberative process may have taken place. According to this official's analysis, if UCSF leaders were in doubt about this, they were pitifully ill-informed about the economy of their campus. (J. Michael Bishop and Bruce Alberts complained in a 1988 letter to Krevans that the Laurel Heights project would be so expensive as to "jeopardize the financial future of the rest of UCSF.")

Communication with the Laurel Heights neighbors broke down because most of the public-relations effort was directed at getting good press and endorsements from business and professional groups. Vocal critics simply ignored the editorialists, and so, apparently, did many of their neighbors. Instead, the community paid increasing attention to UCSF's health-and-safety lapses.

Outreach efforts—including letters, glossy brochures, and meetings—were designed to convince a "scientifically illiterate" community that the university's actions were wise, or at least innocuous. They were not meant to involve neighbors in a decision-making process. The object was community ratification of decisions already taken; failing that, pacification. Throughout the conflict, university officials allowed for narrow flexibility only in how decisions would be implemented, not on the use or design of the Laurel Heights campus. They steadfastly refused to give a single guarantee on any aspect of Laurel Heights development, including the basic issue of capping growth at the site. As outreach efforts looked increasingly like an elaborate smoke screen, the community refused to buy the "trust us" line.

---------------- ର୍ଷର୍ଷର୍ଷ ----------------

The Contradictions of Nimbyism

For its part, LHIA's battle against UCSF became a vendetta, extending far beyond neighborhood borders. After the San Francisco cancer-cluster episode, Laurel Heights activists provided the primary opposition to UCSF's friendly takeover of Mount Zion Hospital, located about a mile southeast of Laurel Heights. UCSF needed the site to expand its compressed clinical programs. And without the university, the most important hospital for nearby Jewish and black residents would probably have closed its doors due to insolvency. Nearly all other community and business associations supported the UCSF acquisition of Mount Zion. Devincenzi also lobbied officials in Marin County, just north of San Francisco, in an effort to keep UCSF from participating in an aging-research center there.

LHIA portrayed UCSF as a cancer and biological warfare factory, positions for which evidence—even anecdotal evidence—was weak at best. These are the politics of intransigence: attacking in any venue, refusing to back down on any point. LHIA relished procedural objections, mounting delay upon delay, slowing down the process long enough to persuade a few more neighbors to join the opposition.

When UCSF's independently conducted, community-monitored environmental assessment of its Parnassus campus was released in September 1989, it indicated that the university's contribution to local toxic pollution was minimal. Sampling for radiation, chemicals, and biological organisms indicated that they had been filtered to a tiny fraction of government-allowed limits. The report estimated that the entire campus emitted about 107 pounds of chemicals into the air a day. The most dangerous of these was ethylene oxide, a gas used in hospital sterilizers. UCSF agreed immediately to add $500,000 scrubbers to remove 98 percent of sterilizer emissions. With the new scrubbers, the mammoth medical center became a less significant health risk than most community hospitals. The worst industrial polluters in the Bay Area discharge up to five tons of toxic chemicals into the air every day, while the filling station that Goyan's dad once operated ostensibly presents a higher cancer risk than the entire UCSF campus.

UCSF hoped that this study would lay to rest accusations that it was a major polluter. Parnassus-area neighbors were, by and large, encouraged, although they withheld judgment until an outside consultant could check the document. LHIA activists laughed off the study as another UCSF sham, irrelevant to the Laurel Heights conflict. An independent review of the study, conducted under the supervision of the San Francisco Department of Public Health by Marc Lappé, professor of health policy and ethics at the University of Illinois and a noted critic of government and corporate polluters, was released in January 1990. Lappé's report affirmed every significant finding of the original study.

LHIA's doubts about UCSF's promises on safety were certainly arguable. The community group did not invent the university's radiation mishaps. It did not dream up the Q-fever episode. To some neighbors, such problems undoubtedly seemed threatening. (And given the Parnassus Heights experience, fantasies of UCSF moving into Laurel Heights in a similarly acquisitive fashion were hardly paranoid.) Yet LHIA never made a meaningful attempt to determine whether research could be conducted safely at the Laurel Heights site. Carr says his group talked about one aspect of UCSF's presentations with a single chemical engineer but consulted no other technical experts. A qualified review of the hazards, supervised by LHIA, could have provided valuable information for confused neighbors. By the standards of the larger community—the city, the state, the nation—LHIA's environmental and health complaints were absurd. In the absence of apparent harm caused by the Parnassus Heights labs, and without an alternate scientific review of the potential hazards of the Laurel Heights project, LHIA indeed appeared irrational or selfish to many outside observers. Coming from affluent Laurel Heights, demands that UCSF move its labs to an industrial area were reminiscent of what such situations have often meant in practical terms—move the risks to where poor people live.

The Fate of Biomedical Research

A 1988 survey conducted by the National Science Foundation showed that nearly half of U.S. universities and medical colleges did not have enough research space to support the needs of their programs in biology and medicine. Those institutions deferred two-thirds of repair and renovation of existing facilities. The National Institutes of Health reported in the same year that only about one-third of U.S. research facilities in biology and medicine were suitable for the most sophisticated research. Budget shortfalls, poor planning, and new regulations for ventilation and handling toxic materials all contributed to the situation.

Nimbyism has also played a role. UCSF experienced an extreme dose, but such opposition is hardly unique. Educational giants around the nation, including Harvard, Yale, MIT, and Columbia, have been confronted by local demands for more control over university growth, based on concerns about property values, land use, environmental degradation, and animal rights. Claustrophobic opponents increasingly raise fears about health dangers as they resist the tightening embrace of large campuses.

Nowhere have these fears been more pronounced than in the San Francisco Bay Area. In 1987 animal rights activists joined a local toxics watchdog group to fight Stanford University's plan to build an animal-holding facility and a basic biological research lab, raising many of the health-related charges pioneered by Laurel Heights activists. In the face of protracted opposition, Stanford agreed to delay the project and prepare a more than $2 million EIR. The project went forward after the EIR supported Stanford's assumptions.

UC's giant Berkeley campus has always had a love-hate relationship with the city it dominates. Because of the university, Berkeley became a dynamic cultural center. Yet the university's exemption from local taxes and planning laws means that as it acquires valuable real estate to feed its insatiable expansion appetite, city revenues suffer. Local residents have challenged campus growth in court. And UC Berkeley's dismal record for care of experimental animals, for which it has been sanctioned by federal agencies, has not helped its reputation. Beginning in 1987, animal rights and antitoxics activists similar to the Stanford coalition emerged to oppose construction of a new animal facility and expansion of campus biology labs. In one demonstration, protesters scaled a 175-foot crane on the construction site, unfurling banners assailing the university for toxic pollution and animal abuse, and for promoting germ warfare—a reference to some military-funded studies slated for the lab. The week-long occupation cost the university $200,000 (not to mention the bad press). The campus was stung by an appellate court ruling that threw out the project's EIR based largely on the Laurel Heights precedent although the facility was ultimately built.

Given the California penchant for political activism and cultural trendsetting, protests of this kind may be expected to crop up there.

Yet in Illinois, New York, Massachusetts, Georgia, and elsewhere, coalitions of local residents, animal rights activists, and environmentalists have recently fought the construction or operation of basic research facilities over fear of environmental and health dangers.

Such cases "reveal a disturbing pattern of assaults on science," according to Stanford University Assistant Vice President Larry Horton. "One thing about the increased activism against research . . . ought to be clear: We will see more of it and it will be an increasingly serious problem. At the very least, it will drain resources away from the direct support of research, raise the cost of doing business and divert funds and energies into methods of coping with public relations and political problems. More seriously, it may result in the direct curtailment or suspension of some kinds of research."

"Above all, the Laurel Heights experience has convinced me that universities around the United States are potentially in deep trouble," Goyan says. "If we lose, what could happen to a Harvard, a Stanford, a Hopkins?" The concern has merit. Just as many major universities show UCSF's proclivity to ignore the social context of their expansion plans, then mishandle the political backlash, frightened and angry community groups all over the country demonstrate LHIA's tenacity and inflexibility.

In a sense, grass-roots control is fundamentally incompatible with basic research. Free collaboration, the essence of science, relies on uniform standards and the ability to share materials across state and national boundaries. Local limitations—whether codified into laws or enforced by the determined litigiousness of a Nimby group—may well become serious obstacles to what science historian Sheldon Krimsky has called "the universality inherent in the pursuit of science."

"Serious environmentalists ought to be very concerned about the manipulation of environmental laws to serve non-environmental concerns," Horton says, be they animal rights as in the case of Stanford, or local control as in UCSF's experience. Horton may be presumptuous to define what is serious or frivolous, but his point deserves consideration. Actions taken in Laurel Heights cost the local community, the university, and the courts an incalculable number of person-hours and many millions of dollars. Is this a rational allocation of society's resources in the face of profound, demonstrably deadly problems of industrial pollution that continue, business as usual? UCSF may be insensitive, elitist, even imperious. But it is not a Rocky Flats Nuclear Plant, whose value to society is at best arguable and transitory, and whose vast danger to its community is a matter of public record. Nor is UCSF an Advanced Genetic Sciences—releasing a proprietary, experimental product that was ʾcontroversial even among experts—directly into the environment.

A great university that contributes much to society has qualitative differences with the other institutions. But UCSF officials—bland, evasive, legalistic in their approach—were archetypes for the universal, faceless "authorities." They did as little as their Rocky Flats or Advanced Genetic Sciences counterparts to attack the real source of their opponents' discontent—their inability to influence meaningfully a large institution whose unilateral actions affect their lives.

Laurel Heights residents converted generic feelings of powerlessness and vulnerability that are endemic to modern society into a belligerent protectiveness of the home environment. In this way, UCSF was hit hard by a revolt against aloof, unresponsive, undemocratic conduct by all manner of institutions that control science and technology. The Laurel Heights Improvement Association response to UCSF may have been extreme or out of proportion to the immediate dangers. But from the community's perspective, why not be extreme? Under existing power relations, nothing else seems to work.

6
The Far-Reaching Impact of Nimby Activism

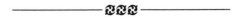

We're losing facilities faster than they're being replaced, whether it's prisons, power plants or hazardous waste treatment plants. . . . We're rapidly getting to the point where we're going to be in a crisis in many of these areas.
——Kenneth Portney,
Tufts University political scientist

Nimby conflicts extend far beyond science and technology. Virtually all ventures—from essential social services and the ugly trappings of industry to prisons and shopping malls—that threaten to increase pollution, noise, crime, or traffic congestion, to deflate property values or undermine aesthetic desirability, may face Nimby opposition. Pick any big-city newspaper at random; on most days it will carry a story about *some* local community opposing *something*. Yet Nimbyism defies quantitative definition. Groups with Nimby characteristics spring up overnight. After their single-issue campaigns end—win or lose—they quickly disband, making them almost impossible to count accurately.

A single Nimby conflict can cost millions of dollars in delays, legal wrangling, missed opportunities, social dislocation, and commercial stagnation. Thousands of such conflicts occur simultaneously around the country—a potentially staggering price tag. Yet,

Nimby groups often defeat unwise, wasteful, unsafe, or profit-gauging ventures that offer little benefit to the larger community. The net economic impact of Nimbyism is far from clear. Industry and government officials focus on the unquestionably significant ways in which Nimbyism makes their jobs more difficult. "We experience [Nimbyism] almost at every turn, every time we do *anything*," laments William Witte, director of housing and economic development in San Francisco. "Cities have always been places of opportunity. . . . That is how the people objecting got here, but they forget that." He was referring to the unremitting disputes in his city and hundreds of others around the country against psychiatric halfway houses, low-income housing, parking lots, fast-food restaurants . . . the list is endless.

David Morell, a former academic who wrote about Nimbyism in toxic-waste cases, is an executive at a major hazardous-waste disposal firm. "The Nimby syndrome has introduced a paralysis in effective corporate response to marketplace incentives," Morell says. He may overstate the case, but fear of Nimby resistance clearly causes companies to overbuild when a project is approved or scale back to avoid rejection. Frank Popper, chairman of the Urban Studies Department at Rutgers University, concurs. Where undesired projects have not been stymied or delayed for years, he says, "they have been built too small, in insignificant numbers or in wrong places. Or they have been made too difficult, controversial or expensive to manage." Kenneth Portney, a Tufts University political scientist who has studied the influence of Nimbyism on the business community, sees no end in sight. "We are totally deadlocked on most of these issues," he says about the siting of many kinds of unwanted but ostensibly necessary facilities.

"Fundamentally, [Nimbyism is] reactionary in its approach," according to Ray Brady, head of research and analysis for the Association of (San Francisco) Bay Area Governments. "It looks at me, myself and mine. We're losing a sense of community responsibility. There are certain things we generate—waste, traffic and so on—and we have a collective responsibility to deal with these things." Allan Mazur, professor of sociology at Syracuse University and a long-time chronicler of technological controversy, goes so far as to compare some manifestations of Nimbyism with the racist communities that fought integration of their neighborhoods during the 1950s. Today's bitter battles against AIDS treatment centers, foster homes, or homeless shelters may be tinged a similar color.

Indeed, Nimbyism substantially undercuts the delivery of social services. Opinion polls show that people want something done about the illicit drug problem. Experience shows that they want it done somewhere else. Neighborhood opposition—not lack of funds—forms the single biggest obstacle to establishing drug-treatment centers in New York, according to rehabilitation officials. And the trend is spreading to other states. Rich communities fear that drug clinics will import crime and violence. Poor areas counter that they have enough trouble as it is and have done their share to cope with urban problems.

In the largest national survey to explore the Nimby phenomenon, conducted in 1990 for the Robert Wood Johnson Foundation, half of the respondents opposed the placement of any kind of mental-illness facility in their neighborhood. (Table 6.1 lists some of the survey's other findings.)

Table 6.1   Nimbyism: Results of a 1990 Survey

Facility	% Who Would Welcome	% Who Would Not Welcome
Homeless shelter	43%	28%
Alcohol-rehabilitation center	42	25
Drug-treatment center	40	31
Shopping mall	36	40
Group home for AIDS patients	29	37
Factory	24	57
Garbage landfill	8	85
Prison	7	79

SOURCE: *Public Attitudes Toward People with Mental Illness* (Princeton, NJ: Robert Wood Johnson Foundation, April 1990), pp. 24–25.

The survey found that even facilities that the vast majority of communities need—such as medical clinics, schools, and day-care centers—would be welcomed by only 58 percent, 65 percent, and 68 percent of respondents, respectively. And surveys generally tend to *understate* the actual degree of local opposition. When communities are confronted with the concrete prospect of a group home or shopping mall—rather than an abstract question on a polling form—they are much more likely to dig in their heels.

-------------------- ৫৫৫ --------------------

The Technological Dimension

As chapters 3–5 describe, Nimby activity against potentially hazardous technological projects has become a typical feature of modern America. Following are just a few examples of the results of Nimby activity in the United States.

No large, fully operational, freestanding, hazardous-waste disposal facility has been established in this country since 1980. Local communities simply refuse to accept them. And during the 1980s, some 14,000 U.S. sanitary landfills (which do not accept hazardous waste) closed, leaving only about 5,500 and generating widespread concern about an impending garbage crisis amid a meteoric rise in disposal costs. EPA analysts predict thousands more landfills to fill up within a few years.

No new U.S. nuclear power plant has been undertaken since 1978, although influences in addition to Nimbyism have played leading roles in this case. (Chapter 3 covers the problems of establishing repositories for weapons-related nuclear waste. The commercial nuclear industry has experienced similar difficulties.)

At least two dozen attempts from 1970 to 1980 (during the height of the energy crisis) were made to find a site for a new oil refinery somewhere along the eastern seaboard. They all failed due to local opposition. No new effort has since been mounted.

Neighbors of metropolitan airports throughout the United States, after enduring years of jet-engine noise, have begun to dictate their own terms on noise pollution. Not a single major airport has been built in nearly three decades, and only one is on the drawing board. That is in Denver, where a substantial buffer zone was added to the design to accommodate local concerns. Demands that officials muffle the din have forced widespread alterations of flight patterns, limited night flights at more than 300 U.S. airports, and quashed plans to add new runways at many of these. The changes have made scheduling nightmares commonplace. Some pilots claim that local noise controls, which require them to reduce power after takeoff, compromise safety. And flight delays cost an estimated $5 billion a year.

While the focus here is on U.S. developments, Nimby actions in Western Europe, Japan, and recently the Soviet Union and Eastern Europe have also become increasingly common. Regarding the establishment of nuclear-waste repositories, for example, local opposition frequently parallels the U.S. experience, particularly in West Germany, Switzerland, and England, which have strong traditions of local autonomy on planning issues. In contrast, community-based resistance to hazardous technologies in France has been relatively quiescent. The French tradition of strong central-government control has largely stifled local input on such issues. Sweden, with its history of political compromise and public participation in national issues, has had an easier time than other nations deciding where to put nuclear waste. The process was helped, however, by the Swedes's unique decision to phase out their nuclear-power industry. In the Third World—a traditional dump site for industrial society's overflow of hazardous waste as well as for surpluses of newly banned drugs and pesticides—some governments have begun to turn away ships carrying lethal cargo, despite the badly needed revenues they offer.

—————————— ꙮꙮꙮ ——————————

Sources of Conflict

The elements of Nimby obstructionism that may be dangerous (such as airplane noise controls), apparently intractable (such as waste disposal), or tragic (such as the blockage of vital social services) have prompted U.S. politicians, bureaucrats, and corporate officials to issue blanket condemnations of Nimbyism. To be sure, Nimby groups sometimes earn the "selfish" label. Although Nimbyism occurs at every social stratum, the affluent have more to lose from any environmental disruption. They have less to gain from economic revitalization that risky or undesirable projects may promise. And wealthy communities have an easier time forcing their will on the powers that be. By design or default, this often pushes less-desirable development into poor people's backyards.

Yet broad-stroke condemnations of Nimbyism as a self-interest phenomenon obscure the reasons why Nimbyism has become a prevalent trend. The social movements of the 1960s and early 1970s steeped an entire generation in distrust for large institutions. The political conflicts of the period forged thousands of savvy, resourceful activists. As social upheaval waned, many former activists adopted the acquisitive "me first" attitude that was emblematic of the late 1970s and 1980s. But they also retained their skepticism of authority figures and their confidence to confront perceived injustice.

Draconian cuts in public and social services (amid record corporate profits) during the Reagan era made problems such as homelessness, inadequate health care, and unemployment more obvious than ever. The desperation of poverty and the rising epidemic of drug addiction drove up crime rates and the general misery index in America's cities. And the AIDS epidemic loaded a major new weight on the already thread-bare social safety net. Meanwhile, the environmental problems discussed in chapter 1 prompted many people to become increasingly sensitive to any environmental insult that hit close to home. In large measure, Nimbyism grew out of the failure by the conventional institutions of liberal democracy to solve—or even contain—these social and environmental problems. They failed to uphold the implicit social contract to care for the sick and the needy and to conserve our natural resources. At the same time, corporations and government agencies gradually monopolized power over decisions regarding the range and extent of social services, the pace and character of urban development, and the introduction and management of technology. People may well be selfish. But their actions stem from justifiable, if sometimes misdirected, outrage about apparently uncontrollable institutional forces that do not run society humanely or effectively. This is not to say that people deserve praise for refusing to allow a homeless shelter, low-income housing project, drug-treatment clinic—or, for that matter, a parking lot, prison, or shopping center—into their neighborhood. But decades of flawed social policy created the Nimby trend. Only social policy that begins to reduce poverty, humanize the urban environment, and restore public confidence in political and economic leaders will end the Nimby reflex.

In disputes involving technology, the selfish label most clearly blames the victims. Nimbyism triggered the waste-disposal crisis. But in light of the disastrous environmental abuses of the waste-disposal industry, and the profligate use of "disposable" resources by our society as a whole, it should hardly come as a shock. Nimbyism certainly circumscribes the ability of oil companies to create refining capacity that may be vital to the short-term energy needs of the nation. Given the record for safety and social responsibility of the major oil companies, however, why should local communities trust that a new refinery would operate without incident? Nimby insistence on noise controls have led to crowded and possibly unsafe airports. Should people who live near airports tolerate stupefying noise levels so that air travelers can fly at more convenient times?

Few communities subscribe to the idea that society does not need drug-treatment centers, sanitary landfills, homeless shelters, or shopping centers. Nimby groups fight projects that they didn't ask for and that no one asked their permission about. They fight for a modicum of control.

Perceptions of health and environmental dangers add an element of fear of the unknown that often mires Nimby conflicts in doubt and confusion. Environmental health problems are so commonplace and their dangers so often uncertain that many people empathize with the victims, or potential victims, of technological hazards who become intransigent obstructionists. Widespread identification with those who oppose apparent environmental dangers has conferred a measure of social acceptance and respectability on Nimbyism as a tool for preserving a community's quality of life against irresponsible or unfair assaults. This engenders a sense of righteousness that has galvanized socially and geographically disparate Nimby groups into a self-conscious trend.

Nimbyism and Environmentalism

"This is a real people's movement, one of the strongest in the country," according to Lois Gibbs, primary leader of the Love Canal uprising who later founded the Washington, D.C.-based Citizen's Clearinghouse on Hazardous Waste. Her organization assists some 5,000 groups—she calls them "environmental justice groups"—working on a range of local environmental concerns. Few of them can afford paid staff and some have only a handful of members. Others run sophisticated operations that can draw 10,000 people to a rally. The Boston-based National Toxics Campaign offered technical assistance to 1,300 such organizations in 1989, up from 600 in 1987. These numbers denote power. But Nimbyism is far too unorganized and amorphous, too varied in its nature and goals to be considered a "movement" in any traditional sense. In fact, if

Nimbyism developed a national leadership structure with an articulated strategy, its distinct power of immediacy would probably dissipate as individual groups adjusted to larger goals.

Yet many Nimby activists who oppose technological projects draw insight and inspiration from the environmental movement. Nimbys and environmentalists would seem natural allies. In practice, as seen in the Rocky Flats controversy, they have had an overlapping yet uneasy relationship. Environmentalists tend toward a big-picture critique of society, or at least hold a vision of sweeping policy reforms designed to preserve the natural environment. In contrast, environmentally based Nimbyism almost always stems from personal experience of technology's intrusions on everyday life. (In this way, Nimbyism more closely resembles shop-floor struggles of industrial workers for better health-and-safety protections.) "[Nimbys] seek personal protection, compensation for loss, and the ability to return speedily to the normative consumptive American lifestyle," writes Michael Edelstein, a specialist on the psychological impact of toxic-waste exposure. "And they join together out of necessity, not voluntarily because of shared ideals."

Nimbyism has little in common with countercultural environmentalists who eat organic vegetables and embrace a back-to-Mother Earth philosophy. In fact, many Nimby activists disdain unconventional ideas. "We're not dope-smoking, hippie environmentalists," argues a pharmacist in Lexington, Tennessee, who organized opposition to a proposed landfill. "We're a new breed. We drive pick-up trucks and wear overalls. And we'll be a lot harder to stop." George Carr, a leader of the group that opposed University of California biomedical labs at Laurel Heights, said this during a public hearing: "You have to take us as we are. Even those of us that might occasionally have one of those God-forbidden cigars. That's us. We're members of the public, and we are not lily-white pure. We're full of contaminants. But we're surviving."

Although the two groups are often ideological opposites, Nimbys may be most similar in style and sensibility to radical environmentalists whose diffuse groups have no clearly defined leadership structure. Some radicals favor *ecotage*—cutting power lines or monkey-wrenching heavy machinery used to clear-cut forests—as the most effective tactic against what they see as nature's imminent demise. (Similarly, animal rights extremists have firebombed research labs.) Nimbys rarely use such tactics, but they share this desperate absolutism. For example, in an effort to add teeth to their demands for relocation, Love Canal residents kidnaped and briefly held two federal officials.

A keen sense of urgency, born of immediate fear, separates Nimbys from mainstream environmentalists. Both groups lobby, but Nimbys are far more likely to hound unsympathetic politicians out of office. Mainstream environmentalists match opponents' scientific firepower to argue a change in course. Nimbys may seek scientific advice, but (as seen in both the Laurel Heights and Rocky Flats situations) they rely on it only reluctantly, distrusting experts' proclivity to compromise. Further, mainstream environmentalists speak the language of the system and adopt the politics of the possible, looking toward gradual change. Their tactics tend to reflect the range of behavior acceptable to established structures for public participation. Nimbys routinely pump up community anxiety about a potential danger as an organizing tool for achieving absolutist goals. (This also serves to counteract the numbing impact that the litany of modern environmental problems has on some people.) And because Nimbys have little or no faith in dominant institutions, they often try to disrupt official proceedings. Corporate and government officials, scientists, and many environmentalists find this willful unreasonableness chilling, largely because they cannot control or channel it.

Urban planners Robert Gottlieb and Margaret FitzSimmons say that the differences between the two groups reflect a split in the direction of environmentalism: "On the one side are national organizations which concern themselves with Nature as outside of human urban patterns; on the other are popular attempts to integrate environmental concerns with community control of everyday life."

From the grass-roots, the large, relatively rich, Washington-based environmental organizations resemble corporations or government agencies—complex bureaucracies that, in their efforts to mold the national environmental agenda, have lost touch with those on the front lines of pollution. The environmental establishment concerns itself with "how best to maintain and rationalize organizational growth, how to secure influence with the centers of power rather than how to build on the culture of protest that characterize[s] single-issue, community-based groups," according to Gottlieb and FitzSimmons. "Computerization of mailing lists took precedence— in fact substituted for—community organizing; the skills of the lobbyist, litigator, and expert were valued over the passion of the outraged [homemaker and] the angry consumer. . . ." Indeed, women often lead Nimby opposition to scientific and technological dangers—as seen at Love Canal, Rocky Flats, Tulelake, and Laurel Heights—by engaging in extraordinary self-education and community-organizing campaigns. The degree to which dominant institutions recoil at Nimbyism may involve an element of sexism.

"The bigger 'movement' may be caught up in making enough money to cover [large institutional] budgets," says Lauri Maddy, a toxic-waste protester who once handcuffed herself to a chair in the Kansas governor's office. "But nobody pays us for 40 hours a week, or over 80. Because most of us living in high-chemical-impact areas came to fighting this [battle] out of self-preservation."

Former EPA Chief William Ruckelshaus and current EPA administrator William Reilly demonstrate the constellation of relationships among industry, government, and mainstream environmentalists. After his second stint at EPA, Ruckelshaus became head of Browning-Ferris, a waste hauler frequently targeted by environmentalists and Nimbys alike. Yet he also serves on the board of the World Wildlife Fund/Conservation Foundation. Reilly, who previously led the World Wildlife Fund/Conservation Foundation, is the first EPA administrator to come from the ranks of the environmental movement. Some former colleagues see Reilly as a smoke screen for business as usual; they call other appointees in environmental jurisdictions "Watt clones," after James Watt, Reagan's interior secretary, who environmentalists widely considered a disaster. To Nimby activists, Reilly and Ruckelshaus may look like they are passing through the same revolving door.

Some of the largest environmental organizations raise hundreds of thousands, even millions of dollars from corporations—including major polluters—every year. They have added corporate officials to their boards. This may or may not be an effective strategy for environmental preservation. In any case, it distances mainstream environmentalism from local activists who seem to reject all institutionally sanctioned versions of reality.

——————————— ଓଓଓ ———————————

The Evolution of Nimbyism?

Despite the divergence in environmentalism—or because of it—Nimbyism exerts growing pressure on the environmental movement. Until recently, national environmental organizations had been able to ignore grass-roots environmentalists. Now they do so at their peril. Mainstream organizations increasingly see Nimbyism as a force to be reckoned with—a force that shares some goals with environmentalists but rarely works hand-in-glove with them. "A reordering of priorities, a rethinking of strategy and tactics is taking place throughout the entire environmental movement because of the increased activism by the very people who are most at risk," according to Gerry Poje, chief environmental toxicologist at the National Wildlife Federation. "Here in Washington it is becoming increasingly obvious that true change will occur at the local level."

Can a social force based largely on individualism and that draws its strength and identity from decentralization and personal experience be transformed into a coherent, organized approach to remaking our technological society? Some environmentalists believe Nimby power can be harnessed. All over the nation, antitoxics coalitions share technical and logistical assistance, and they promote regional strategies to resist toxic-waste facilities and other polluting industries. California Communities against Toxics, for example, boasts representatives from 100 communities. A handful of umbrella groups have emerged, including the National Toxics Campaign and the Citizens Clearinghouse on Hazardous Wastes. Greenpeace (one of the few large environmental organizations that rejects corporate funds) also works closely with local groups. These organizations loan consultants, promote leadership skills, prepare fact sheets and position papers on scientific issues, and hold training and organizing conferences. They preach reduction, recycling, and reuse of toxics in an overall effort to draw local activists into a national movement. And they enjoy considerable success in helping Nimby groups recognize the relationships between their own situations and those of other communities.

Operating in isolation, Nimby groups stymie desirable or benign facilities along with the truly ill-conceived ones. They may complicate or delay serious efforts to solve environmental problems, even as they force corporations and regulators to perform at a higher standard. But as a social and political trend, some environmentalists see Nimby gridlock—the consequence of a multitude of communities rejecting any plan regardless of its characteristics—as a way to force changes in how society as a whole chooses and manages certain technologies. The national umbrella organizations have effectively adopted the gridlock approach by opposing almost all available technologies for hazardous-waste disposal. *Niaby*—not in anyone's backyard—or *Nope*—not on planet earth—may slowly be supplanting *Nimby*.

Gridlock sometimes leads to caution; government, industrial, and scientific leaders must rethink and open the process for deciding when and how new technologies will be introduced or old problems solved. By slowing technological decisions to a socially acceptable pace, Nimby gridlock may improve long-term prospects for responsible development of controversial technologies, such as genetically engineered microbial pesticides. But will it do so without choking off creativity? Nimby gridlock has compelled the Department of Energy's weapons complex to reduce the volume of waste it produces. But if the agency ever comes up with a workable siting plan, will any community accept the nuclear garbage?

Consider the archetype of Nimby gridlock; hazardous-waste disposal. Historically, short of irresistible legal, political, or economic pressure, major polluters have rejected the massive source-reduction and recycling that may be the only ecologically viable, long-term solution to the toxic-waste problem. As Niaby efforts foreclose the business-as-usual approach, that day draws closer. Or does it?

Portney, the Tufts professor, has studied hazardous waste throughout the 1980s. "I don't see the chain of events occuring that would [vindicate the gridlock strategy]. I don't see companies trying to build [waste-disposal] facilities, being turned down, then turning to source-reduction," he says. Where reduction is taking place, it is more a matter of economics—saving on disposal and liability expenses.

Allan Mazur considers "not in anyone's backyard" to be "pure rhetoric"—a simple defense against the selfishness charge. "As soon as an area is off the list [of candidates for an unwanted facility], it fades out of the picture," he says. Noble Niaby aspirations suddenly disappear. Meanwhile illegal, dangerous "midnight dumping" by unscrupulous waste haulers runs rampant. Government fiats that create new dump sites may not be far behind.

"People are mixing tactics with policy. When you stop up a toilet, the need to go to the bathroom doesn't go away," says Richard Gimello, who started out as a Nimby, then Niaby activist in the late 1970s. He fought to gain a tough toxic-waste siting law in New Jersey, and ultimately became director of the siting commission the law established. Gimello held that job for nearly eight years (during which time, due to community pressure, not a single new facility was built). In 1990, he went to work for the waste industry. Gimello argues that the "constipation approach" overlooks the eminent manageability of much of the hazardous-waste stream and ignores recent improvements in technology. "[Activists] still pretend that hazardous-waste facilities that are planned and built today are the hole in the ground that Love Canal was."

Still, with their commitment to national strategies and grassroots, democratic involvement, environmental coalitions and umbrella organizations could eventually stimulate more flexible, discriminating, solution-oriented approaches to the war on waste. More important, their efforts could help resolve a wide range of dilemmas posed by health and environmental hazards. But that goal depends on sweeping changes in our society's approach to risk and power in matters of science and technology.

7

Toward Democratic Decision Making about Science and Technology

We should remember that risk assessment data can be like the captured spy; if you torture it long enough, it will tell you anything you want to know. —William Ruckelshaus, administrator, Environmental Protection Agency

The controversies highlighted in this book share a central feature with a multitude of similar conflicts between local communities and those who control science and technology: Opposing sides look at the same or similar information, then draw opposite conclusions about a technology's safety or wisdom.

For millennia, people have tried to predict the likelihood that a particular project will cause harm. The Asipu people, who lived in the Tigris-Euphrates Valley nearly 5,000 years ago, provided methodical risk assessments. Babylonian leaders consulted the Asipu when pondering such diverse questions as where to place a major new building and with whom to arrange a marriage. The Asipu carefully evaluated and recorded the factors involved in each problem, then they plotted each factor within a range of likely scenarios based on the various choices. The option that involved the best ratio of positive to negative factors—tempered by divine guidance—was then recommended to the client.

Only in the last decade, however, have risk assessment and its progeny, risk communication and risk management, grown from the colorless pastimes of statisticians to diversified, flourishing growth industries, peopled by academics, regulators, and public-policy specialists. The new risk analysts produce mounds of studies and scholarly journals, form professional societies, and hold frequent meetings. More significant, the government now offers substantial grants to study the subject of risk.

Meanwhile, social researchers labor to divine how the public will react to new or troublesome technologies. Consultants claim to have magical abilities to help the unruly masses understand the overriding benefits of one risky project or another. One might presume that this frenzied activity has helped the public decide what to fear; how to balance danger with opportunity. Just the opposite has occurred: People are more confused than ever. Part of the reason lies in how risks are perceived and measured.

As discussed in chapter 1, in the 1980s people began to see the world as a risky place and becoming even riskier. Using survey data, researchers have constructed a taxonomy of risk perception. For example, voluntary hazards, such as smoking, generate less fear and concern than imposed hazards, say, breathing car exhaust. A familiar chemical plant that has belched a foul odor for decades fades into the background, while a proposal for a state-of-the-art hazardous-waste facility touches off a civil war. Common hazards do not stand a chance in a fear competition with exotic hazards, regardless of countervailing evidence. Accident-prone though they may be, power saws are part of everyday life. Not so laboratory experiments using recombinant DNA, which are not known ever to have harmed anyone seriously. Catastrophes, such as an airplane crash that may kill hundreds of people at a stroke, generate a terror well beyond the fear of automobile collisions—in aggregate, a far greater killer.

———————— ଙଙଙ ————————

Risk and Rationality

The incidence of dangerous outcomes often has little impact on people's perceptions of risks. Clearly not all fears are rational, particularly in an actuarial sense. By failing to put risk in perspective, many risk analysts claim, people routinely engage in dangerous behaviors while they resist relatively benign and demonstrably beneficial technologies.

Yet there is more to risk than a body count. Quantitative comparisons of hazards mean little outside of their political, social, and economic contexts. For example, what is *voluntary risk?* Can most people freely choose not to drive in a car-dependent culture? Someone angered by toxic contamination of drinking water might be informed that the danger is no more likely to cause harm than eating peanut butter (which contains a naturally occurring carcinogen) or, for that matter, than being struck by lightning. Such comparisons make risks seem ubiquitous, random, unavoidable, even trivial. They cast the concerned party in the role of an inconsistent alarmist. More important, many risk comparisons ignore the economic underpinnings of the equation. Corporations do not profit from lightning strikes, but they make a fortune from polluting industries.

Risk analysis was conceived, in part, to help society decide how to mitigate potential hazards. But the risk industry more often functions to stem the "mindless fear of science and technology" that slows or stymies technical innovation and hampers the smooth progression of profitable enterprise. Consider the terms used by risk analysts. *Risk,* for example, is preferred over *hazard;* the obscure replaces the obvious. Risk emphasizes doubt of harm. It prompts "excruciatingly detailed inquiry with dozens (if not hundreds) of fascinating dimensions," in the words of science historian Langdon Winner. "Faced with uncertainty about what is known concerning a particular risk, prudence becomes not a matter of acting effectively to remedy a suspected source of injury, but of waiting for better research findings. . . . Action tends to be postponed indefinitely," Winner argues. *Risk analysis* implies a willingness to weigh gain against loss, and the term rejects value judgments regarding social need, life-style, or community preservation. In other words, it subtly limits debate. It evolves easily to *acceptable risk*.

Risk analysts, regulators, and corporate officials also favor the term *priorities*. We should rank our risks and deal with them in order, they argue. EPA considers such problems as air pollution, atmospheric ozone depletion, and global warming our most urgent environmental hazards. Yet the cleanup of toxic-waste dumps, judged a far less significant problem by EPA, consumes vastly greater funds because the immediate neighbors of these dumps raise hell about them. The cleanup of hazardous-waste sites is the highest environmental priority of the general public. Is this a distortion of priorities caused by local shortsightedness? Discounting for a moment that, to people who live near a leaky dump, global warming may seem abstract at best, the term *priorities* itself obfuscates and limits the issue. *Priorities* implies an arbitrary limit to resources— that we cannot clean toxic dumps *and* protect the ozone. The term suggests an acceptable allocation of effort to environmental safety. And why should people take EPA priorities seriously when they rarely see those priorities reflected in decisive policy? The government routinely sabotages or moderates efforts to curb emissions of pollutants that cause acid rain, global warming, and other pressing problems, in deference to complaining industries.

Quantitative risk analysis promises certainty in a haze of intimidating numerical specificity. It is a false promise, however, because scientific abilities develop unevenly. The science of measurement, for instance, has recently yielded ways to detect the presence of some toxic substances down to parts per trillion. Yet the sciences of assessment—toxicology and epidemiology—lag far behind. (The primitive state of epidemiology has stimulated many local communities to conduct their own informal studies—barefoot epidemiology—when officials deny the presence of health effects in defiance of citizens' common-sense observations.) Consequently, when scientists say that a particular pollutant will cause one more cancer per million people over 70 years (such statements are the stock in trade of risk analysis), their conclusions are often based on dubious extrapolations from uncertain data.

Social scientists Michiel Schwarz and Michael Thompson tell an anecdote about a complex, expensive computer model constructed by an international scientific institute to plot the world's energy future. The model's conclusions were endorsed by some of the world's leading scientific societies and relied on by major nations to plan their energy policies. It was later shown that the model's scenarios were "hard-wired" to "far from explicit assumptions that had, in fact, provided the cultural cohesion for the project." The 4,200 variables considered by the analysis proved irrelevant to the result.

Risk analysis, like most human endeavors, depends on the assumptions of its practitioners, assumptions rarely shared by people affected by a technological hazard. A precursor and close relation of risk analysis, cost-benefit analysis, used mainly to oppose environmental and occupational-health regulation, suffers from similar limitations. These social regulations have been estimated by conservatives to cost $100 billion a year or more; a figure liberals consider a ludicrous exaggeration that ignores the fiscal benefits of cleaner air and water and healthier workers. Efforts to assign a dollar value to human life also reflect the subjectivity of cost-benefit calculations. In 1985 three federal agencies variously estimated a life to be worth from $400,000 to $3.5 million.

Rules for risk assessment "are a manual of defaults," according to Ellen Silbergeld, a toxicologist for the Environmental Defense Fund. "In the absence of data we will assume X." Waste incinerators emit dioxin, the highly toxic chemical that destroyed Times Beach, Missouri. Scientists can detect the presence of minute amounts of dioxin in the environment. But how much dioxin may the outlying community breathe safely? No one knows, so EPA sets limits based on its best guess (a level that allows incineration). Industry might guess a higher amount, local communities one far lower. While a few products of technology, such as DDT and leaded gasoline, carry such obvious and well-documented dangers that scientists almost unanimously oppose their use, there is little consensus on the vast majority of technology-derived threats. In two critical areas, low-level radiation and chemical carcinogens, esteemed scientists within and across fields of study routinely take opposite positions.

"Science thrives on uncertainty," two-time EPA Chief William Ruckelshaus points out. "The greatest triumph of a scientist is the crucial experiment that shatters the certainties of the past and opens up rich new pastures of ignorance. . . . *Of course* scientists will disagree on issues involving the advancing edge of research; that is what they do for a living." And disputes within the scientific community go beyond collegial disagreements about the nature of reality. Scientists play for high stakes—grants, prestige, and power.

The range of *structural uncertainties* in risk analysis—inherently limited tools and data, conflicts of interest, disparate assumptions, and veiled self-interest—are either ignored or treated by risk analysts as mere *technical uncertainties*. The general public's widespread suspicion of technocrats suggests that many people perceive this contradiction.

Local activists who attack official risk estimates (usually without a carefully articulated analysis of their own) are often called "antitechnology" or "antiscience." The labels stick as long as the debate is denuded of its political context and instead is directed exclusively to technical questions that are discussed in technical language and answered with facts accessible to and interpretable by experts only. As community members acquiesce to this mode of reasoning (and despite the rise in locally based environmental protests, most do), they become dependent on experts. The process insidiously leads people to doubt their own intuition and to discard their own experience.

"Statements by experts have their proper place—most often in pointing out the technical or logical fallacies in arguments put forward by others," argues science historian and journalist David Dickson. "They are seldom valid as a basis for either making or justifying social and political decisions." This describes most technology-related risk conflicts today: They are social and political choices defined as technical choices.

The emphasis on science over politics in risk decisions arises, in part, from a growing fear of "excess democracy," sometimes blamed by those who control technology as the source of the Nimby phenomenon. As seen in chapters 4 and 5, technocrats regularly offer nightmarish visions of a scientific and economic standstill— virtually an end to progress—to prevent "scientific illiterates" from gaining any direct control over technological management. "A multitude of people are now able to participate in the decision-making process—without adequate knowledge," Jerome Wiesner, former president of the Massachusetts Institute of Technology and science advisor to Presidents Kennedy and Johnson, said ominously. "This leads to a paralysis of decision making. What we need is reestablishment of a governmental mechanism to . . . provide environmental protection and . . . at the same time permit the evolution of technical processes that are required for industry." No one has framed the prevailing view more bluntly than John Kemeny, who chaired the presidential commission that reviewed the Three Mile Island nuclear accident. "Jeffersonian democracy cannot work in the year 1980," he said, "the world has become too complex."*

Such cynical appraisals exaggerate the effectiveness and wisdom of technical expertise. More important, they imply that the current system by which corporations and government officials choose and manage technology is both optimal and immutable. The Kemenys

---

*French political theorist Andre Gorz predicts "the rise of electrofascism" in any society that becomes heavily dependent on such an extravagantly dangerous and delicate technology as nuclear power. Overwhelming security and safety needs in a nuclear society would require "a caste of militarized technicians" to run the plants, transport, store, and protect the ever-growing mountain of waste for hundreds of thousands of years. "The all-nuclear society is a society full of cops," agrees another French analyst. "There can't be the slightest self-management in a society based on such an energy choice."

and Wiesners fail to ask whose interests are served by the consolidation of technological decision making in a few hands.

———————— ⚝⚝⚝ ————————

A Clash of Cultures

"Life's Risks: Balancing Fear against Reality of Statistics." This 1989 headline in the *New York Times* inadvertently caricatures one model for viewing technological hazards: statistics as "reality." Advocates of the other model could be expected to counter with the old saw about the three kinds of lies: lies, damn lies, and statistics.

Science historians Sheldon Krimsky and Alonzo Plough describe this dichotomy as emerging from opposing rationalities—technical and cultural—each with its own logic based on independent criteria (see table 7.1.) Although in any specific disagreement over technological risk the models may overlap, their inherent contradictions make conflict inevitable.

Cultural rationalists see their opposites as unfeeling, counterintuitive, and autocratic; limited to quantitative analysis; and usually serving the interests of those who control or profit from a controversial technology. The cultural model of risk comes from the personal experiences and shared history of those who are subject to the hazards. Scientists and engineers have been terribly wrong in the past, and may well go wrong again, cultural rationalists reason. The cultural model depends on popular wisdom. "Given the choice, it errs on the side of caution rather than recklessness, of safety rather than profits," according to Dickson. "It does not require definitive or conclusive evidence of a hazard before taking preventive action." Most important, the cultural model places political decisions about how to cope with risky technologies in the hands of those subject to the hazards.

Practitioners of the technical model view the cultural approach as emotional rather than objective, highly inefficient, and a drag

Table 7.1   Characteristics of the Technical and
Cultural Rationality of Risk

Technical Rationality	Cultural Rationality
Trust in scientific methods, explanations, and evidence	Trust in democratic explanations, and evidence process, with widest possible participation and openness
Appeal to authority and expertise	Appeal to folk wisdom, peer groups, and traditions
Boundaries of analysis narrow and reductionist	Boundaries of analysis broad; include liberal use of analogy and historical precedent
Risks depersonalized, with emphasis on statistical probability	Risks personalized, with emphasis on family and community
Focus on consistency and universality	Focus on particularity, with less concern for consistency
Only risks that can be specified and measured are relevant	Unanticipated or unarticulated risks are also relevant

SOURCE: Adapted from Sheldon Krimsky and Alonzo Plough, "The Emergence of Risk Communication Studies: Social and Political Context," *Science, Technology and Human Values* 12, no. 3 and 4 (Summer/Fall 1987):9. Reprinted by permission of Sage Publications, Inc.

on progress. Technical rationalists estimate risks based on defined principles, scientific norms, and logical consistency, and they use this "to fine-tune the regulatory apparatus so that it presents the minimal burden to the corporate sector," Dickson says. Technical rationalists agree that the public must be protected from undue risks. But they oppose costly safety measures whose necessity has not been scientifically verified—which is only rarely possible. Like their counterparts, technical rationalists may err on the side of caution. But they use equal caution to avoid overestimating risks in ways that create obstacles to profitability. Technical rationalists "listen to complaints from those who claim to have suffered from the consequences of corporate actions, but then use scientific experts to certify these claims before accepting that they have any significance," Dickson adds. Finally, the technical model gives responsibility for controlling risks to corporate or government decision makers.

Both the technical and the cultural approaches influence risk assessment and management. Both suffer from blind spots that have economic or ecological consequences. But the technical model—as the model of those in power—has been by far the more destructive in terms of social disruption, environmental degradation, and health effects. Its weaknesses, failures, and contradictions have provoked the outcry by local communities all over the country. Not surprisingly, the cultural rationalists—Nimby activists among them—are not always coherent, consistent, logical, or "responsible." To adopt such qualities implies trust in the technical model, or competition on the terms of the technical rationalists—something local communities can do only from a position of weakness.

———————— ଷଷଷ ————————

Consistency of Conflict

At first glance, the cases in chapters 3, 4, and 5 look vastly different: The technologies appear to present a wide range of danger levels, from deadly plutonium processing and unknown environmental effects of recombinant organisms to relatively benign and well-understood biomedical experiments. The political, economic, and social functions of the sponsoring institutions also vary greatly: a secretive government agency at the center of the national security apparatus building weapons of mass destruction; a profit-seeking corporation on the cutting edge of agricultural science; a public university conducting basic research and providing clinical care while advancing its own prestige and influence. Yet these three institutions exhibited remarkably similar behavior in several key areas.

Candor: Each institution—deliberately, inadvertently, or carelessly—withheld critical information until all major initial decisions had been made. The secrecy mandated by law at Rocky Flats was interpreted by plant officials as a license to lie about gross environmental hazards. Officials of Advanced Genetic Sciences (AGS) concealed many decisions as trade secrets or merely to skirt controversy in its work on ice-minus. University of California at San Francisco (UCSF) administrators deliberated about what to do with the newly acquired Laurel Heights property behind closed doors. A lack of openness greatly inflamed each of these conflicts.

Approach to communication: All three institutions began with a general disregard for, or complacency about the views of local residents. Only after community groups voiced health or environmental objections did Rocky Flats, AGS, and UCSF officials attempt to reach out to the communities. The primary form of this outreach was public-relations efforts, which amounted to a simple "Trust us; we are the experts." Further, the project sponsors uniformly described hazards as nonexistent or miniscule, regardless of conflicting or missing evidence. They compared their work to everyday hazards, such as cigarette smoking, that were of little relevance to the hazards in question. Officials in each case downplayed or ignored the uncertain risks of their projects until after Nimby groups had generated substantial support, and then only when outside scientists or regulators supported community positions. As their credibility eroded, the three institutions accused the opposition of ignorance, scientific illiteracy, antiscience attitudes, or lack of insider knowledge; the latter was true by definition and design. Public outreach was described as "educational" or an "exchange of information." But the primary impetus of the institutions was to placate or persuade opponents, or to satisfy legal requirements.

Attitude toward the community: Each institution's officials acted at first as if they could operate in a world apart, independent of social context; able to plan and enlarge their operations and initiate controversial activities regardless of the neighbors' views. When compelled to take notice, Rocky Flats, AGS, and UCSF scientists and administrators consistently patronized their opponents. Officials exuded their unshakable belief in the inherent superiority of their goals over concerns raised by community activists.

Attitude toward hazard control: All three institutions took advantage of gaps and disarray in the regulatory apparatus, attempting whenever possible to operate independently. In each case, the strategy backfired. When gaffes, carelessness, and arrogance came to light, each institution was subjected to far more stringent regulations than before. Rocky Flats, AGS, and UCSF officials took affirmative steps on health and safety only after they had been chastised by the regulators and stung by the ground swell of opposition. While protesting that their operations had always been perfectly safe and well run, these officials finally adopted "model" or "state-of-the-art" health and safety approaches.

The Nimby opponents to Rocky Flats, AGS, and UCSF also showed strikingly similar features.

Attitude toward authority: Each Nimby group displayed resolute distrust for institutions. This distrust went beyond Rocky Flats, AGS, and UCSF, extending to regulators, local government, and the business community. Each Nimby group worked or interacted with established environmental or activist groups, but usually with reluctance. (At Rocky Flats, in particular, many peace and environmental activists were viewed by the Nimbys as counterproductive.) The prevailing perspective among the Nimbys was that they could count on only themselves and their neighbors.

Tactics: The Nimby activists used strident, hyperbolic presentations. They raised worst-case scenarios and risk analogies with powerful emotional appeal: Ice-minus field tests and biomedical research were compared to a nuclear meltdown. (AGS and UCSF considered such analogies ignorant fear-mongering because of their dissimilarity with the technologies at issue. Cultural rationality views the precedents of other technologies that were once described as safe but later proved disastrous as essential information. "Analogies are generally dismissed by those who seek hegemony over technological decisions," Krimsky says. Those who create and manage technology prefer sterile, ahistorical expert analysis.) The Nimbys displayed uncompromising fury—such as shouting down speakers at public events—and thereby made each environmental review painfully slow. They fed local fears and used this as their most effective organizing tool.

Attitude toward science: Most of the principle Nimby activists in each case harbored grave fears and a sense of increasingly compelling urgency. They were self-taught; poring over relevant reports, memos, newspaper articles, and whatever else they could get hold of. Deeply skeptical of scientific data, the Nimbys dwelled on the irregularities and uncertainties that attend any complex scientific undertaking. Some of the activists became confused about technical details and occasionally put out flawed information. This may have been due, in part, to their reluctance to seek expert assistance, preferring to rely on their own common sense and research ability. And while the activists cared little about abstract notions of national security, commercial competitiveness, or scientific advancement, in no case did they oppose science or technnology per se. Rather, they opposed the impact of specific, potentially hazardous technologies on their lives and challenged the exclusive right of large institutions to choose, introduce, and operate those technologies. The Nimbys wanted to stop the process in order to examine whose interests were being served, and to assert some degree of control.

The similarities among the three institutions and among the Nimbys who opposed them do not mean that the situations were equivalent or should be judged on the same terms. Yet the consistent approach used by the corporate entities across so-called "objective" risk levels shows the pervasive influence of the technical model of risk management. And the consistent approach used by the Nimby groups shows the broad popular appeal of the cultural model. Bridging the two opposing rationalities presents a daunting challenge because our society, as alternative-energy proponent Amory Lovins argues, "has mechanisms only for resolving conflicting interests, not conflicting views of reality."

Rigidities on each side, which led to the bitterness of the conflicts, were direct consequences of disparities in power. Officials at Rocky Flats, AGS, and UCSF began with total control over the technologies and tried to maintain that control at every turn. The Nimbys, with justification, believed that they could force due consideration of local concerns in only one way: through aggressive and provocative, if sometimes unfocused, defiance.

--------------- ଙଙଙ ---------------

Failing to Meet the Challenge

Risk analysis on the technical model failed to help resolve any of the conflicts profiled in this book. These are typical failures. The history of corporate and government responses to Nimbyism suggests why the technical model of risk management has become increasingly unworkable and difficult to enforce in the Nimby era.

Years ago, unwanted or unpleasant facilities were simply crowded together in poor or industrial areas. Zoning regulations encouraged the creation of now-infamous strips of fast-food restaurants, groups of polluting industries, waste-treatment plants, and pockets of sex businesses amid neighborhoods in decline. As poor people began to rebel against this manifestly unfair practice, and as the range of unwanted facilities expanded, the concentration strategy became impractical or impossible in most areas.

For a time, developers assumed that by keeping quiet about potentially controversial or undesirable projects until they were in place, or were so far along as to appear inevitable, they could simply sneak a project in through the backdoor. The California Department of Corrections, for example, once converted a Southern California health club into a work-furlough program for convicts. The agency left the sign, "Aerobics and Nautilus Unlimited," in place.

As recently as 1979 EPA recommended this "low-profile approach" in relation to siting toxic-waste dumps in relatively remote areas. Such methods were often successful in the 1960s and early 1970s. But aside from being unethical and undemocratic, secrecy or deceit stands little chance of long-term success today. The unpredictability of responses by surprised and angry neighbors outweighs any advantages of the approach.

Legal fiat has sometimes been used with limited success to site unwanted social services. Resistance to group homes for the mentally retarded has been so intense that by 1988, 37 states had enacted laws forbidding zoning restrictions against placing the homes in single-family neighborhoods. Once these laws are in place, communities often grow accustomed to the unwanted arrivals. In at least two cases, however, in New York and California, neighbors set fire to the facilities. Even without such an extreme response, the long-term costs for forcing a facility in an area that doesn't want it can be high—deep community disaffection and intransigent resistance the next time around. "The old process of decide, announce, and defend doesn't appear to be possible anymore," says Ray Newton, director of planning in Jacksonville, Florida.

Indeed, when local residents feel sufficient fear of technological hazards, they can usually convince or threaten elected officials into blocking unwanted projects. In North Carolina, for example, the legislature empowered a statewide board with local representation to decide where to place hazardous-waste dumps. The board duly deliberated, then made a selection. The chosen community organized such strong opposition that it was not only able to prevent the site development but also caused the legislature to scrap the board and repeal the law establishing the procedure. According to the National Conference of State Legislatures, many states have passed laws that forbid the storage of high-level radioactive waste and the movement of such waste across their territory (even though such transport restrictions violate federal statutes). Michigan had agreed to host the repository for low-level radioactive waste from seven Midwest states. But after local communities blocked all proposed sites, the state legislature established such stringent criteria for waste storage that it soon became clear that no site in Michigan would ever prove acceptable.

New technologies are sometimes promoted as solutions to the problems of older technologies, or to encourage the acceptance of social necessities. Highways could be constructed with better noise baffles. Recombinant bacteria could neutralize toxic waste or consume oil spills. And in areas where residents reject the building of new prisons, convicts might be confined to their homes and monitored by irremovable, radio-transmitter ankle bracelets. But consider the flaws of these examples. Quieter highways might promote increased urban sprawl. The experience of ice-minus casts doubt on any biotechnology-based approach to pollution. And electronic monitoring promotes a worrisome "Big Brother" aspect to incarceration. A technological fix rarely eliminates a problem at its social or economic roots; technology often changes the intensity, form, or location of undesirable side effects. (Recall that nuclear power was promoted as a clean alternative to oil.) More important, belief in the technological fix undermines the basis for designing for safety in the first place.

--------------- ෨෨෨ ---------------

Involving the Public

The pitfalls of coercion, secrecy, and the technological fix suggest some basic prerequisites for resolving Nimby conflicts: tough, well-enforced pollution controls, health standards, and building codes; and early, extensive public involvement in the siting process. But these actions must be taken in good faith. Attempts to manipulate or placate the public in pursuit of a predetermined goal—the bread and butter of public relations—exacerbated local fears of ice-minus field tests and UCSF's biomedical research. At the other end of the spectrum, the decision makers, who quite reasonably fear rejection, rarely give a local community direct control over the fate of a controversial project.

Between these two extremes lies a spectrum of consultation and negotiation. At pro-forma public hearings or community meetings, bureaucrats typically count heads and faithfully note people's comments (dismissed later as inconsequential or irrelevant to the narrowly defined purpose of the hearing). Activists often describe these same events as little more than prettying-up the "decide, announce, defend" strategy. The hearings usually have little bearing on essential decisions about the project's character; still less on its acceptance or rejection. This is why the Citizen's Clearinghouse for Hazardous Wastes defines *public hearing* as "an event where the public speaks and the officials don't listen."

Environmental impact reports (EIRs), also ostensibly designed to promote an early, effective public role in technological decisions, arguably have the opposite effect. On the one hand, Nimby groups challenge EIRs as a stalling tactic against regionally needed, locally unwanted developments. On the other, EIRs require environmentalists and Nimbys alike to conduct endless analysis of voluminous documents, distracting them from challenging the regulators and the corporate entities that produce EIRs. These typically low-quality reports—formulaic descriptions rather than scientific assessments of technology—are produced to justify rather than enlighten decisions. "Whether [EIRs] have improved the quality of decision-making or whether the same effects could have been achieved at much lower cost through alternative, more direct means of public participation—remains an open question," David Dickson says.

The California Environmental Quality Act proved itself to be part of the problem in the Laurel Heights conflict. The primary terms of the law—*significant impact, mitigation,* and *alternative*—carry legalistic meanings barely related to the common definitions of these words. The results: Communication chasms separate environmental law experts from the community; and input from thoughtful, yet naive members of the public often falls flat because it is irrelevant to law. The draft EIR released by UCSF in October 1989 ran 750 pages, most of it highly technical. Anyone but the most disciplined readers found the document opaque. The detail and length of the EIR was clearly mandated by the state Supreme Court. "But what good is it to open your books if they are incomprehensible?" commented an exasperated Bruce Spaulding, the UCSF official responsible for preparing the tome. Only the most militant opponents took the time and energy to study the EIR seriously, and local residents logically looked to them for guidance. Moreover, the law that mandated the EIR was written to protect the environment from unsound development, but it complicated creative approaches to comprehensive environmental and community preservation—approaches addressing the overall well-being and quality of life of citizens and their communities—by forcing costly "mitigation" of often trivial "impacts."

In a growing number of cases, however, genuine efforts to open up a dialogue with the widest possible audience have helped avoid Nimby battles. "We have found that community opposition to social services is almost universally confined to a vocal minority of people who are in very close proximity to the site," says Michael Dear, an urban geographer at the University of Southern California. "What participation does is bring the supporters of the project out also." In this way, genuine communication is a hopeful approach; it assumes that most people are thoughtful and flexible. Jacksonville's Newton says his department has gained substantial cooperation by using a mediated negotiation to give the community some latitude in defining the nature and dimensions of such projects as road development. The keys to success, he advises developers and government officials, are these: Make a meaningful effort to accommodate local concerns regarding the design and operation of the development, and show the kind of behavior you hope for in the community.

Yet these techniques have rarely found similar success in controversies involving health and environmental risks. In a much-publicized 1983 case, for instance, EPA went to extraordinary lengths to involve the public in a decision involving an arsenic-spewing copper smelter owned by Asarco, Inc. in Tacoma, Washington. EPA was deliberating whether to require pollution controls that Asarco officials insisted would force them to close the plant as unprofitable. In an elaborate series of educational meetings and public hearings, EPA asked Tacoma residents to build a consensus on the jobs versus health issue. "True public involvement meant forcing the public to confront the trade-offs involved in this risk-management decision," said then-EPA administrator William Ruckelshaus. Not surprisingly, the public wanted jobs *and* health. EPA called the Tacoma case an example of successful risk communication. But the stark choice was little better than blackmail. "EPA . . . failed to offer any alternative regulatory schemes which would require Asarco to amortize the cost of necessary pollution control equipment against the stream of profits it . . . earned over the past several decades of [poorly controlled] plant operations," noted one commentary at the time. Risks were communicated, but risk managers ignored the pivotal stumbling block to effective community involvement—Asarco and EPA retained all the power. Ultimately, Asarco closed the plant for economic reasons unrelated to the pollution problem.

In conflicts that involve health and environmental risks, the fears are too great, the scientific uncertainties too disconcerting for Newton's approach to be effective. Consequently, another strategy for overcoming Nimby opposition has become increasingly popular—one that focuses on compensation or economic incentive. Communities or municipalities are beginning to expect a quid pro quo for accepting low-level nuclear waste dumps, factories, shopping centers, and a wide range of other developments. The price may be a new fire truck or local road improvements. For instance, when the power company in upstate New York was allowed to build a $600 million power line, it gave $12 million in grants to communities that the line transversed. Jacksonville might finance a new park, with features at least partially decided upon by the community, in exchange for an agreement to host a new landfill. Or a developer might certify that a percentage of new jobs will be offered to local residents. Some states use a twist on the compensation theme—taxing hazardous-waste facilities or other locally unwanted land uses, then turning most of the revenues over to the host communities—while officials of the Dallas Airport take the compensation strategy to its logical conclusion. In their eagerness to build two new runways, they are considering cash payments to nearby residents for air rights, and guarantees on local property values. Similarly, Kodak plans to offer guarantees for residents near its manufacturing facilities in Rochester, New York.

Compensation will work some of the time. If communities see no other choice, especially when times are so hard that a community faces economic extinction, money or jobs can be the most powerful motivation. Every so often, an isolated desert town finds within its desperation a great love for nuclear waste or nerve-gas incineration. These are rare cases, however. A community in Illinois responded to a $25 million offer to expand an existing landfill more characteristically: "No thanks."

Plans for buying cooperation nearly always break down in the face of large or uncertain dangers. What is a fair price for possible health problems? You can compensate people for aesthetic disadvantages, inconvenience, and economic dislocation. You can ensure their property values, and perhaps even coax or shame them into compassion for drug addicts or the mentally ill. "But the studies have shown that you can't compensate people for [feelings of] lack of safety," says Donald MacGregor of Decision Research, a risk-consulting firm in Eugene, Oregon. "You cannot work the risk angle to get any movement in the public. Once a project is seen essentially in terms of its risk, you're lost." For example, 14 states offer economic incentives to communities that accept hazardous-waste facilities. Exactly zero plants have been built in those states since the incentive plans were enacted.

Even when compensation succeeds in individual cases, it fails as a comprehensive solution. Locally unwanted development is everywhere. If compensation becomes standard operating procedure for placing new facilities, can it be long before communities that have suffered for years or decades with old hazards begin to demand similar treatment? Moreover, risk compensation sends a corrupting message to developers: Don't worry about maintaining the highest possible pollution and safety controls; public health is a commodity that can be bought or sold.

Allan Mazur, a sociologist who studies technology-related controversy, says this about compensation: "It's like legalized prostitution . . . a way of keeping projects out of rich areas." Compensation can succeed only by being undemocratic. It shows the cynicism that has crept into the risk debate. Proponents of compensation assume people will never voluntarily meet the challenges of public involvement in risk decisions. As a long-term strategy— and many risk-management theorists believe it represents the only realistic option—compensation equals abdication.

Some more recent proposals begin to address the question of fairness, however. Kenneth Portney, a Tufts University political scientist, proposes "risk substitution." Under this plan, a modern toxic-waste facility, for example, might be located at the site of a long-standing, leaky dump after the developer cleans up the old dump. The community still ends up with a hazard, but one that is more carefully constructed, more safely operated. Similarly, New York City has initiated (though not yet implemented) an innovative plan known as "Fair Share," designed to distribute locally unwanted development equitably. City governments generally tend to buy the cheapest possible property for siting everything from landfills to bus garages to group homes. These properties are invariably in poor areas. Fair Share addresses this problem by balancing cost effectiveness against community preservation and requiring an equitable balance of burdens throughout the city's neighborhoods. The plan mandates intensive public deliberation on siting decisions and greater government accountability when new facilities have negative effects.

Another proposal, put forth by Frank Popper, chairman of the Urban Studies Department at Rutgers University, is based on a point system for sharing and trading unwanted facilities. A waste dump might be worth six halfway houses. A coal-fired power plant could earn as many points as five trailer parks. Regional bodies would first negotiate point values, then the unwanted facilities would be sited in ways that required each community to absorb a roughly equal number of points. "The point system merely brings out into the open and routinizes [what has been] done covertly, semi-randomly, often unfairly and corruptly," Popper says.

Some combination of these various proposals—always involving intensive community involvement, mitigation of hazards, regional planning, and efforts to promote fairness—could help de-escalate knee-jerk rejections of social services and projects that do not present significant health or environmental dangers. But they are not effective long-term approaches to Nimbyism in relation to science and technology. All of these techniques strive to make palatable technology in general, including technologies like massively polluting industries and high-level nuclear-waste dumps, which ultimately cannot be sustained ecologically, socially, or economically. The schemes also reinforce the idea that corporations and large government agencies should control all significant decisions about science and technology. Such reforms will never stem the tide of local community uprisings spawned by outrage over powerlessness. And because the proposals fail to place some scientific resources under the direct control of the communities subject to the potential hazards, the public remains ill-equipped to make thoughtful choices about which technologies to discard and which to retain.

Of course, scientific and technological choices descend through the greater structure of corporate and governmental power. People will probably tend toward rigidly protective postures about technological intrusions into their backyards as long as they continue to feel impotent to influence actions of, say, General Motors or General Electric, or to puncture the bloated budget of the Department of Defense. As long as government and industry make what are widely considered irresponsible, unfair, or dangerous decisions with impunity, local communities are unlikely to moderate their blanket opposition to potential risks. UCSF's biomedical labs will continue to look remarkably similar to the Rocky Flats bomb factory. Nimby obstructionism inevitably will go on until overall decision-making structures become responsive to local concerns and values. Nimbyism may even be a precondition to changes in those structures.

Therefore, society would do well to stop trying to "solve the Nimby problem" and to begin exploring ways to make Nimbyism unnecessary. This will require a radical reappraisal of the relationship between the public and the entire scientific and technological enterprise.

———————— ଌଌଌ ————————

A New Politics of Technological Choice

Nimbyism tests the burden of proof regarding scientific and technological risk. Formerly, victims were compelled to prove harm. Increasingly, scientists and technocrats take the defensive in efforts to prove safety. But this effect has been limited, haphazard, and often disruptive without social gain. To prepare the ground for a consensus on risks and benefits—one based on trust and shared power—the burden of proof must be shifted deliberately, methodically, and definitively. The following ideas are not like the recipes of a cookbook; recasting an implicit social contract is an uncertain process. Instead, they offer a vision of political conditions that would support flexible, discriminating, and reasonably efficient public involvement in decision making regarding science and technology.

Aggressive outreach: Nimby opposition arises spontaneously. Potential opponents of a project can rarely be identified by targeting local officials or established community organizations, or by appointing blue-ribbon panels. Actions of this kind more often inflame opponents rather than assuage their fears. The grass roots must be contacted on the assumption that the neighbors of a proposed project will establish their own agenda. (UCSF and AGS for example, admitted that they made a critical error in failing to reach out directly to the residents of Laurel Heights and Prunedale at the outset.) "You have to have a presence in the community" from the very beginning, says Richard Gimello, who began as a Nimby activist, then became a toxic-waste regulator, and recently began to work for the waste industry. "You have to be able to go to the ugly public meetings and take a beating," yet keep a blank slate with regard to community demands. In bridging different views of reality, everything must be open for discussion.

Full disclosure: Secrecy in any form is the enemy. Only rarely can restrictions on public access to environmental data be reasonably justified. The right-to-know provisions of the Superfund toxic cleanup law, despite flaws and lax enforcement, hint at what is possible. That law requires some 1.5 million industrial facilities, businesses, and farms to notify their respective communities of toxic releases. It also mandates broad public access to company files on the types, quantities, and locations of hundreds of toxic substances. Where citizens have been able to obtain data, they have often publicized gross pollution problems that regulators ignored or overlooked.

Beyond talk: Corporate and government officials often grow exasperated when extensive public discussion on siting has little impact on Nimby standoffs. Communication may air concerns, but if local communities are to become legitimate participants in the management of dangerous or risky projects, they must have direct oversight powers. Authorized, trained community representatives should be given carte blanche for enforcing specific, prenegotiated performance standards.

A new measure of health and safety: Although implementing the preceding ideas may ease certain Nimby conflicts, only the adoption of public- and worker-interest standards on health and safety can begin to address the source of Nimbyism. Such standards would dictate caution in projects with unknown effects. In practical terms, greater caution would mean spending the time and money—more than scientists or engineers may consider necessary—to find the best technical approach to limiting environmental hazards or to appraise their health effects. In the long run, however, little would be lost by institutionalizing a go-slow approach designed to build public support.

Under community-based standards, the most controversial or dangerous projects would be sited in or moved to remote areas. There is no good excuse for keeping a Rocky Flats in a major metropolitan area; no valid scientific rationale for testing ice-minus in the agricultural heartland. If economic burdens for removing such technologies from population centers are considered prohibitive, the technologies themselves are probably not sufficiently valuable to retain.

The object of risk management must be redefined from mere minimization of technology's "negative externalities" to a just, ecologically sound, democratically determined distribution of scientific and technological hazards and benefits. Risk assessment based on community standards should be able to answer the following questions to the satisfaction of those subject to the risk: Who gains and who loses if a project goes forward? What is "acceptable" risk?

Nimbyism will recede only when the public becomes confident that technocrats consider health and safety as important as intellectual, economic, and military goals. This includes stronger health and environmental regulation. As noted in chapter 2, corporate officials routinely warn that the world as we know it will end if stringent pollution controls are established and enforced. The government normally responds by sculpting health and environmental policy to fit the profit strategies of industry. Yet when threats of economic dislocation have been resisted—such as in some clean-air provisions for factories and automobiles—industry usually has responded with remarkable resilience. In the 1970s, for example, corporations tenaciously fought the promulgation of tough regulations for reducing emissions of vinyl chloride, a carcinogenic material used in plastics production. In meeting the regulations, however, the industry discovered techniques that drastically cut manufacturing costs.

No matter how carefully technologies are evaluated or policed, however, error, incompetence, and corruption will never be completely eliminated. In such cases, the public has a right to expect that polluters will pay the full cost of eliminating health hazards—without passing those costs along to victims via price or tax hikes. The agencies or corporations that have a history of poor environmental performance should be barred from involvement in major new ventures that pose serious environmental risks. It appears doubtful, for example, that DOE will ever convince any state or local community that it can build and maintain an acceptable structure for storing long-lived nuclear waste. That task should be turned over to an institution with a better track record. By the same token, companies or agencies that use potentially hazardous or poorly understood technologies should conduct rigorous, ongoing medical monitoring and epidemiological studies in outlying areas, with direct oversight by local citizens. Such studies could lay to rest health concerns, or reduce the prospect that years later a polluter could plausibly dispute anecdotal evidence of harm.

Clearly, worker- and community-interest standards on health and safety would require reordered priorities, including substantial increases in environmental health expenditures. The profits of General Electric Corporation, one of the nation's major polluters, reached nearly $4 billion during fiscal year 1989. EPA's entire budget for that year was only $5.6 billion. Given the massive economic and social costs of environmental disasters and mismanagement, these figures hardly reflect a thoughtful allocation of resources for gaining public confidence or preserving the environment. And recall that the United States spends about one-thousandth as much on predictive ecology as it does on biotechnology research and development. Yet many biotechnology executives complain that overregulation stifles the industry. They give little consideration to the prospect that effective, comprehensive regulation might bring products more speedily to a more accepting, confident public.

Industry often criticizes regulation as a drain on efficiency. Neither capitalism nor the technical model of risk assessment is inherently efficient, however. For example, vast sums have been spent to develop nuclear power, a costly, potentially catastrophic technology that generates, along with energy, apparently insoluble environmental problems. Solar power, a nonpolluting and safe technology, may or may not be a reasonable alternative. Little has been invested in finding out, however, because solar's decentralized nature makes it less amenable to centralized control by corporate owners; control that is essential to a stable flow of profits.

Just as such considerations distort energy-development choices, corporations create a multitude of profitable products that pose health dangers or risks, yet are wastefully redundant or fill no demonstrable need. "Industries producing plastics, pesticides, and petrochemical[s] have been largely unchallenged," urban planners Robert Gottlieb and Margaret FitzSimmons point out. Environmentalists have "failed to undermine the common presumption that corporate values—the right to profit, private sector control of production decisions, the use of advertising to create new markets and consumer preferences—are natural and necessary parts of the economy. In many cases, unless consumers, workers, and communities have the right to judge the social character of products or technologies that affect them, they will not be able to form a meaningful assessment of risks and benefits.

Under such scrutiny, some businesses inevitably would fail because of their inability to conduct operations safely or to produce socially valuable goods. The widespread ancillary costs of allowing unsafe or useless enterprises to continue—health problems, environmental degradation, public cynicism, and mounting resistance to relatively benign and genuinely needed technologies or services—testify to the bankruptcy of current risk-management and regulatory policies. These ancillary costs make transitory economic dislocations pale in comparison. Ultimately, the nation cannot afford to base its economy on industries or products that ignore basic public-health and environmental standards or that fail the test of social worth.

─────────── ಚಿಚಿಚಿ ───────────

Effective Public Participation

The preceding reforms could begin to alter the power relations that have made Nimbyism a practical necessity for local communities. To function productively in a more powerful role, however, the public will need to refine its ability to evaluate difficult choices that must be made under conditions of substantial uncertainty; to use the valuable aspects of the technical model of risk analysis—specificity, rigor, and logic—while avoiding delusions of false certainty. For this, local communities will require allies from the world of science. But such alliances do not form easily. Scientists may see recalcitrant communities as ignorant spoilers. And the people most vulnerable to the hazards of science and technology are usually the most alienated from scientists, whom they view as tools or apologists of the power structure that creates the problems.

As discussed in chapter 2, most scientists do not dwell on the power relations that affect their work. The cherished myth of science as the free, self-directed pursuit of natural truths has considerably greater durability in the scientific community than among the general public, whose ears are pricked up for signs of collusion among the creators, purveyors, and regulators of technology. Scientists' freedom to run their own labs, universities, and research institutes with relative immunity from government meddling obscures powerful, often unwise, political and market influences over the course of research funding and, consequently, the overall directions and priorities of science. These influences effectively make most scientists political captives.

In 1981 meteorologist James Hansen told the *New York Times* what was then considered provocative—the world is getting warmer due to a greenhouse effect. The Department of Energy, which had funded Hansen's research, promptly cut him off. "[DOE] saw these climate concerns as [examples of] environmentalists blocking economic and industrial progress without sufficient basis, and felt that it would only give more publicity to these concerns," Hansen said. His comments had entered the realm of advocacy on a hot political topic. Hansen's case was unusual only because it was publicized widely. Scientists who lose funds for speaking their minds usually scramble quietly to find other support or backtrack to less controversial studies.

The trademark of science—dispassion—lies at the root of the issue. One research proposal, for example, describes radioactive-waste drums leaking on the ocean floor and disturbed by newly discovered currents, not as a profound hazard of radioactivity working its way up the food chain in ever greater concentrations, but as "a powerful tool for the study of the way in which marine organisms react with their environment." There is no cause for alarm implicit in these bland words, merely an interesting scientific question. Sociologist Chandra Mukerji points out that while such dispassion legitimates scientists' results as objective in the eyes of other scientists and members of the general public, it also prevents scientists from taking explicit policy positions. Scientists have positions, she adds, "but these are given to the government, rather than presented in the political arena as the voice of science. . . . So scientists who promise (explicitly or implicitly) to sustain their dispassion in the face of potentially highly politicized questions also show themselves capable of exercising skills useful to the state." This process is "the opposite of ventriloquism," Mukerji continues. "Scientists do not send their voices out to speak through the mouths of mute government officials. Government officials [and more overtly, corporations] extort the language of science and scientists' analytic skills to do their political jobs. Scientists are made mostly mute, except when politicians find their voices useful." Scientists who advocate for their own beliefs or identify themselves with opponents of technological ventures are often seen as "political." Their credentials may be questioned, their reputations tainted. (The fate of the Los Alamos National Laboratory researcher who discovered a link between cancer and low-level plutonium exposure in Rocky Flats workers [see page 65] illustrates the risks scientists run when they violate this tacit agreement.)

To be sure, there has always been a minority of scientific gadflies and independent-minded researchers who spontaneously align themselves with local activists. For example, the Boulder Scientists group, described in chapter 3, provided a counterpoint to Rocky Flats and EPA. And the Citizens Clearinghouse on Hazardous Wastes, the National Toxics Campaign, Greenpeace, and the Ralph Nader-initiated Public Interest Research Groups are beginning to make technical expertise accessible at the local level. But mainstream scientists will become effective allies for local communities only when those scientists begin to recognize the poor bargain they have struck with their patrons. For funding and the ability to control their immediate research projects, scientists have traded political cooperation and acquiescence on the larger scientific directions. Scientists have given away what they honor above all else—genuine scientific freedom. Acting in their own self-interest means that scientists must reclaim their voice. And science will become an effective tool for the public to judge hazards by nature and degree only through a parallel democratization of the scientific enterprise; through a sharing of power. This will mean a retreat from conventional definitions of *scientific literacy* discussed in chapter 1, which are based on panic about the nation's ability to compete in the scientific, technological, and economic arenas. Formal scientific training alone will do nothing to build genuine public confidence in science without emphasis on the uncertainty of science and the politics of technical controversy. And, of course, scientists themselves will have to be educated on these matters.

The process cannot start without money, though. To build trust, communities (and, for that matter, workers) need financial resources to hire their own scientific help. Since 1986 EPA has offered technical-assistance grants to community organizations that monitor hazardous-waste sites on the Superfund National Priority List (sites considered most hazardous by EPA). These grants have sometimes enhanced a community's authority with both the polluter and the government. The problem is their $50,000 limit. For a Superfund site like Rocky Flats with an estimated $1 billion-plus cleanup cost, the grant is ludicrously low, almost to the point of subterfuge. Eleven states offer technical-assistance grants to communities proposed as hosts for toxic-waste dumps. In New Jersey, local groups have been given up to $400,000 for this purpose. In each case, the siting proposal failed. But "[Nimby] outrage didn't defeat any site in New Jersey," says Richard Gimello, who headed the state commission that oversaw the process. "What killed them was elaborate technical evaluations." The process became one of negotiation between participants who shared power.

These examples were not the first government subsidies of this kind. In the late 1970s Senator Edward Kennedy promoted "Science for Citizens," a program designed to fund citizen groups that were challenging decisions about controversial technologies. The program was so watered down by the time it became law, however, that little of Kennedy's original intent survived. The Science for Citizens experience reflects the importance of diversifying the source of such grants to prevent technical knowledge from being held captive by political pressures. The corporations, government agencies, and universities that propose risky or controversial projects should incorporate adequate grants for affected local communities into every new proposal, to be administered through a mutually acceptable third party.

For the scientific process itself to become less directly identified with corporate and government interests, it too must be opened to greater public involvement. This does not mean that community representatives should dictate to individual scientists or infringe upon the creative autonomy that effective research requires. Rather, it means "that the criteria by which priorities and practices are decided should be open to discussion at all levels," in the words of David Dickson, "that the chances of individual scientists being allowed to build research empires whose top priority becomes economic profitability or institutional survival should be minimized, and that scientists should accept the many ways in which decisions made inside the laboratory have important social dimensions that should not be resolved behind closed doors."

In some fields, such as biomedical research funded by the National Institutes of Health, nonscientists play an advisory role in overall funding directions. This process can be expanded in that agency and extended to others. Only by building the kind of community-based standards described earlier into the overriding priorities of research will the scientific community be able to penetrate the barrier between technical and cultural rationality.

Of course, public participation could create more restrictions on science. Public participation takes time; projects would sometimes lag. But the experience of laypeople in helping to develop rules for recombinant DNA experimentation, and as members of research safety and ethics committees, indicates that the public can directly participate in evaluating science without harming research. Moreover, public accountability—particularly when research funding is overwhelmingly derived from taxes—is hardly a radical notion. And the probable increase in informed public support engendered by participation could pay substantial dividends to the research community. An extensive public role in determining research directions could also generate more socially useful priorities than those dictated by government (with its overriding value on military power) or business (with its overriding value on profitability).

———————— ඞඞඞ ————————

Democracy, Responsibility, and Trust

"A failure of trust courts chaos," William Ruckelshaus has said. To a degree, Nimbyism represents a chaotic backlash to a system that has been allowed to go on too long without a democratic rudder. Without trust, people withdraw consent.

In a complex technological society, the definition of *community* must ultimately expand beyond one's backyard. No magic will convert local obstructionism into creative participation in decisions about science and technology. Gradual confidence building, based on the kinds of reforms suggested here, could begin to renew trust and ease the crisis of technological choice.

People have a responsibility to learn to distinguish between what is important and what is trivial; to balance danger and necessity. But to do this, the general public must be treated as a resource for solving complex problems, rather than shunned as an obstacle to expedient solutions. The public must be valued as a key actor in a social process, rather than despised as an inconvenience or labeled "Luddite." People may be fearful, but they do not want a fail-safe society. They want to feel secure, in control of their lives, and they want to see that their influence amounts to more than a cipher.

Three recent national surveys confirm what may seem like a common-sense observation: American youths are profoundly alienated and nihilistic. They see figures of authority as liars and hypocrites; politics, international affairs, and public involvement of all kinds as irrelevant to their lives, which are increasingly caught up in the pursuit of personal fortune. Their fears of nuclear war, of environmental collapse, and of violence and drugs in the streets mirror their cynicism about the ability of our political culture to solve these problems. These young people are a time bomb—a sign of growing public disengagement that could soon make genuine democratic involvement in decisions about environmental health and safety impossible.

The most hopeful aspect of Nimbyism—a determination to be part of the process; in effect, to end alienation—can help build a healthier and more robust democracy.

Source Notes

(Note: Magazine page numbers refer to the first page of the article.)

Chapter 1

Pages 1–4: Ruckelshaus quote is from: *New York Times,* 19 June, 1988. Sources regarding the UCSF background appear in the source notes for chapter 5. Quotes from residents' attorney and Krevans are from: *Science* (11 March 1988), p. 1229. The information on Luddism is drawn primarily from: *Democracy* (Spring 1983), p. 8; and Malcolm I. Thomas, *The Luddites* (London: David and Charles Archon Books, 1970). Kennedy and Baltimore quotes are from: *Technology Review* (May/June 1989), p. 23. Waste Management Forum quote is from: *Toxics Watchdog,* newsletter of the Toxics Cordinating Project, San Francisco (June 1988), p. 1.

Pages 5–7: Lasch quote is from his book: *The True and Only Heaven: Progress and Its Critics* (New York: Norton, 1991), p. 111. Regarding the 1957 poll, see: U.S. Congress, Office of Technology Assessment, *The Regulatory Environment for Science: A Technical Memorandum* (February 1986), pp. 130–32. Regarding Minamata, see: *New York Times,* 16 January 1991. Carson's book is: *Silent Spring* (Boston: Houghton Mifflin, 1962). Dickson quote is from: David Dickson, *The New Politics of Science* (New York: Pantheon, 1984), p. 223. Regarding Seveso, see, for example: *Time,*

14 August 1978; and *Newsweek*, 10 May 1982. Regarding Love Canal and Times Beach, see, for example: *New York Times*, 21 May 1980 and 8 April 1986, respectively.

Pages 8–9: Krimsky quote is from: speech, College of Marin, 14 May 1986. The 1980 poll and the first 1983 poll are from: *Public Opinion* (March 1986), pp. 21, 28. The 1986 poll is from: *U.S. News & World Report* (19 May 1986), p. 19. Regarding the second 1983 poll, see: Office of Technology Assessment, *Regulatory Environment*, p. 133. Regarding the polls on proximity to nuclear and chemical facilities, see: *Risk Analysis* (vol. 3, no. 4, 1983), p. 245; and *U.S. News & World Report* (19 May 1986), p. 19. Regarding the 1990 poll, see: *New York Times*, 17 April 1990.

Pages 9–13: The 1984 survey is from: James A. Davis and Tom W. Smith, *General Social Surveys Cumulative File, 1972–1984* (Ann Arbor: Inter-University Consortium for Political and Social Research, 1984), p. 152. Regarding 1990 studies of youthful alienation, see: *New York Times*, 28 June 1990. For an insightful analysis, see also: *Risk Analysis* (vol. 9, no. 4, 1989), p. 543. Lasch quote is from his book: *The Culture of Narcissism* (New York: Warner Books, 1979), pp. 21, 141. For Nimby profile, see: California Waste Management Board, *Waste to Energy: Chapter 3a: Political Difficulties Facing Waste-to-Energy Conversion Plant Sitings* (Sacramento, California: State of California, 1984), pp. 17–30. Regarding racism in dump siting, see: General Accounting Office, "Siting of Hazardous Waste Landfills and Their Correlation with Racial and Economic Status of Surrounding Communities: (1 June 1983). Regarding the Toxic Avengers, see: *Mother Jones* (April/May 1990), p.17. *Newsweek* quote is from the 24 July 1989 issue, p. 26. Edelstein quote is from his book: *Contaminated Communities: The Social and Psychological Impacts of Residential Toxic Exposure* (Boulder: Westview Press, 1988), p. 195.

Chapter 2

Pages 16–20: Noble and Lord Byron quotes, and portions of the Luddism analysis are derived from: *Democracy* (Fall 1983), p. 71. Thomis quote is from: Thomis, *The Luddites*, p. 59. Regarding Silicon Valley groundwater, see: *San Jose Mercury News*, 1 February

1986; and *San Francisco Chronicle,* 15 December 1988. The 1985 poll is from: *Public Opinion* (February/March 1986), p. 29. The 1989 poll and the MacGregor and Whelan quotes are from: *San Francisco Chronicle,* 30 October 1989, 10 March 1989, and 17 October 1988, respectively. Regarding National Safety Council report, see: *New York Times,* 7 October 1990. Regarding "safety taxes," see Peter W. Huber, *Liability: The Legal Revolution and its Consequences,* (New York: Basic Books, 1988). Regarding "cancerphobia," see: *Wall Street Journal,* 14 December 1988.

Pages 21–23: Regarding the Bush report and American research after the Second World War, see: Vannevar Bush, *Science—The Endless Frontier* (Washington, D.C.: National Science Foundation, 1980; reprinted from Office of Scientific Research and Development, 1945). See also: Dickson, *New Politics,* pp. 26–28; Office of Technology Assessment, *Regulatory Environment,* pp. 13–19; and Don K. Price, "Endless Frontier or Bureaucratic Morass?" in Gerald Holton and Robert S. Morrison (eds.), *Limits of Scientific Inquiry* (New York: W. W. Norton, 1979), p. 77. Regarding funding trends from 1940 to 1960, see: Office of Technology Assessment, *Regulatory Environment,* pp. 11–12; for 1986 figures, see: National Science Foundation, *Science and Engineering Indicators* (Washington, D.C.: National Science Board, 1989), p.91. Regarding the controversy surrounding the Mansfield Amendment and related issues, see: Office of Technology Assessment, *Regulatory Environment,* p. 21; Stanton A. Glantz, et al., "DOD Sponsored Research at Stanford, 1971," in Martin L. Perl (ed.), *Physics Careers and Education* (New York: American Institute of Physics, 1978), pp. 109–22; and *Science* (22 November 1974), p. 706.

Pages 23–25: Glantz quote is from: Perl, *Physics,* p. 115. Glantz and Albers quote is from: *Science* (22 November 1974), p. 706. The Mukerji quotes are from her book: *A Fragile Power: Scientists and the State* (Princeton, N.J.: Princeton University Press, 1989), pp. 11, 191, 9, 88, and 197, respectively.

Pages 26–27: Sinsheimer and Oppenheimer quotes are from: *Ethics* (October 1980), pp. 111 and 103, respectively. Regarding public concern about the conduct of research, see, for example: Office of Technology Assessment, *Regulatory Environment,* pp. 22–

26; and Barbara J. Culliton, "Science's Restive Public," in Holton and Morrison, *Scientific Inquiry*, pp. 147–56. The best source on CIA and DOD mind-control experiments is: John Marks, *The Search for the "Manchurian Candidate"* (New York: McGraw-Hill, 1980). Bok quote is from: Sisela Bok, "Freedom and Risk," in Holton and Morrison, *Scientific Inquiry*, p. 118. The National Academy and Baltimore quotes are from: Dickson, *New Politics*, p. 233 and 221, respectively.

Pages 28–29: Three excellent sources on social regulation and deregulation are: Dickson, *New Politics; Health/PAC Bulletin* (July/August 1980), p. 1; and Richard Kazis and Richard L. Grossman, *Fear at Work: Job Blackmail, Labor and the Environment* (New York: Pilgrim Press, 1982). Regarding social regulations, see also: Office of Technology Assessment, *Regulatory Environment*, pp. 21–22. Dickson quote is from: Dickson, *New Politics*, p. 271. Regarding the effects of Reagan era deregulation, see: Dickson, *New Politics*, pp. 288–89; *Science* (22 May 1987), p. 904; and *Washington Post*, 25 April 1986.

Pages 29–31: Background on Bacon is from: Richard Foster Jones (ed.), *Francis Bacon: Essays, Advancement of Learning, New Atlantis, and other Pieces* (New York: Odyssey Press, 1937), pp. xv–xxix; and Dickson, *New Politics*, pp. 323–24. Morrison quote is from: Holton and Morrison, *Scientific Inquiry*, p. xi. Roszak quote is from his book: *Where the Wasteland Ends* (New York: Doubleday, 1972), pp. 167–68. Wiesner quote is from: *U.S. News & World Report* (11 August 1980), p. 66. Noble quote is from: *Health/PAC Bulletin* (July/August 1980), p. 1.

Pages 31–32: Roszak quote is from: Roszak, *Wasteland*, p. 257. Miller study is: "Scientific Literacy," paper presented at the Annual Meeting of the American Association for the Advancement of Science, 17 January 1989. Political cartoon is from: *San Francisco Chronicle*, 5 February 1989. Poll is reported in: *New York Times*, 25 October 1988. Regarding ignorance about the war in Nicaragua, see: *Public Opinion* (August/September 1983), p. 21.

Pages 33–36: Roszak quote is from: Roszak, *Wasteland*, p. 258. Noble quote is from: *Democracy* (Spring 1983), p. 8. Wiesner quote is from: *U.S. News & World Report* (11 August 1980), p. 66.

Regarding the *Washington Post* sabotage and Noble anecdote, see: *Democracy* (Fall 1983), p. 71. Dickson quote is from: *Democracy* (vol. 1, no. 1, 1981), p. 61.

Chapter 3

Pages 37–39: Michels quote is from: *Science* (21 July 1972), p. 208. Descriptions of Gabel and of cancers and malformed animals are from: *Dark Circle*, documentary film (aired on Public Broadcasting System, 1989). Other Gabel information is from: *Sunday Camera Magazine* [Boulder, Colo. (17 April 1988)], p. 6; *Boulder Daily Camera*, 1 October 1985; and *Denver Post*, 1 October 1985. Hurst quotes are from: interview, 27 December 1989; and untitled personal statement, 12 June 1989.

Pages 39–40: Information on Rocky Flats security, size, and products is from: Rockwell International/Department of Energy, *The Rocky Flats Plant* (Washington, D.C.: Government Printing Office, 675-464, 1989), p. 12; Rockwell/DOE, "Security" (undated flier); *Denver Post*, 11 June 1985; and *Rocky Mountain News*, 11 December 1988. Regarding the founding and early history of Rocky Flats, see: Marcia Klotz, *A Citizen's Guide to Rocky Flats* (Denver: Rocky Mountain Peace Center, 1988), pp. 1–3. Regarding the nature and effects of plutonium, see: Klotz, ibid., p. 7; Judy Danielson, et al., *Local Hazard, Global Threat* (Denver: Rocky Flats Action Group, 1977), pp. 2–3; *Science* (5 November 1971), p. 569; and Niels D. Schonbeck (Metropolitan State College, Denver), "Plutonium Hazards and the Proposed Rocky Flats Incineration," April 1987 (unpublished), pp. 7–8.

Pages 41–42: *Denver Post* and *Rocky Mountain News* articles were published 12 and 13 September 1957, respectively. Holme report is described in: *New York Times*, 15 February 1990. Shift captain quote and background on 1957 fire are from: Carl J. Johnson, "Comments on the 1957 Fire at the Rocky Flats Plant, in Jefferson County, Colorado," 26 September 1980 (unpublished). Other sources on 1957 fire include: *Los Angeles Times*, 7 September 1969; and *Washington Post National Weekly Edition*, 26 December 1988. Primary sources on 1969 fire are: *Los Angeles Times*, 7 September 1969; *Washington Post National Weekly Edition*, 26

December 1988; *Science* (5 November 1971), p. 569; *New York Times*, 15 February 1990; and Klotz, *Citizens' Guide*, pp. 4–6. Love quote is from: *Los Angeles Times*, 7 September 1969.

Pages 42–43: Primary sources on Carl Johnson and his findings are: *Sunday Camera Magazine* [Boulder, Colo. (17 April 1988], p. 6; Carl Johnson, "Epidemiological Evaluation of Cancer Incidence Rates for the Period 1969–1971 in Areas of Census Tracts with Measured Concentrations of Plutonium Soil Contamination Downwind from the Rocky Flats Plant," a report to the Jefferson County Board of Health, et al., 9 February 1979 (unpublished); *Science* (6 August 1976), p. 488; Klotz, *Citizens Guide* pp. 7–8; and Danielson, *Local Hazard*, p.5.

Page 43–46: Regarding AEC site selection, see: *Washington Post National Weekly Edition*, 26 December 1988; *High Country News*, 19 December 1988; and *Bulletin of the Atomic Scientists* (December 1989), p. 18. Regarding Denver-area growth, see: *Science* (5 November 1971), p. 569; and *Denver Post*, 13 November 1987. Regarding landowner lawsuits, see: *Science* (5 November 1971), p. 569; and *Westword*, 4–10 March 1987. Sources for HUD-warning section are: Klotz, *Citizen's Guide*, p. 9: *Denver Post*, 25 September 1978; HUD, "Rocky Flats Advisory Notice" (8RF-1), 1 March 1979; HUD, news release (8-020-79), 27 February 1979; HUD, memorandum (8H), 7 January 1981; Colorado Department of Health, memorandum, 12 April 1979; *Westword*, 4–10 March 1987; and interview with EPA official Nathaniel Miullo, 15 June 1990. "Public to Frolic" headline is from: *Rocky Mountain News*, 26 January 1985. Regarding annexations by nearby towns, see also: *Arvada Sentinel*, 5 February 1987; *Denver Post*, 1 March 1987; *Westword*, 7–13 September 1988 and 14–20 June 1989; and *Rocky Mountain News*, 4 August 1989. "Imagine a great" quote is from: *Boulder Daily Camera*, 5 August 1989.

Pages 46–48: Smith quote is from: interview, 29 December 1989. Activist quote is from: interview with Jan Pilcher, 29 December 1989. Regarding 1982 rally and 1983 encirclement, see, respectively: *Westword*, 23–29 August 1989; and *Rocky Mountain News*, 16 October 1983. Regarding radioactive soil episode and Glenn comments, see, respectively: *Denver Post*, 27 September 1984 and 26 September 1986. Wirth findings are reported in: *Rocky Moun-*

tain News, 14 April 1985. Sources for water supply section include: *Rocky Mountain News,* 13 November 1973; and *Denver Post,* 17 January 1986 and 28 March 1987. Regarding W-470, see: *Rocky Mountain News,* 27 November 1986; and *Sunday Camera Magazine* (18 January 1987), p. 3. Regarding incinerator announcement, see: *Denver Post,* 28 January 1987.

Pages 48–51: Pilcher background and quotes are from: interview, 29 December 1989. Bernard quote is from: interview, 10 October 1989. Towne quote is from: *New York Times,* 23 April 1987. Skaggs endorsement is reported in: *Boulder Daily Camera,* 22 February 1987. CARFC quote is from: Jan Pilcher, "Briefing: Incineration of Hazardous Radioactive Waste at the Rocky Flats Nuclear Weapons Plant," February 1987 (unpublished), p. 5. Skaggs meeting is reported in: *Rocky Mountain News,* 13 March 1987.

Pages 51–53: For Blue Ribbon Brigade background and quotes, see: *Denver Post,* 24 June 1987. Regarding letters to officials, see: *Boulder Daily Camera,* 19 March and 8 April 1987. Boulder Scientists report is: Joe Goldfield, et al., "Papers on: The Proposed Rocky Flats Incineration of Mixed, Low Level Radioactive Wastes," April 1987 (unpublished). Scientists' quote is from: Goldfield, ibid., p. 1. Sources on early use of incinerator and later incinerator fire include: *Boulder Daily Camera,* 7 June and 29 October 1987; and Rockwell International, "Unusual Occurrence Report " (RFP 87-3-776 87-1), 30 September 1987, pp. 1, 3.

Pages 53–56: Batley information is from: *Dark Circle,* op. cit. "Psychiatrist" quotation is from: *New York Times,* 6 August 1989. Seeman background and quotes are from: interview, 28 December 1989. "22 studies," "Crude disposal," "Savannah River," and "From 1957" quotations are from, respectively: *New York Times,* 11 October, 8 December, and 1 October 1988; and *New York Times Magazine* (11 March 1990), p. 50.

Pages 56–59: Background on Grice is from: *Westminster Sentinel,* 28 September 1989. "Energy Secretary," "Energy officials," and "Colorado's Rocky Flats" quotations are from, respectively: *San Francisco Chronicle,* 28 June 1989; and *Denver Post,* 23 March and 30 January 1990. Hurst quotes are from: interview, 27 December 1989; and untitled personal statement, 12 June 1989.

"Thousands of people" quotation is from: *New York Times*, 17 October 1988. "During the first" quotation is from: PBS *Nova*, 13 February 1990. Elofsen-Gardine quotes and background are from: interview, 27 December 1989. "Government officials" and "The Energy Department" quotations are from, respectively: *New York Times*, 15 October 1988 and 1 July 1989.

Pages 59–62: Regarding Rocky Flats cleanup costs, see: *Rocky Mountain News*, 1 July 1988 and 20 January 1989. Physicians group quote is from: *Denver Post*, 27 October 1988. Regarding congressional report, see: General Accounting Office, "Nuclear Health and Safety: Summary of Major Problems at DOE's Rocky Flats Plant" (GAO/RCED-89-53BR), October 1988; and *New York Times*, 27 October 1989. Regarding the machine shop scandal, see: *New York Times*, 6 November 1988. Regarding groundwater contamination and "irreversible contamination" report, see, respectively: *Rocky Mountain News*, 7 December 1988 and 9 February 1989. Regarding FBI raid, see: *Denver Post*, 7 and 9 June 1989; and *New York Times*, 10 June 1989. Regarding earthquake threat, see: *Rocky Mountain News*, 16 June 1989. Sources for criticality hazard are: "An Assessment of Criticality Safety at the Department of Energy Rocky Flats Plant, Golden, Colorado, July–September 1989" (contract DE-AC01-88EH79081, Task 20), pp. ES-1–ES-5; *Denver Post*, 30 March 1989; and *New York Times*, 15 June 1989 and 29 March 1990. Regarding Rockwell lawsuit, see: *New York Times*, 22 September 1989. Regarding Rockwell bonuses, see: General Accounting Office, "DOE's Award Fees Do Not Adequately Reflect ES&H Problems" (GAO/RCED-90-47), October 1989. Landowner and worker lawsuits are reported in: *Denver Post*, 31 January 1990. Regarding ongoing production versus safety conflicts, see: *New York Times*, 25 October 1990.

Pages 63–65: Regarding the Hanford dose reconstruction, see: Technical Steering Panel of the Hanford Environmental Dose Reconstruction Project, "Initial Hanford Radiation Dose Estimates," 12 June 1990. Alvarez quotes are from: interview, 7 June 1990. Iacobellis comments are from: *Wall Street Journal*, 30 August 1989. Simonson quote is from: interview, 28 December 1989. DeBoskey information is from: *New York Times*, 18 November 1989. DOE study is published in: *American Journal of Epidemiology* (vol. 125, no. 2, 1987), p. 231. Wilkinson comments are from: interview, 14 June 1990. Studies of other DOE workers are described in: *San Francisco Chronicle,* 3 August 1989.

Pages 66–72: Regarding report on AEC exposures, see: *New York Times,* 19 December 1989. First Alvarez quote is from: PBS, *Nova,* aired 13 February 1990. Hurst boast is from: interview, 27 December 1990. Grice quotes are from: *Westminster Sentinel,* 28 September 1989. Pilcher, Seeman, and Elofsen-Gardine quotes are from, respectively: interviews, 29, 28, and 27 December 1989. Miullo and Hurst quotes are from, respectively: interviews, 2 January 1990 and 27 December 1989. Second Alvarez quote is from: interview, 7 June 1990. Schonbeck quote is from: interview, 4 January 1990. Sources regarding 1989 demonstrations include: *Westword,* 23–29 August 1989; and *Colorado Daily,* 18–20 July 1989. Experienced activist guote is from: *Westword,* 23–29 August 1989.

Pages 72–74: Figures on Rocky Flats waste volume are from: Rockwell International/Department of Energy, *The Rocky Flats Plant,* op cit., p. 9. Regarding WIPP problems, see, for example: Scott Saleska, et al., *Nuclear Legacy* (Washington, D.C.: Public Citizen Critical Mass Energy Project, 1989), pp. vii-10–vii-14. Quote from DOE memo is from: "Briefing for Mary L. Walker [assistant secretary, environment, safety and health]," 14 July 1986, p. 4. Andrus quote is from: *Rocky Mountain News,* 12 November 1989. Regarding rebellion of state governors, see: *New York Times,* 17 December 1988, 6 May 1989, and 9 September 1989; *Rocky Mountain News,* 18 December 1988; and *Denver Post,* 6 and 12 October 1989. Regarding Trinidad protests, see: *Rocky Mountain News,* 25 October and 2 November 1989.

Pages 75–77: Alvarez quotes are from: interview, 7 June 1990. Watkins quote is from: PBS, *Nova,* aired 13 February 1990. Regarding DOE releases of records to independent researchers and the Department of Health and Human Services, see: *New York Times,* 18 July 1990 and 5 January 1991. Pilcher quotes are from: interview, 29 December 1989. Regarding the new Savannah River complex, see: *New York Times,* 10 November 1990.

Chapter 4

Pages 78–80: Hyer quote is from: U.S. Congress Office of Technology Assessment, *New Developments in Biotechnology*, vol. 3, *Field-Testing Engineered Organisms* (May 1988), p. 43. Lindow quotes and background are from: *San Francisco Examiner/Image* (10 August 1986), p. 19; and interview, 28 August 1989. Regarding the science of ice-minus, see: DNA Plant Technology Corporation, *Frostban: A Natural Approach to Frost Protection* (Oakland, Calif., undated pamphlet). An excellent chronology of Lindow's regulatory experience can be found in: Sheldon Krimsky and Alonzo Plough, *Environmental Hazards: Communicating Risks as a Social Process* (Dover, Mass.: Auburn House, 1988), pp. 113–19.

Pages 80–82: Regarding the ideas of Roszak and Marcuse, see, for example: Theodore Roszak, *Where the Wasteland Ends* (New York: Doubleday, 1972); and Herbert Marcuse, *One Dimensional Man* (Boston: Beacon Press, 1964). Rifkin quotes are from, respectively: *San Francisco Chronicle*, 30 September 1987; and *New York Times Magazine*, 16 October 1988. Gould quote is from: *New York Times Magazine*, 16 October 1988. Commoner quote is from: *San Francisco Chronicle/This World* (7 June 1987), p. 17. Mitchell quote is from: *Daily Californian*, 21 November 1984. Krimsky quote is from: speech, College of Marin, 14 May 1986.

Pages 83–84: Information on Lindow's links to AGS, and Suslow background and quotes are from: interview, 29 August 1989. Regarding the legal battles surrounding the Sirica decision, see: *Daily Californian*, 13 April and 30 May 1984; and *New York Times*, 17 May 1984. The best source on the original nature, development, and enforcement of NIH recombinant DNA guidelines is: Sheldon Krimsky, *Genetic Alchemy* (Cambridge, Mass.: MIT Press, 1982). Regarding approval of the AGS test by RAC, see: *New York Times*, 2 June 1984. Suslow quotes are from: interviews, 29 August 1989 and 11 September 1989.

Pages 84–86: Regarding EPA's first rules on the release of recombinant organisms, see: EPA, "Microbial Pesticides; Interim Policy on Small Scale Field-Testing," *Federal Register,* 17 October 1984, p. 40659. For an excellent analysis of EPA's role, see:

Genewatch [Council for Responsible Genetics, Boston (vol. 5, nos. 2–3)], p.1. Colwell's quote is from letter in: *Science,* (3 July 1987), p. 10. Regarding information on USDA's action, see: General Accounting Office, *Biotechnology: Agriculture's Regulatory System Needs Clarification* (GAO/RCED-886-59), March 1986, pp. 50, 52; and *New York Times,* 4 April 1986. Regarding industry qualms about federal regulatory confusion, see, for example: *New York Times,* 13 April 1986.

Pages 86–89: Information on the safety of small genetic changes is from: *Science* (18 September 1987), p. 1413; and speech by Sheldon Krimsky, College of Marin, 14 May 1986. Schroth quote is from: interview, 18 May 1986. Colwell quote is from: *San Francisco Examiner/Image* (10 August 1986), p. 19. Information on natural strains of ice-minus and AGS strategy are from: interview with Suslow, 29 August 1989. Quote from Harvard and Brandeis professors is from: *New York Times,* 31 May 1986. Baltimore quote is from: *Genewatch,* op. cit. Regarding critics' comments about the possible dangers of the test, see, for example: *Science* (18 September 1987), p. 1413; *Science* (3 March 1989), p. 1141; Office of Technology Assessment, *New Developments in Biotechnology: Background Paper: Public Perceptions of Biotechnology* (May 1987), pp. 3,86; and EPA, Transcript of Proceedings, Subpanel of the FIFRA, Scientific Advisory Panel Meeting, 22 January 1985, pp. 9–10, 34, 44. Brill quote is from: *Issues in Science and Technology* (spring 1988), p. 44. The possible effects of ice-minus on rainfall are described in: *Science,* 27 September 1985; and *Science News* (4 May 1985), p. 282. Arguments against rainfall hypothesis can be found in: *Science* (18 September 1987), p. 1413.

Pages 89–90: Krimsky quote is from: speech, College of Marin, 14 May 1986. Alexander comment is from: interview, 8 May 1986. EPA panel quote and conclusions are reported in: EPA, "Review of the Advanced Genetic Sciences' (AGS) Proposal to Conduct Small-Scale Field Studies with a Genetically Altered Microbial Pesticide" (undated), pp. 1–2. The 1986 OTA poll data are from: U.S. Congress, Office of Technology Assessment, *Public Perceptions,* pp. 64, 86–87, 90.

Pages 91–95: Church background and quotes are from: interview, 19 August 1989. For further background, see: Krimsky and

Plough, *Environmental Hazards*. Church opinion piece is from: *San Jose Mercury News*, 23 March 1986. Regarding the 27 January board of supervisors meeting and decision, see: *San Jose Mercury News*, 28 January and 12 February 1986. Shipnuck quote is from: *Multinational Monitor* (28 February 1986), p.12. Packard and Karas conflict is from: House of Representatives hearing, " 'Ice-Minus': A Case Study of EPA's Review of Genetically Engineered Microbial Pesticides" (4 March 1986), p. 120. Oakland *Tribune* quote appeared: 21 August 1986. Lindow quote is from: *Daily Californian*, 26 February 1986.

Pages 95–98: Sarojak quote is from: *San Francisco Examiner/ Image* (10 August 1986), p. 19. Suslow quotes and background are from: interview, 29 August 1989. Regarding the AGS scandal, see, for example: *Washington Post*, 26 and 27 February 1986; and *New York Times*, 27 February 1986. Church, Bedbrook, Colwell, and first Schatzow comments are from: House of Representatives, " 'Ice-Minus': A Case Study," op. cit. pp. 122, 27, 89, and 85, respectively. Second Schatzow comment is from: *New York Times*, 25 March 1986.

Pages 98–99: Cowen quote is from: *Salinas Californian*, 8 March 1986, the same article that broke the story of the test-site location. Suslow quotes are from: interview, 29 August 1989. Church quote is from: interview, 19 August 1989. I learned the details of the prevalent conspiracy theory in a letter, undated, from Ed Waldin, a concerned resident of Monterey County.

Pages 100–101: Bouckaert quote is from: *Wall Street Journal*, 3 March 1986. Regarding the Wistar Institute incident, see: *New York Times*, 11 November 1986, 22 January 1988, and 4 February 1988; and *Science* (12 October 1989), p. 1192. Regarding Oregon State University incident, see: *New York Times*, 13 November 1986. Regarding "Coordinated Framework," see: Executive Office of the President, "Coordinated Framework for Regulation of Biotechnology" (June 1986). Kingsbury quote is from: *New York Times*, 11 November 1986. For an analysis of "Coordinated Framework," see: *The Nation* (25 October 1986), p. 400. King quote is from: *New York Times*, 22 May 1986.

Pages 102–3: Krimsky and Plough quote is from: *Environmental Hazards* p. 106. Regarding the formation of local opposition in

Tulelake, see: Krimsky and Plough, *Environmental Hazards* pp. 82–84. Church quotes are from: interview, 19 August 1989. Edgar quotes are from: interview, 14 September 1989.

Pages 105–7: Suslow quotes are from: interview, 29 August 1989. AGS efforts to gain approval and opposition efforts are reported in: *San Francisco Examiner*, 18 January 1987; *San Francisco Chronicle*, 11 February, 19 March, and 18 April 1987; *San Jose Mercury News*, 18 February 1987; and *Oakland Tribune*, 15 April 1987. Church quotes are from: interview, 19 August 1989. Greens' spokesperson is quoted in: *San Francisco Chronicle*, 18 April 1987. The AGS test is described in: *San Francisco Chronicle*, 25 April 1987. Edgar quote is from: interview, 14 September 1989. The Lindow test and post-test vandalism are reported in: *San Francisco Chronicle*, 30 April 1987 and 27 May 1987, respectively.

Pages 107–8: Regarding the outcomes of the AGS and Lindow experiments, and the recurrence of vandalism, see: *San Francisco Chronicle*, 9 June 1987, 2 December 1987, and 16 November 1988. Bedbrook quote is from: *New York Times*, 18 January 1988. Background on the AGS purchase is reported in: Oakland *Tribune*, 27 February 1989. Information on the marketing of natural *Pseudomonas* strains is from: interview with Suslow, 29 August 1989. Church quotes are from: interview, 19 August 1989. Regarding EPA spending on biotechnology risk assessment, see: *Genewatch*, op. cit.

Pages 108–12: Regarding frost and potato conditions in Tulelake, see: Krimsky and Plough, *Environmental Hazards,* pp. 101–02. Brill quote is from: *Issues in Science and Technology* (Spring 1988), p. 44. Lindow quote is from: *Daily Californian*, 26 February 1986. *The Economist* quote appeared 8 March 1986, p. 85. Regarding Kingsbury resignation, see: *Science* (7 October 1988), p. 28. Edgar quote is from: Krimsky and Plough, *Environmental Hazards,* p. 101. Church, Reber, and Suslow quotes are from interviews, 19 August, 7 August, and 29 August 1989, respectively. Mazur quote is from: presentation at the Annual Meeting of the American Association for the Advancement of Science, 17 January 1989. Panetta quote is from: House of Representatives, " 'Ice-Minus': Case History," p. 97. Regarding OTA poll, see: Office of Technology Assessment, *Public Perceptions,* pp. 27, 30, 50, 53, 63.

Pages 113–15: Colwell quote is from: *San Francisco Chronicle,* 5 September 1988. The Ernst and Young surveys, which include profit figures for biotechnology companies, are reported in: *San Francisco Chronicle,* 20 September 1989 and 19 September 1990. Regarding Monsanto Corporation spending, see: *New York Times Magazine* (10 June 1990), p. 26. First Suslow quote is from: speech, College of Marin, 14 May 1986. AGS losses are reported in: Association of Bay Area Governments, "Biotechnology in the Bay Area" (September 1988), p. 4-D-1. Second Suslow quote is from: interview, 29 August 1990. Regarding history of agricultural technology, see, for example: *New York Times,* 18 and 23 March 1986. Recent government report is: U.S. Congress, Office of Technology Assessment, *Technology, Public Policy, and the Changing Structure of American Agriculture* (March 1986).

Pages 115–17: Regarding the controversy surrounding bovine growth hormone, see, for example: *New York Times,* 24 August 1989 and 28 April 1990; and *Science,* 17 November 1989 and 24 August 1990. Church quote is from: interview, 19 August 1989. Primary sources for information on status of field testing: interviews with EPA officials Beth Anderson and Bill Schneider, 14 September 1990. Rifkin quote is from: *Science* (28 October 1988), p. 503. Suslow quote is from: interview, 29 August 1989. For OTA poll, see: *Public Perceptions,* pp. 4-5.

Chapter 5

Pages 118–21: Mansbach quote is from: UCSF-Laurel Heights, *Site Development Plan: Final Environmental Impact Report* (June 1986), p. 183. Goyan quotes and background are from: interview, 21 November 1989; and UCSF press release, 9 September 1979. Primary sources for UCSF history section include: UCSF-Laurel Heights, op. cit., pp. 30–31; *San Francisco Chronicle/This World* (8 October 1989), p. 13; and *UCSF Alumni News* (Fall 1989), p. 2.

Pages 121–22: Incendiary flier quote is from: Inner Sunset Action Committee, "Open Letter from the Residents of San Francisco's Communities" (undated). Local resident quote is from: *San Francisco Chronicle,* 6 August 1975. Regarding Mount Sutro Defense

Committee suit, see: *Synapse* (UCSF student publication), 5 August 1975, 8 January 1976, and 8 January 1987; "Statement by Robert L. Derzon, UCSF Hospitals and Clinics Director," 8 February 1977; Resolution of UC Board of Regents, "Designation of Open Space Research, Alteration of Campus Boundaries, Commitment of Houses to Residential Use, Authorization to Negotiate Sales of Properties and Commitment of Transportation Studies," 21 May 1976; and UCSF, *1982 Long Range Development Plan Final Environmental Impact Report* (September 1982), pp. 53–56.

Pages 123–24: Krevans quote is from: *Synapse*, 10 January 1985. Carr quote is from: *San Francisco Chronicle*, 25 December 1984. Krevans letter to Carr, dated 26 December 1984, is reprinted in: UCSF-Laurel Heights, op. cit., p. F-209. Neighborhood meeting description and Jordan Park quote is from: *San Francisco Chronicle*, 5 February 1985. Carr letter to Krevans, dated 8 February 1985, is reprinted in: UCSF-Laurel Heights, op. cit., p. F-210.

Pages 125–27: Carr statement is from: UCSF-Laurel Heights, op. cit., p. F-37.Gwyn quote is from: UCSF press release, 18 June 1986, p. 4. Gwyn interview took place on 22 May 1990. Krevans response to Carr letter, dated 12 March 1985, is reprinted in: UCSF-Laurel Heights, op. cit., p. F-211. Verges quote is from: *San Francisco Chronicle*, 12 June 1986. Krevans letter to neighbors is dated 11 July 1986.

Pages 127–30: Critic's comment was made at 21 April 1989 public hearing. Baltimore and Kennedy quotes are from, respectively: *Technology Review* (May/June 1989), p.23; and (November/December 1981), p. 58. Regarding changing ideas about safe levels of radiation exposure, see, for example: Arthur Upton, et al., *Health Effects of Exposure to Low Levels of Ionizing Radiation* (Washington, D.C.: National Academy Press, 1990). Regarding the development of the recombinant DNA guidelines, see: Krimsky, *Genetic Alchemy*. Regarding the biotechnology poll, see: Office of Technology Assessment, *Public Perceptions*, op. cit., p. 53. Regarding general fear of AIDS, see, for example: *San Francisco Chronicle*, 13 October and 29 November 1989. The AIDS study cited is from: *Journal of the American Medical Association* (13 October 1989), p. 1949. Regarding medical-waste scandals, see: *New York Times*, 27 June 1989 and 17 July 1990. Regarding university lab safety, see: *Business Week* (2 May 1988), p. 58. Lab survey data is from: NIH, *The Status of Biomedical Research Facilities: 1988* (January 1989), pp. 30–31.

Pages 130–31: Regarding industry-academic conflicts of interest, see, for example: *New York Times*, 12 June 1989; and *Forbes* (28 November 1988), p. 204. Baltimore quote is from: *Technology Review* (May/June 1989), p. 23. Figures on Harvard scientists are from: *The Nation* (30 October 1989), p. 477. Figures on industry support for biotechnology are from: *Science* (17 January 1986), p. 242 and (13 June 1986), p. 1361.

Pages 131–33: Principle sources for animal rights section are: Growth of movement and militant actions: *New York Times*, 27 August 1987 and 14 January 1989; *San Francisco Examiner*, 26 April 1987; and *Newsweek* (26 December 1988), p. 50. Research rules: *New York Times*, 3 February 1986; and *Science* (4 November 1988), p. 662. Boston episode information: *Boston Herald*, 26 February 1989; and interview with Aaron Medlock, New England Anti-Vivisection Society, 22 September 1989. California episode information: Larry N. Horton, associate vice president, Stanford University, speech at the Annual Meeting of the American Association for the Advancement of Science, 17 January 1989. Carr quote is from: interview, 2 November 1989.

Pages 134–38: Carr background and quotes are from: interview, 2 November 1989. Regarding 33 radiation violations, see: *Synapse*, 30 April 1987 and 13 March 1986. Primary sources regarding biological warfare flap are: UCSF press release, 9 March 1987; *Synapse*, 23 April 1987; letters to community from Krevans, 14 August 1987 and 19 January 1988; letter from Jere Goyan to Agabian, 3 June 1985; and letter from Goyan to dean of UC Berkeley, School of Public Health, 12 August 1985. Devincenzi quote is from: *Science* (11 March 1988), p. 1229.

Pages 138–41: Devincenzi quote is from: *San Francisco Progress*, 12 July 1987. Court of Appeal quotes and conclusions are from: Decision, Case AO36955, 9 July 1987, pp. 10–11, 13–14, 21–24, 26–27. Krevans quote is from: UCSF press release, 17 July 1987. Van de Kamp quotes are from: Amicus Curiae Brief, Case S001922, 16 December 1987, pp. 8, 18. Coalition quote is from: *Synapse*, 21 January 1988. UCSF economic data is from: UCSF, "UCSF

Economic Impact" (February 1988). Regarding poll, see: UCSF, "UCSF and Laurel Heights—How San Franciscans View the Issue" (February 1988).

Pages 141–43: Regarding faculty report, see: *Synapse*, 11 February 1988. Regarding health and safety incidents, see: *Synapse*, 15 and 22 October 1987, 28 January 1988, and 10 November 1988. Regarding the childhood cancer outbreak, see: San Francisco Department of Public Health, "Report on Cancer Incidence in San Francisco" (24 October 1988); and follow-up, "Study of San Francisco Residents 0–4 Years of Age Diagnosed with Cancer between 1981–1987" (undated). See also: *San Francisco Chronicle*, 26 October 1988; and *San Francisco Examiner*, 2 December 1988. Krevans quote is from: UCSF press release, 3 June 1988.

Pages 143–47: Supreme Court quotes are from its decision: Case S001922, 1 December 1988. Schulman quote is from: interview, 2 December 1988. Verges comments at later forum are from: UCSF-Laurel Heights, "Environmental Impact Report, Verbatim Comments, Vol. A: Hearing Transcripts" (April 1990), p. 401. Smith comments came at information meeting, 13 November 1989. Regarding petition signatures, see: *San Francisco Chronicle*, 26 December 1989. The breech of contract and EIR decisions are, respectively: San Francisco Superior Court, Cases 862850, 23 November 1990; and 920851, 11 January 1991.

Pages 148–50: Rolinson comments are from: interview, 4 December 1989. Bishop and Alberts comments are from: letter to Krevans, 10 February 1988. Spaulding quotes are from: interviews, 25 and 31 October 1989, and 20 November 1989.

Pages 150–54: Goyan comments are from: interview: 21 November 1989. Krevans quote is from: *Science* (11 March 1988), p. 1229. Bishop and Alberts letter is dated 10 February 1988. Regarding UCSF environmental study, see UCSF press release, 1 September 1989. Lappé study is: Marc Lappé, Ph.D., "Final Evaluation: Adequacy of Radian Corporation's Report on the Environmental Impacts Posed by University of California, San Francisco," 25 October 1990. Carr comment regarding failure to seek expert help is from: interview, 2 November 1989.

Pages 154–57: Regarding research space crisis, see: NIH, op. cit., pp. 26, 28; National Science Foundation, *Scientific and En-*

gineering Research Facilities at Universities and Colleges: 1988 (NSF 88–320), September 1988, pp. 29, 36; and Association of American Universities and National Association of State Universities and Land-Grant Colleges, "University Research Facilities: A National Problem Requiring a National Response" (June 1989), p. 7. Information on Stanford lab and all Horton quotes are from: Larry N. Horton, speech at the Annual Meeting of the American Association for the Advancement of Science, 17 January 1989. Regarding opposition to UC Berkeley, see, for example: *East Bay Express*, 2 December 1988; and *Daily Californian*, 22 February 1989. Goyan quote is from: interview, 21 November 1989. Krimsky quote is from: speech at the Annual Meeting of the American Association for the Advancement of Science, 17 January 1989.

Chapter 6

Pages 158–61: Portney and Morrell quotes are from: *New York Times*, 19 June 1988. Witte and Brady quotes are from: *San Francisco Chronicle*, 17 November 1987. Popper quote is from: Frank J. Popper, "LULUs and Their Blockage: The Nature of the Problem, the Outline of the Solutions," in Joseph DiMento and LeRoy Graymer (eds.), *Confronting Regional Challenges: Approaches to LULUs, Growth, and other Vexing Governance Problems* (Cambridge, Mass.: Lincoln Institute of Land Policy, forthcoming). Mazur's views are from: interview, 31 July 1990. Regarding drug-treatment centers, see, for example: *New York Times*, 30 September 1989. Regarding the 1990 national survey, see: *Public Attitudes toward People with Mental Illness* (Boston: Robert Wood Johnson Foundation, April 1990), esp. pp. 8–9, 23–25, 42.

Pages 161–62: Regarding Nimby actions in Europe, see, for example: *Environment* (October 1987), p. 14; *San Francisco Chronicle*, 9 August 1990; *Risk Analysis* (vol. 9, no. 4, 1989), p. 463, and (vol. 9, no. 2, 1989), p. 215. Regarding efforts by Third World nations to reject toxic cargo, see, for example: *The Amicus Journal* (Winter 1989), p. 9; and *New York Times*, 5 July 1988. Regarding the failure to build new hazardous-waste dumps and nuclear power plants, see: *Omni* (September 1989), p. 60. For figures and predictions on the garbage crisis, see, for example:

Newsweek (27 November 1989), p. 66; and *Forbes* (28 November 1988), p. 172. Regarding attempts to build oil refineries, see: DiMento and Graymer, *Confronting Regional Challenges.* For figures on airport noise battles, see: Dimento and Graymer, *Confronting Regional Challenges; Omni* (September 1989), p. 60; and *New York Times,* 17 April 1990.

Pages 165–66: Information on Citizen's Clearinghouse for Hazardous Waste is from: interview with Lois Gibbs, 20 July 1989. Regarding the National Toxics Campaign, see: *New York Times,* 2 July 1989; and National Toxics Campaign: "Taking Action Now to Stop the Spread of Toxic Killers in Your Community" (undated pamphlet). Edelstein quote is from: Michael R. Edelstein, *Contaminated Communities: The Social and Psychological Impacts of Residential Toxic Exposure* (Boulder: Westview Press, 1988), p. 166. Pharmacist quote is from: *Wall Street Journal,* 18 April 1983. Carr quote is from: UCSF-Laurel Heights, "Environmental Impact Report," (Vol. A, Hearing Transcripts, April 1990) p. 379.

Pages 166–69: Regarding radical environmentalism, see, for example: Christopher Manes, *Green Rage: Radical Environmentalism and the Unmaking of Civilization* (New York: Little, Brown, 1990). The Love Canal kidnaping episode is described in: Nicholas Freudenberg, *Not in Our Backyards!* (New York: Monthly Review Press, 1984), pp. 188–89. Gottlieb and FitzSimmons quotes are from: "A New Environmental Politics?" paper distributed for discussion at International Green Movements Conference, April 1986. Maddy quote is from: *The Nation* (27 March 1989), p. 403. Regarding the EPA revolving door and corporate donations to environmental groups, see, for example: *Mother Jones* (April/May 1990), p. 23; and *New York Times,* 29 October 1989. Poje quote is from *New York Times,* 2 July 1989.

Pages 171–72: Portney, Mazur, and Gimello quotes are from: interviews, 30 July 1990, 31 July 1990, and 9 August 1990, respectively.

Chapter 7

Pages 173–77: Ruckelshaus quote and Asipu material are from, respectively: *Risk Analysis* (vol. 4, no. 3, 1984), p. 157, and (vol.

5, no. 2, 1985), p. 103. Regarding the taxonomy of risk perception, see, for example: *Science* (17 April 1987), p. 280. For good discussions of faulty risk comparisons, see: *Science, Technology, & Human Values* (Summer/Fall 1987), p. 70; and *Health/PAC Bulletin* (July/August 1980), p. 1. Winner quote is from: *Science for the People* (May/June 1986), p. 5. Regarding EPA priorities, see: *Science* (10 August 1990), p. 616, and *New York Times*, 29 January 1991. Schwarz and Thompson anecdote is from their book: *Divided We Stand: Redefining Politics, Technology and Social Choice* (Hertfordshire, Eng.: Harvester Wheatsheaf, 1990), pp. 83–85.

Pages 177–79: Regarding cost-benefit analysis examples, see: Dickson, *New Politics*, p. 286; and *U.S. News & World Report* (16 September 1985), p. 58. Silbergeld quotes are from: *New York Times*, 24 January 1988. Ruckelshaus quote is from; *Issues in Science and Technology* (Spring 1985), p. 19. Regarding the structural uncertainties of risk analysis, see: Schwarz and Thompson, *Divided We Stand*, pp. 142–43. Dickson quote is from: Dickson, *New Politics*, p. 53. Wiesner quote is from: *U.S. News & World Report* (11 August 1980), p. 66. Kemeny quote is from: *Democracy* (vol. 1, no. 1, 1981), p. 61. Quotes from Gorz and other French analyst are from: Andre Gorz, *Ecology as Politics* (Boston: South End Press, 1980), pp. 106–109.

Pages 180–81: Headline appeared in: *New York Times*, 8 May 1989. Chart is adapted from: Krimsky and Plough, *Environmental Hazards*, p. 306. Dickson quotes and much of this analysis are from: *Democracy* (vol. 1, no. 1, 1981), p. 61. See also: Dickson, *New Politics*, pp. 262–65, 288–89.

Pages 184–86: Krimsky quote is from: speech, College of Marin, 14 May 1986. Lovins quote is from: Schwarz and Thompson, *Divided We Stand*, p. 33.

Pages 186–88: Regarding aerobics club ruse and zoning laws on group homes, see: *Time* (27 June 1988), p. 44. Regarding EPA's low-profile approach and the failures of legal preemption, see: David Morrell and Christopher Magorian, *Siting Hazardous Waste Facilities: Local Opposition and the Myth of Preemption* (Cambridge, Mass.: Ballinger, 1982), pp. 126–27, 185. Regarding fires at homes for the mentally retarded, see: *Time* (27 June 1988), p. 44. Newton quote is from: interview, 31 July 1990. North Carolina anecdote is from: interview with Kenneth Portney, 30 July 1990. Nuclear waste example is from: interview with Cheryl Runyon, National Conference of State Legislatures, 31 July 1990.

Pages 189–91: Citizen's Clearinghouse on Hazardous Wastes quote is from: "Everyone's Backyard," CCHW newsletter (March/April 1990), p. 22. Regarding environmental impact statements, see: *Science* (7 May 1976), p. 509, and (17 February 1978), p. 743. Dickson quote is from: Dickson, *New Politics*, pp. 258–59. Spaulding and Dear quotes, and Newton comments are from, respectively: interviews, 20 November, 1 August, and 31 July 1990. Regarding Asarco case, see: Krimsky and Plough, *Environmental Hazards*, pp. 200–12, 216, 220; and *Los Angeles Times*, 13 August 1983. Ruckelshaus and unnamed quotes are from, respectively: *Issues in Science and Technology* (Spring 1985), p. 19; and *San Jose Mercury News*, 11 December 1983.

Pages 191–95: Regarding economic incentive examples, see: *New York Times*, 19 June 1988 and 17 April 1990. Illinois example is from: *Newsweek* (27 November 1989), p. 66. MacGregor quote is from: interview, 3 July 1990. Regarding the failure of economic incentives in siting hazardous-waste sites, see: New York Legislative Commission on Toxic Substances and Hazardous Wastes, "Hazardous Waste Facility Siting: A National Survey" (June 1987), pp. 16, 19. Mazur and Portney quotes are from, respectively: interviews, 31 and 30 July 1990. Regarding New York's Fair Share plan, see: Office of the Mayor, press release 248–90; and letter from Mayor David Dinkins to Richard L. Schaffer, chairman of City Planning Commission, both 18 July 1990. Regarding Popper's point system, see: Frank J. Popper, "LULUs and Their Blockage: The Nature of the Problem, the Outline of the Solutions," in Dimento and Graymer, op. cit. For a good critique of various incentives and burden-sharing plans, see: Schwarz and Thompson, *Divided We Stand*, pp. 59–60.

Page 196. Gimello quote is from: interview, 9 August 1990. Regarding right-to-know provisions, see: *New York Times*, 14 February 1987 and 24 March 1991; *Christian Science Monitor*, 29 April 1987; and *Journal of Commerce*, 1 July 1988.

Pages 196–99: Regarding effective industry adaptation to tough regulations, see, for example: *Newsweek* (24 July 1989), p. 24.

General Electric profit and EPA budget figures are from, respectively: interviews with GE and EPA spokespeople, 29 August 1990. For a good analysis of the solar versus nuclear issue, see: *The Nation*, 30 April 1990; and Gorz, *Ecology as Politics*, esp. pp. 18–20. Gottlieb and FitzSimmons quote is from their paper: "A New Environmental Politics?" distributed at the Conference on International Green Movements, April 1986, p. 10.

Pages 200–203 Hansen quote is from: *Science* (11 May 1990), p. 672. Regarding the radioactive-waste research proposal, see: Mukerji, op. cit., p. 77. Mukerji quotes are from, respectively: Mukerji, op. cit., pp. 77–78, 198, and 202–03. Regarding EPA technical-assistance grants, see: EPA Office of Public Affairs, "Note to Correspondents" (R-234), 1 December 1989; and "Fact Sheet: Revisions to TAG Interim Final Rule" (undated). Gimello quote is from: interview, 9 August 1990. Regarding Science for Citizens, see: *Science* (15 October 1976), p. 306; and Dickson, *New Politics* pp. 230–31.

Pages 203–5: Dickson quote is from: Dickson, *New Politics*, p. 327. Ruckelshaus quote is from: *Risk Analysis* (vol. 4, no. 3, 1984), p. 157. Regarding national surveys about the attitudes of youths, see: *New York Times*, 28 June 1990; and *San Francisco Chronicle*, 7 August 1989. For an excellent analysis of youthful alienation, see: *New York Times*, 27 December 1989.

Index

229